The Forgotten Hero of Gettysburg

The Forgotten Hero of Gettysburg

A Biography of General George Sears Greene

David W. Palmer

To order additional copies of this book, contact:
Xlibris Corporation
1-888-795-4274
www.Xlibris.com
Orders@Xlibris.com
25546

CONTENTS

Preface 9

Acknowledgements 13

Chapter One: The Second Battle of Gettysburg 17

Chapter Two: Rhode Island and Young George 21

Chapter Three: West Point—Shaping the Future 25

Chapter Four: Life in the Regular Army 30

Chapter Five: A New Challenge 34

Chapter Six: Railroads 41

Chapter Seven: New York and the Drift towards Civil War 47

Chapter Eight: Save the Union 52

Chapter Nine: Greene Enters the War 65

Chapter Ten: The Maryland Campaign 77

Chapter Eleven: Expeditions in Virginia 98

Chapter Twelve: "Winter Quarters" 113

Chapter Thirteen: Chancellorsville 118

Chapter Fourteen: Papa make them trot again 131

Chapter Fifteen: Culp's Hill: July 2nd 145

Chapter Sixteen: Culp's Hill: July 3rd 195

Chapter Seventeen: Get that gun out of the water 208

Chapter Eighteen: Your Obedient Servant 224

Chapter Nineteen: No Profession was more Honorable 238

Chapter Twenty: A Priceless Heritage 250

Appendix A: Civil War Medical Treatment of Jaw Fractures 263

Appendix B: The Death of Preston King 265

List of Abbreviations 267

Endnotes 269

Bibliography 315

Index 331

To My Sister, Gale Delana Palmer
Her Love And Spirit Lives On

Preface

There are many individuals in history who have contributed to their nation and go unnoticed. It is not only what they have done or said, but what was not done or spoken of that can make that person in history remembered or forgotten. This can be said about General George Sears Greene.

In July of 1996, my friend and I took a trip west to Gettysburg to spend the day. Since we had been to the visited areas of the park (Ex. Pickett's Charge, Little Round Top), why not go to Culp's Hill? It was here that I saw his statue for the first time. He looks towards the Confederate line with right arm pointing out, showing his men where to concentrate their fire. Observing the statue and the area, many questions came to mind. How did he get to be in this part of the battlefield? Did his men feel isolated here (like I did)? Who was George Sears Greene? Why was he not awarded the Medal of Honor? Did this 62 year-old brigade commander win the Battle of Gettysburg for the Union?

By September 1998, after helping a fellow Civil War friend with research on General Barksdale, I decided to embark on the task of writing about Greene's life. Despite a long life, he is not well remembered by the American public. More people know about the Gettysburg citizens John Burns and Jenny Wade! I hope my efforts here will bring him out from under the shade of the trees and into the rays of the sun.

He was "perhaps the best of the six native Rhode Islanders who attained Union generalship" writes one person.[1] Another author speaks of Greene as "a fine General" and in need of a long-overdue biography[2] The challenge is finding those resources. Perhaps that is part of the reason for no full-length biography of him since his death in 1899. Many records were lost over the years due to fire, water damage, or indifference from companies that built the railroads, water works, and worked the coal mines in the 1800's. This involves George Sears Greene as a Civil Engineer.

As for the Civil War, Greene's soldiers did not get into print in comparison with other Army of the Potomac soldiers. As of this writing, those regiments that were under Greene's command the longest, only the 60th New York and 149th New York have had regimental histories published from his brigade. There are none from the 78th, 102nd, and 137th New York regiments. Even more surprising is the omission of published letters or diaries as a book or in journals over the years. In fact, you could make the argument about "the 12th Corps being neglected" as one Civil War writer states.[3] This is beginning to slowly change. In recent years, new regimental histories have been published on the 27th Indiana and 66th Ohio (this was under Greene's command when he took control of the division at Antietam). Books on Antietam and Culp's Hill by prominent historians Stephen W. Sears and Harry Pfanz has helped us to understand the complexities of these battles and give them a voice among their fellow comrades.[4] And finally, the Gettysburg Magazine, published by Morningside House Inc. has been a valuable source this last decade for scholars and students in showing why Culp's Hill was the key to deciding the fate of the Confederacy.

The focus of this book is Greene. The words of those he served with are being printed here for the first time in many cases. He was disciplinarian to some and an agreeable gentleman to those in higher authority in civil and military affairs. What he worked so hard for and received in life was the respect of his peers. This goal was achieved. This was his Medal of Honor.

David W. Palmer
Clifton Heights, PA
July 17, 2000

Notes: Preface

1. Mark H. Dunkelman to Author, February 8, 2000
2. Wilber D. Jones, Jr. to Author, (postmarked) November 26, 1999
3. Ibid
4. Sears, Stephen W. Landscape Turned Red: The Battle of Antietam Ticknor & Fields, 1983; Pfanz, Harry Culp's Hill & Cemetery Hill University of North Carolina Press, 1994.

Acknowledgements

During my research into Greene's life, a fellow author told me that he considered writing a biography the hardest thing to write about. Whether true or false, the groundwork for putting the pieces of the puzzle together of that person's life comes from those individuals and institutions who helped make it possible. I am most thankful to everyone for their assistance and encouragement with special recognition for the following:

Lynn Kennedy for your insight and knowledge of sources for Greene's tenure with the 2nd Massachusetts. Your time in helping me answer my questions while dealing with your father's illness has not been forgotten.

Dennis Buttacavoli for sharing letters from your collection that gives the general public a better understanding of what soldiers went through on the battlefield and for advancement in the military ranks.

Robin Moore and Jeff Ollis for their assistance with the 149th New York Regiment in using Oliver Ormsby letters and diary and the transcribed letters that Robin patiently worked at when it seemed to be unreadable, along with being given the wrong soldier's name in verifying its authenticity.

Judy Coy for sharing Charles Engle's letters and interest in my project.

Joseph Pierro for his advice and various people he directed me towards since those days when I began thinking about Greene in 1998. My knowledge for learning of the past has reached a higher level due to your friendship.

Rob McVeigh for your reading and suggestions of improvement to first draft of manuscript and computer knowledge to guide me along. We never could have guessed my friend, that trip to Gettysburg was the beginning of an odyssey to learn about Greene.

Kurt Kablec and Sandra Putney for your efforts in tracking down old newspaper articles, letters, and enthusiasm in looking for sources to get his story written.

Jerry Shippee for researching Greene's letterbook and finding those "needles in the haystack" items to shed light on his earlier life.

Mac Wyckoff for his knowledge of Kershaw's South Carolinians fighting against Greene's men at Antietam and permission to use quotes from his books.

My appreciation goes out to the many libraries and historical societies who contributed to my manuscript including the following: Antietam National Battlefield Park, Gettysburg National Military Park, Henry E. Huntington Library, Kennebec Historical Society, Massachusetts Historical Society, National Archives and Records Administration, New York Public Library, New York State Archives, Ogdensburg Public Library, Rhode Island Historical Society, St. Lawrence County Historical Association, United States Army Military History Institute, and the United States Military Academy.

During the time when I sought out assistance to make corrections on the manuscript, I cannot forget to mention my appreciation to the Writers' Workshop of Delaware Valley and Eric J. Wittenberg. They pointed out the errors that many first-time authors get trapped in and helped to guide me back in the right direction.

Finally, I wish to thank the relatives of George Sears Greene who provided me copies of articles and pictures of him and family members. Their kindness to an inquisitive stranger about their relative shows me that the General would be proud of his future generation of Greenes. For John G. Greene, Edward Hasse, and Joan Pierpont his story can finally be told.

And to my Mom, Vema E. Palmer, who shared my interest in Greene, listening to my endless talks about new discoveries and disappointments of materials, reading every chapter to check for errors of sentence structure and spelling, and co-designing the dust jacket cover, your love and faith in me has blessed my life to meet the challenges of each day. The words "thank you" are not enough.

List of Illustrations

Section One: The Early Years
Section Two: Civil War
Section Three: Progress & Reflection

Maps

Antietam: Morning and Early Afternoon
   of September 17th................................between pp. 76 & 77
Chancellorsville: Morning of May 3rd......between pp. 117 & 118
Culp's Hill: Evening of July 2nd..............between pp. 144 & 145
Wauhatchie: October 29th Midnight........between pp. 223 & 224

All maps have been drawn by the author and researched thoroughly to show Greene's position only, except Antietam, where notes were necessary for the reader because of the movements of both armies across the battlefield.

Chapter One

The Second Battle of Gettysburg

From the end of the battle of Gettysburg in July 1863 until the present time, arguments have been rife about who was responsible for victory and who was to blame for obscuring the facts. The soldiers continued their efforts to educate the general public in letters, diaries, newspapers and in later years with speeches and reunions. While pride was the motivating factor in the beginning, how history would judge them became the driving force to preserve their stories. George Sears Greene knew this only too well.

Culp's Hill was Greene's shining moment and according to William Monroe Balch, a historian in the 1930's, Greene was aware of what those men did for the Union. Balch said "Gettysburg won the Civil War. George S. Greene won Gettysburg. At leas[t] Gettysburg could not have been won without what Greene's brigade did on the 2nd of July, 1863. The battle was at no other time so nearly lost as it was in that emergency when old George Greene and his men did the impossible and saved the day that won the war."[1]

To establish the truth of this statement, Greene had to get recognition from Meade, Commander of the Army of the Potomac, for being present on the battlefield in the Official Records. On October 1, 1863, the War Department received General George Gordon Meade's official report of the Battle of Gettysburg. Among the errors in the report for the Twelfth Corps was the failure to give credit to Greene's brigade. "The line of the extreme right was held by a very much reduced force," since the left of the Union line was sent elements of the Twelfth Corps as Meade stated. This reduced force that General Meade neglects to identify was Greene's brigade.

Greene did have support to fight this injustice. His superiors, Generals Slocum and Williams wanted changes made to the report. "It beats all in blunders and partially," wrote Williams to his daughters.

Recovering from his wound in Tennessee, Greene received a letter from General Slocum on this matter:

Tullahoma Dec. 30th 1863

Dear General

Your favor of the 23rd has been received. I enclose a copy of a letter which I send to General Meade by the mail of today. I wish you would try to see Meade after he gets my letter and talk this matter over and learn what he intends to do. He must write to the Sect. of War on the subject. My Corps is together again. Geary having been ordered to Bridgeport & Stevenson. I feel confident that everything will work out in the end and I am very anxious you should return to the Corps before the spring campaign opens. I will endeavor to give you a position more agreeable to you than the one you have held heretofore.

So don't make arrangements which will take you away.

Williams has gone on leave. Please let me hear from you.

Yours Truly,

H. W. Slocum[4]

This was good medicine for the mental anguish Greene felt for himself and his men. That letter to Meade shows Greene's brigade "maintained its position and held the enemy in check until the return of Williams Division."[5] Given the corrected facts (and delayed reports from the Twelfth Corps), Slocum made this statement to Meade: "Your report is the official history of that important battle, and to this report reference will always be made by our Government, our people, and the historian, as the most reliable and accurate account of the services performed by each corps, division, and brigade of your army. If you have inadvertently given to one division the credit of having performed by another, you do an injustice to brave men and defraud them of well-earned laurels. It is an injustice which even time cannot correct. That errors of this nature exist in your report is an indisputable fact."[6]

Meade defends himself for not giving Greene's brigade credit and tries to lay the blame on Slocum.[7] He wrote to General Halleck (after writing to Slocum & Williams) that same day, February 25th 1864, asking for Halleck to have the corrected versions of the July 2nd participation of Greene's brigade and the Twelfth Corps entered in the Official Records.[8] Despite the ill feelings that Meade and Slocum were beginning to develop from blaming each other, the opposite was true of Greene and Meade.

They were similar in many ways. Both were well-respected and considered disciplinarians, graduates of West Point, engineers, and family men. Greene understood the adjustments for Meade in a new command. He felt Meade will resolve the matter for all concerned. To Greene's satisfaction, it came in a letter from his commander:

Hd. Qrs. Army of the Potomac
March 10th 1864

Brig. Gen. G.S. Greene
Washington DC.

General,

I could not procure from General Halleck a copy of my letter my report of the battle of Gettysburg, but have had one made on my return, from the original, which I send herewith. I trust it will prove satisfactory to you, altho' I have not made such particular mention of your services as they undoubtedly deserved and it would have gratified me to do had my report been other than a general one.

I take this occasion to say that as God is my witness, I had no intention of doing injustice to you or any other man in the 12th Corps or any other Corps.

Very Truly Yours
Geo. G. Meade
Maj. Gen.[9]

With earlier testimony given by Meade giving credit to Greene's brigade during the congressional investigation into the Gettysburg Campaign, Greene's silence enables Meade to stay with the Army of the Potomac.[10] The atmosphere in Washington was "a political witch hunt." Meade knew the cruel game of politics.

There was a group of anti-Meade Army officers and politicians that blamed him for errors at Gettysburg and sought his removal from command. He was sincere to Greene, but needed his silence if he [Meade] was to keep his enemies from using the Culp's Hill report to attack him. "My enemies consist of certain politicians who wish me removed to restore Hooker; then of certain subordinates whose military reputations are involved in the destruction of mine," Meade wrote to a family member and described "a class of vultures who in Hooker's day preyed upon the army, and who sigh for a return to those glorious days. I expect to retain my place, but I am anxious about my reputation."[11]

All indications are that Greene would have been given the support of Colonel Kane, Generals Howard, Slocum, and Williams if he testified to the Congress. It is probable that Meade may have resigned afterwards or Ulysses S. Grant, the new Commander-in-Chief, could have him placed on assignment (leave of absence). He would have suffered the same fate as McClellan, Burnside, Butler, and Sigel. General George Sears Greene's actions helped retain Meade's place in the Army of the Potomac and caused little harm to his reputation. The Union shall be the greatest beneficiary of them all.

Chapter Two

Rhode Island and Young George

The history of Greene's family in the New World began with John Greene's departure from England in 1635 to Boston (part of the Massachusetts Bay Colony). He wanted to practice his religion without persecution and came to befriend a man who shared his feelings named Roger Williams. In time, Williams had challenged the Massachusetts Bay Colony's leadership and was forced to leave. John Greene and those followers of Williams strived to establish a new colony called Rhode Island. John Greene's son was Lieutenant-Governor and in the following generations, the name Greene would be recognized for the distinguished offices that these men held; Governor, Lieutenant-Governor, a U.S. Senator, and Justice of the Supreme Court. Besides the political arena, two of young George's ancestors, Major General Nathaniel Greene and Colonel Christopher Greene, were recognized for their contributions during the War of the Revolution.[1]

In 1772, George's father, Caleb Greene was born. He was a ship-master in his youth and became a ship-owner and merchant, living in the village of Apponaug, in the town of Warwick. The several hundred acres that Caleb owned dated back to 1640 when that land was purchased by John Greene from Miantonomah, the Indian Chief.[2] He raised from the Soil such crops as corn, oats, hay, and wheat. Caleb had a small cotton-cloth factory located on his property that worked by water power. This was the start of New England's growth in manufacturing of cotton cloth. Caleb saw the need for jobs and the money that could be made from this industry. His grandson, Francis Vinton Greene explained, "The cotton was brought in Caleb's ship from Baltimore, and on their return voyage they carried cotton cloths and occasionally the anchors and chains which were still made at the iron works at Coventry, established by Nathaniel Greene's father fifty years before."[3]

With good fortune smiling on Caleb, he met and fell in love with Sarah Robinson Wicks.[4] They were married in 1795 and Caleb had a 2 1/2 story, center chimney house built in Apponaug. Here in the southwest room on the second floor, on May 6,1801, a son, George Sears Greene was born. His middle name was given to honor Caleb's best friend, George Sears, who died the year before. George was one of nine children of Caleb and Sarah. As time went by, four of these children died before the age of two.[5]

Young George began his education at the village school at Apponaug and then move on to the grammar school at Warwick.[6] Many of those schoolmates and playmates that George sat in class and played outdoor games with were also from merchant families. The economy in trade goods depended on freedom of trade on the high seas. A visit by young George to the wharfs gave the appearance of a city of tall ships, with sailors and dock men working like ants, unloading such items as tea, whale oil, and cotton. Although he was too little to understand, this busy activity at the wharfs was declining and influenced his father's business and George's future.

While the new American Republic was growing, it became more involved with restriction of free trade in the Atlantic Ocean due to the war between England and France. Each one wanted to stop the other from receiving goods from any country. The main antagonist would be England's navy. Shipping was intercepted before they approached ports in Europe and sailors were sometimes removed and impressed into the British navy. President Thomas Jefferson decided to attack this violation of America's neutrality (despite the British frigate's attack on the American ship Chesapeake, killing or wounding twenty-one Americans), not by war, but with the passing of the Embargo Act of 1807.[7]

Jefferson felt the need to protect American interest without giving in to those who cried for war. The Embargo Act prevented trade of American goods to the world and Jefferson believed isolationism was the remedy to cause the British merchants economic hardship and make them approach their government to end their navy's impressments of American seamen. Not only did this policy fail to bring about change in England's conduct, it caused widespread suffering in America. While Jefferson saw his own native Virginia hurting (ex. Tobacco market), the New England merchants were affected the most.

They were outspoken, calling it Jefferson's "dambargo."[8] Ships stayed tied up to the wharfs. Greene's father would see financial reverses and with the War of 1812, the family joined others in dire straits.

Young George was sixteen when he was sent to Wrentham Academy and the next year he attended the Latin grammar school in Providence. This school was near Brown University, where the family had planned for George to further his education. However, George had to change those plans because of the slow recovery of the family's finances.[9] With his education on hold, Greene began looking for employment.

He must have felt that the best way was to learn a trade. Many local boys dreamed about being sailors and living the adventures on the open seas. With the war over, commerce was slowly recovering to the area. He tried to be an apprentice on an East India merchantman, but with the captain's next voyage, he decided against taking any apprentices.

Greene chose to travel to New York City to find employment. He felt the city had more opportunities for a young man than New England could offer. This proved to be true in shaping his future. Greene obtained work in the Pearl Street office of a Mr. Henry Jacobs, a dry goods merchant.[11] It is likely that Greene's father, Caleb, sent with him a letter referring to his character and knowledge of the mercantile business.

During his tenure at the store, Greene met the Superintendent of the United States Military Academy, Major Sylvanus Thayer. It was not unusual for Greene to see officers from West Point come into New York for business or entertainment. It is even possible he had a discussion with them about how to gain admittance into

West Point. This meeting with Major Thayer was no accident. It is fair to speculate that young George began to think about West Point, where you received a free education, upon his rejection as an apprentice.

Since he did not have political connections, his reasoning was to be in New York City and meet those people who could help him.

Here was the chance of a lifetime! Impressed with the young man, Thayer submitted George's name to the Secretary of War to be a cadet at West Point. He would reply from Warwick in April 1819 to the Secretary's letter: "Sir, I received on the 17 inst your letter of the 24th concerning—That I was appointed a cadet in the service of the United States and have accepted the appointment. Your order will be obeyed early in June. I would request that an error in my name as addressed might be corrected as signed by adding 'Sears'."[12]

After passing the examination, George Sears Greene, the grandson of Nathaniel Greene of Revolutionary fame, entered the Academy on June 24, 1819.[13] This boat trip up the Hudson river to the village of West Point was a rare opportunity for this 18 year old adolescent and showed him another world that Caleb's business and the economy of New England had little to offer in stability. He wanted to honor his family's name and show Major Thayer that he made the right choice.

Chapter Three

West Point—Shaping the Future

After visiting his family back home and making preparations to leave for West Point, Greene recalls those days later in life. "I first set foot on this plain [West Point], coming from Rhode Island to Connecticut by stage, thence by steamer to New York, where we took the Albany steamboat. We were landed at the North dock by a yawl towed by a long line from the steamer, which paid out the line till the yawl reached the dock at which the landing took place. Not more than two to four minutes was occupied in landing and receiving passengers, when the tow-line was hauled in by machinery on the steamer, carrying the embarking passengers." This young cadet described West Point, with the river and the surrounding mountains as "beautiful and grand."[1] Major Thayer understood the impression the area made on new arrivals.

Sylvanus Thayer was known in history as "the father of West Point." Only with the institution for two years before Greene's arrival in 1819, he worked hard to provide academic and disciplinary procedures for the cadets and get rid of the political favors and incompetence that had existed.[2] Greene studied many subjects such as chemistry, mineralogy, drawing, philosophy (moral and political), physics, topographical drawing, and engineering (civil and military). Most of the time was spent on mathematics and French.[3] This is due to the heavy influence from the recent Napoleonic Wars in Europe.

During Greene's tenure at the Academy, Major Thayer did not have cavalry instruction or horses for artillery drill for the cadet's training. They would improvise their own method as related by

Greene, "we drew the guns about the plain in field manoeuvers by bricoles, a wide endless leather strap over our shoulders with a rope and hook for harness. We acquired good knowledge in the handling of guns, but our horse practice was not of much value as instruction in that line, though it gave us good physical training."[4]

Greene lived under Thayer's system, as many cadets in the future continued at West Point, in the following manner: Five-thirty a.m., you were awakened and had your breakfast, then attend classes and study until One o'clock in the afternoon; next will be a break for lunch and then commence to study again until four; before having dinner at Six, you could write letters and read. The rest of the time was spent in study until lights were ordered out at Nine-thirty that evening. Often, the cadets continued to study afterwards by candle light.[5] Greene, no doubt, hid the light from his candle so he could learn more and avoid getting any demerits.

Although we don't know of any demerits, Greene had done well in his first year (Fourth Class) being ranked ninth out of Eighty-six cadets. [6] It is interesting to note that of the cadets who were found deficient and turned back that year was Dixon S. Miles (No. 65), who was admitted the same day as Greene and will cross paths again during the early part of the Civil War.[7]

Each summer, it was the custom of the Academy to have a practice march. Rising at Five-thirty a.m., Greene will march up the Hudson to Rhinebeck in 1819 with his fellow cadets. The next year will be south to Philadelphia and in 1822 to the north to the city of Boston. Not all of this marching was by foot as half of the distance was by transportation from boats.[8]

"When the river was closed by ice," stated years later by Greene, "the only communication with New York and the outer world was by a mail coach on the east side of the river, at a speed of three or four miles per hour." During his years at West Point, Greene never forgot one night taking in the view up the river; "I once saw a grand lunar rainbow, in all its splendor, stretched across the river from mountain to mountain, a phenomenonseldom seen by moonlight, and this one was unrivalled for its extent and beauty."[9]

With much of the cadets schedule laid out, there was little time for other activities. Many of their official duties were relaxed on Sundays (despite being required to attend the Episcopal service at the chapel) which gave them the opportunity to pursue some form of entertainment.[10] For Greene and the rest of the cadets, the place to go was Benny Haven's, a local tavern, just a few miles from the Academy. Many of their visits were after-hours and it seemed that the officials had turned a blind's eye to their ventures. Here one could enjoy the taste of buckwheat cakes and roast turkey and toast each other with beer or whiskey. Despite the official stance that West Point took against this behavior, Benny Havens became a cadet institution until after the Civil War.[11] Strong bonds of friendship were forged from those social activities and Greene did not let it interfere with his studies.

In his second year (Third Class), out of sixty-three cadets, Greene was ranked fourth and remain there in the third year (Second Class) when his class dropped down to forty-three.[12] He was being recognized by his peers, being quartermaster-sergeant and quartermaster of the battalion.[13] During his fourth year (First Class), Greene was honored for his work ethic by being the acting assistant professor of mathematics and finishing in his class with the rank of second of the thirty-five that had remained in his graduation on July 1, 1823.[14] He was the 327th graduate from the United States Military Academy.[15]

George Sears Greene had made friends and was well acquainted with some of those cadets who became general officers in the Civil War. In his own class was Hannibal Day (No. 23) and future Union Adj. General Lorenzo Thomas (No. 17). Others include Joseph K. Mansfield, David Hunter, David Vinton (his best friend), Dennis Hart Mahan, and Albert Sidney Johnston. In the years ahead, Day and Vinton will come into Greene's life and shape his future.[16]

The day of graduation, he was brevetted Second Lieutenant in the U. S. First Artillery and then promoted to the same grade in the Third Artillery that very day. Because of Greene's rank (No. 2), it was the usual procedure that the top cadets went into the Engineers, but it has been suggested that he chose the artillery. The reason is because vacancies were so few in 1823.[17]

Like all graduating cadets, Greene will enjoy a furlough before his next assignment. It was the standard practice for one to be apart from the academy for a few years and then come back from the army to serve as instructors. This was not to be Greene's beginning in the army. The years 1823-1827 (with one exception) was spent at the U. S. Military Academy as an Assistant Professor of Mathematics and as Principal Assistant Professor of Engineering.[18]

Why was Greene made an exception? Clearly, the Superintendent, Sylvanus Thayer was the one who had Greene assigned this tour of duty. His instincts about the 18 year old had proved correct. This young man was recognized for his learned skills in mathematics and could have been an engineer already, if not for the few vacancies available. Perhaps he was trying to compensate Greene. Better yet, why not use his skills to teach the other cadets for the future (at this time, West Point was more of an engineering school).

The one exception mentioned earlier in teaching at the academy was his posting to Fort Monroe in Virginia, from June 16, 1824 to October 6, 1824, as Assistant Instructor of Mathematics in the Artillery School for Practice.[19] This temporary duty had not changed his outlook for a career in the army, but one event that year was significant and serve him in his thoughts of America's future. Whether by accident or design (Sylvanus Thayer?), George Sears Greene was presented to General Lafayette, who was winding up his tour of America in 1824, for the Yorktown celebration that Lafayette had participated.[20]

Here was a living link to his grandfather, General Nathaniel Greene and the Founding Fathers. We can only imagine the stories he shared with Greene about him. George never forgot their meeting.

Another link to the Founding Fathers was Greene's visit with his fellow cadets to the home of John Adams. They had paid their respects to the former president, living in nearby Quincy, after their march to Boston during the summer encampment. The great statesman spoke to Greene and the other cadets that day like a father advising his son: "I congratulate you on the great advantages you possess for attaining eminence in letters and science as well as arms. These advantages are a precious deposit for which you are responsible to your country."[21]

During his days as a teacher at West Point, Greene taught mathematics and engineering to a cadet from Virginia who recently met Lafayette in Alexandria. His name was Robert E. Lee. We do not know Greene's perception of this young student, but Lee's tutorage under the professor and assistant professor resulted in being credited fourth in mathematics with a rating of 197 from a possible 200 in his first year. Lee's academic standing and conduct could have been given a recommendation by Greene to Sylvanus Thayer for his teaching position in mathematics was given to Lee upon returning to the barracks on September 1, 1826.[22] The teacher and student will meet again, but against each other on the field of battle to preserve their way of life that had divided a nation.

After a brief time of ordnance duty, Greene will leave West Point and have good memories of those who helped him and use his skills in whatever future was ahead in the Army or in civilian life. In possession of the education he wanted, Greene felt secure about his future and showed others that given the chance, his hard work will be beneficial for all.

Chapter Four

Life in the Regular Army

The United States had a small army in comparison to their fellow counterparts in Europe. Unlike the continent of Europe which had large standing armies to strengthen their government's foreign policies, America did not have its army carry out functions in that manner. The only foreign power that America was concerned about was England. With Canada (a providence under the British Crown) sharing the northern border with America and England's navy guarding the Atlantic ocean, the U. S. government did not want the Eastern seaboard to be exposed to invasion. The memories of the War of 1812 with England were still fresh and particularly in New England. Here was Lieutenant Greene's next assignment.

Greene is reunited with his regiment at Fort Wolcott, Rhode Island in November 1827. The following years were spent on garrison duty from 1828 to 1836 at Fort Sullivan in Eastport, Maine, with the exception of his service as a recruiting officer 1829-30 at Fort Independence, Massachusetts.[1] During his time in Massachusetts, Greene was promoted on May 31, 1829 to First Lieutenant in the U. S. Third Artillery.[2] He held that rank for the next seven years. For a young man serving in the Regular Army, garrison duty did not provide the challenge to grow (as Greene had at West Point) or acquire rapid promotions. Unless an officer died or resigned, you could stay at the same grade for years. Another way was for new regiments to be created, but that took an act of Congress and there was no pressing need to have this implemented.

Despite this problem, the Secretary of War, Lewis Cass was attempting to create a better environment for those soldiers in garrisons. During Greene's tenure, the two issues in question was the abuse of alcohol and the need for religious instruction. Cass felt that chaplains should be appointed to military posts and the daily liquor ration be ended.[3]

He recommended that tea, coffee, and sugar be issued and army sutlers not be allowed to sell liquor. This was accepted by Congress. This was an issue the lieutenant had to deal with since his Colonel (N. B. Buford) was on furlough. Greene assumed the duties of Acting Assistant Quartermaster on March 1, 1831 and began hearing at the fort some grumbling among the men. He felt that Cass should have made an exception for the surgeon's use, complaining that "no whiskey will be registered for issue on this post on any account, whatever."[4] Greene could appreciate the Secretary's efforts to improve life in the army for the present and future.

With Greene's posting to the New England area, he was reunited with his best friend from West Point, David H. Vinton. Graduating in 1822, Vinton in 1828 had renew his friendship with George in Rhode Island.[5]

No doubt they asked each other what they were doing currently and reminiscences about their cadet days at West Point. It was at this time that he met David's sister, Elizabeth Vinton. Perhaps Greene knew about her from letters that David had shared with him as cadets or even met briefly on a visit during the summer break. In any event, they fell in love and were married on July 14, 1828 in Pomfret, Connecticut.[6] Elizabeth gave birth to three children over the next four years: Mary Vinton, George Sears and Francis Vinton.[7]

Since Greene had his wife and three children to love and care for (and with improvements in the army), garrison life was tolerable. However, before Greene's son Francis was born, his world started to collapse around him. On June 6, 1832 three days after her birthday, Mary Vinton died.[8]

Greene had wanted to have Elizabeth with her relatives during this time of her pregnancy and requested a leave of absence two weeks later for two months, with application for two months after its expiration. [9] They needed to have the support of their families, but if Elizabeth was having a difficult pregnancy before Mary's death, Greene wanted to have enough time with her before resuming his duties.

Greene had the support of Captain Childs, who commanded his company, after the birth of his son, saying "the health of my family will not admit of their accompanying traveling at the expiration of my present furlough." This request was granted in August by special order and by mid-September he had notified will notify the Army of moving from Pomfret, Connecticut to Warwick, Rhode Island (to be with his parents and sibling). [10]

Despite the time away from Fort Sullivan, Greene had to send in a notification of the garrison's expenditures for fuel and outfits to his commanding General Thomas J. Jessup during the first quarter of 1832. Also during his absence, repairs were being made to the Block House and the Hospital. Greene had been upset that Jessup should think he was lax in his duty. He told his commander that it was the responsibility of his replacement and "I did not think that any further orders were necessary for me." [11]

Recovering from giving birth to Francis and Elizabeth leaning on her husband in their grief over Mary, tragedy shall visited them again, with the death of George Sears on October 7, 1832. [12] Unable to get another furlough, Greene will resume his duties on the first of November and just try to face each day with hope. This proved to be more difficult than he could have imagined. By the year's end, on the day after Christmas, his wife Elizabeth will be dead and Francis shall join her on February 22, 1833. [13]

The question begs to be answered: Why did George Sears Greene lose his wife and three children and he was spared their fate? One source does suggest that they all died of a fever within that time period, but that is very unlikely. [14] The most reasonable cause of death for the children was tuberculosis. The disease was easily transmitted among people and it attacked the lungs. Children and adults, who were in delicate health bore the most chance of getting it. Since Mary was care for by her mother during her pregnancy, Elizabeth could have inadvertently passed it on to

George Sears and with the slow recovery from child birth and the stress of losing two children, her immunity was weak and the disease would contributed (with the other factors) to her death.

Greene survived because of his good health and les exposure to the children and his wife. The doctor or medical surgeon kept them isolated from the garrison in the fort to keep the disease from spreading. When not on duty, Greene was likely told by the doctor to limit his time with his family (to prevent the disease from affecting him). His body was strong due to his exposure over the years as a boy who played with the other kids at the docks, living in New York City where sanitary condition bred diseases, and traveling to other areas building up his immunity to resist those diseases that were prevalent in his time.

With his family taken from him, George Sears Greene faced the worst moment of his life. Where or who could he turn to for help? The feeling of guilt being left behind, anger towards God or for not feeling like you did enough to help them may be some of the grief he expressed to the chaplain at Fort Sullivan (a recent policy implemented by the Sec. of War). It is possible he may have reached out to his parents, who could relate to the loss of children. No one could have blamed him if he had turned to drinking to relieve his suffering. It is a testament to Greene's character and the human spirit that he did not become part of the alcohol abuse problem that Lewis Cass was attempting to change in the army.

He used as therapy for his pain and isolation at Fort Sullivan studying books and courses in law and medicine. After three years of study (including engineering), Greene was qualified for taking the examinations and enter those professions.[15] His engineering was his strong interest however, and it may have been a factor in requesting a leave of absence in the autumn of 1835.[16] The army was not advancing his skills by remaining at Fort Sullivan, slow in giving promotions, and perhaps the memories of Elizabeth and the children made him realize it was time to move on with his life. He sent in his resignation, which took effect on June 30, 1836.[17] At 35 years of age, George Sears Greene looked at his future as a new challenge.

Chapter Five

A New Challenge

It was a new challenge, a fresh start in life that George Sears Greene was looking for when he left the army. Certainly, his 17 years in the Army from West Point to his career as an officer should be an asset to the civilian world in the growing economy. Greene's entrance in the civil engineering field had kept him busy with different projects until the beginning of the Civil War. The need for civil engineers grew in the 1830's and 1840's as the towns in the East were growing and looked to expand their products in the open market. While canals by river transportation was the main method for to move goods, the beginning of the 1830's saw the advent of the steam engine and railroads.

This growing demand to connect towns by railroads had given Greene his first job in Massachusetts. He was an assistant engineer on the Andover to Wilmington line, and went into the cities of Boston and Charlestown on a regular basis.[1] When Greene was in Maine (possibly surveying an extension of the line), he met a 28 year old woman named Martha Barrett Dana, who had been visiting the area with her father.[2] The meeting revived feelings he had only shared with Elizabeth. Greene used his trips into Charlestown (where father and daughter resided) and Boston (Samuel Dana practiced law) to get better acquainted. Her father, Samuel Dana, was a prominent and influential man, whose family had descendents that came from England in 1640. He served Massachusetts with several terms in the Assembly, the State Senate, and Congress.[3] He was aware of his daughter's interest in this Civil Engineer and learned much about him. Martha probably saw many traits of her father in George. Samuel approved of his good, moral character and secure that Greene could provide for their future. With her father's death in November 1836, Martha was drawn closer to George in her grief, which he understood her feelings only too well. For the second time in his life, George Sears Greene fell in love and married Martha in her hometown, Charlestown on February 21, 1837.[4]

While Greene was getting ready for their wedding, his professional career was taking off. In January 1837, the former Senator and Governor of South Carolina, Robert Y. Hayne became the president of the Louisville, Cincinnati, and Charleston Railroad Company.[5] Internal improvements were a concern for western settlers and Hayne had a great interest in the problems of communication and transportation. Greene had accepted an assignment as assistant engineer on Hayne's project. He helped to survey and locate the route for a railway from Charleston, S.C. to Cincinnati, Ohio.[6]

For Greene's part, he surveyed and located the route, beginning near Asheville, North Carolina, down the majestic valley of the French Broad River to the Tennessee River, and moved across the Cumberland Mountains into Kentucky.[7] To be involved in this great project that encompassed five states not only benefited the nation, but it made Greene a better engineer (dealing with various geological terrains). He had been in the Lexington, Kentucky area when Martha gave birth to their son on November 26, 1837.[8] They named him George Sears Greene.[9] Although one child could never replace the one that died, Martha knew George suffered over the loss of his children by Elizabeth Vinton. He may have asked her or she suggested that they name their son after him. Either way, it was part of the healing process for him and the newlyweds were happy.

The work on the line continued with other teams surveying to Cincinnati and from North Carolina to Charleston. Hayne wanted to bring the economic wealth of the West (predominantly Ohio & Indiana) to the South, thereby creating strong economic ties with the Southern ports and Europe. Another benefit was to be less isolated politically and avoid the Nullification Crisis of 1832 that South Carolina had endured.[10] Despite Greene's efforts to make Hayne's dream come true, it did not become reality. It was a combination of the economy (recovering from the Panic of 1837), politics, and the death of Robert Y. Hayne on September 24, 1839.[11] No doubt disappointed that the project came to an end, Greene was recognized by this peers in the civil engineering field and companies inquired about his services.

With little George in tow, the family arrived in Allegheny County, Maryland to call home until the end of 1845. Just east of the town of Frostburg, they lived on the lands of the Maryland Mining Co.[12] It was Greene's task to survey the coal mines in the Frostburg-Mt. Savage-Cumberland area and complete the portion of the Baltimore—Ohio (B&O) Railroad west of Cumberland. This area of Western Maryland was growing as a community and how the coal mines, railroads, and clay furnaces affected future generations.

His work began with the Cumberland Coal & Iron Co. in surveying the adjacent farmland around their property for seams of coal. This process required Greene to contact the lawyer to discuss possible buyouts of farmers such as Harding, Powell or Williams. "Now is the time to make conditional contracts to advantage," he told Cumberland's lawyer, because upon further developments, he believed the area "contained not less than 38,00000 tons of Coal."[13]

The company had discussed about expenses in their last meeting (which Greene had participated) and were cautious about paying too much for the lands if there are only small amounts of coal to be obtained. Sounding more like a businessman, Greene made his feelings known "I consider the whole of the purchases of the greatest importance to the company as giving us the advantages of all the valuable coal & iron in the Coal Field, which with exception cannot be excelled by any property in their region."[14]

Greene heard the stories and talked to those men who lived in the coal mines and felt morally responsible to improve life in the area (with his family Greene could socialize more than constantly moving around with Hayne's railroad project). Initially, coal was packed in "hogsheads," taken by wagons to Cumberland and dumped onto coal barges on the Chesapeake and Ohio Canal. Work was halted in the winter because of the canal being frozen, bringing hunger to many a miner's family. You had children moving like ants over the hills searching for the spring poke plant that came to the surface so there could be more food on the table. If he was lucky, a miner could make $3.00 a month in the winter. He knew when the Canal was free from ice, those long days of 14 to 16 hours (after walking 2 to 7 miles to the mines), 6 days a week over the summer provided food for the winter.[15]

The building of the railroads that Greene help connect with the coal mines, iron ore and clay furnaces brought changes. Work was no longer scarce and became very busy with railroads able to move coal easier to market than by wagons and canals that depended on good weather. Also, round hoppers on flat cars and dumped from the sides replaced the wooden barrels that held the coal.[16] George and Martha had to make adjustments in their new home. Martha gave birth to their second child, a boy, who was named Samuel Dana (after her father) on February 11, 1840 in Cumberland.[17] Now with his family growing and feeling secure about his staying here (unlike the Hayne project), Greene must have discussed with Martha about George Jr. being baptized.

Religion was not an issue between George and Martha, but Greene's children from Elizabeth had been on his mind. Were they saved? He could not see that they shall leave this world before their lives had begun. If he did not discuss his feelings with Martha, then Greene could have made her believe it was her idea to have little George baptized. The y asked friends from the community (no doubt George would have some workers or company men) to share in this festive day. In the town of Frostburg, on August 23, 1841, the Bishop of Maryland, William Robinson Whittingham looked out to those in the congregation (with proud Mom and Dad by his side) and with an outstretched arm say these words:

> "In the name of the Holy and ever blessed Trinity, God the Father, Son and Holy Ghost, and conformably with the godly order and administration of the Catholic Church of Christ in these United States of America, George Sears Greene has this day received the seal of confirmation by laying on of hands with prayer having openly before the Church, ratified, confirmed and solemnly assumed his baptismal vows and obligations in presence of me."[18]

By the beginning of 1842, Greene had once again been blessed as Martha gave birth to their third son, Charles Thruston Greene, on March 5th.[19] This happy event added to Greene's civil engineering results put forward that year in the map from the surveys of the part of the Frostburg Coal Field. He displayed the coal openings by drifts, with the figures listing the thickness of the seam in feet. Also shown are the Iron ore openings and Superior Fine Clay (including the outcrop of Limestone). Finally, Greene makes notes on the B&O Railroad (that brought all these commodities together for the marketplace). He wrote: "The grade on the Balt. & Ohio Railroad will be about 26 feet to the mouth of Jennings Run, thence about 80 ft. per mile to the mouth of Trotter's Run, thence about 130 ft. per mile to the mouth of Cranberry Run. The line of the Baltimore & Ohio Railroad has not been definitely Located. But the route has been surveyed and the location will not vary materially from the route indicated."[20]

Greene knew the area well, with its names (Ex. Trotter) dating back to Colonial times from families who settled there or Indians who had stayed among the white settlers. In a few cases, the named area was a recent memory. Jennings Run was named after the geologist who had discovered ore deposits about 20 years ago.[21] The B&O Railroad people were pleased since work was started on its construction right away. At this time, an editorial from the American Railroad Journal had stated that there was no firm in the United States capable of manufacturing heavy-edged rail. The British dominated the rail market in the U.S. and the B&O used their rails until they bought it from the Mt. Savage rolling mill.[22]

Built in 1843 by the Maryland & New York Iron & Coal Company, the Mt. Savage rolling mill was a fine counterpoint to its British competition. It had 3 trains of rollers, 17 puddling furnaces, 6 reheating furnaces, and 3 special facilities for sheet iron production. Coal gas (produced at the mill) was used as fuel in the Siemens type furnaces. Here, too, Cannon balls were produced in large numbers. Given the mills output of rails for the B&O and other railroads in 1844, the need for imported products to the United States declined.[23] This lowered the cost for the B&O railroad and Greene didn't have to wait for supply of rails so construction could proceed.

Many of those working in the rolling mills, clay furnaces, coal mines, and railroads were immigrants. Greene saw they didn't always get along with each other. One incident is related here: "When the railroad from Cumberland to Mt. Savage was built, a massive man (6ft. 4 in.) weighing 240 pounds was hired for foreman. His name was Eckhart. Fights broke out between the fighting Irish and stubborn Germans, but then the huge Mr. Eckhart waded in with bare fists, and if the fighting resembled a small battle, he resorted to a heavy club. Lumpy heads and bruised backs gave evidence of a brisk hour of fighting."[24]

Greene's civil engineering efforts for the B&O Railroad the Frostburg—Mt. Savage—Cumberland area in 1845 had another benefit to the local economy. The B&O instituted passenger service, with three trains operating out of Cumberland each day connecting to Mt. Savage.[25] These early days of travel into the coal fields were remembered by William Cullen Bryant: "At Cumberland, you leave the B&O Railroad, and enter a single passenger car at the end of a long row of empty coal wagons, which are slowly dragged up a rocky pass beside a shallow stream into the coal regions of the Alleghenies."[26] It seemed like this part of Western Maryland became an industrial oasis and blueprint for the rest of America.

George Sears Greene had another mouth to feed with the birth of his daughter, Anna Mory Greene, on October 19, 1845 in Cumberland.[27] The work for Greene on the B&O and the coal fields was finished.

Unlike the Hayne project, his contribution to the growth of the industries in the area and a better life for its citizens became a monument to those future generations. It was a happy time for George and Martha during their stay in Western Maryland, with the growth in their family (Samuel Dana, Charles, and Anna) and making friends in the five years of being part of the community. The demand for railroad building continued and town officials looked to expand their markets. Greene did not have to wait long. He started the year 1846 by going back to the New England area with his family where it all began.

Chapter Six

Railroads

Like a later generation that saw the growth of the West with new towns, population shifts in different regions, and sound economics, this was made possible due to the presence of the railroad. The days of isolation for towns in the East were changing with many of those in financial circles (banks, merchants), local government, and industry wanting to be part of the expansion of railroads in America's Industrial Revolution.

With Greene's return to the New England area, he was employed with the Boston & Providence Railroad.[1] The time with them, however, would be short due to developments in Maine. Towns along the coastline were attempting to create or improve existing rail lines. One of those recent companies created was the Kennebec and Portland Railroad. A meeting was held in the town of Gardiner, at the Gardiner hotel on June 18, 1845. Citizens came from Augusta, Hallowell, Gardiner, Pittston, Bowdoinham, Brunswick, Bath, Portland and even from Boston.[2] This was followed by a second meeting held at the Court House in Augusta on July 7, 1845. the discussion was building the railroad from Augusta to Portland, with a branch to Bath.[3]

A reporter for the Kennebec Journal wrote: "The meeting, though not a crowded one, was of a highly respectable character comprising many of the heaviest capitalists and most influential citizens in the towns above named, and moreover exhibited a degree of spirit and enthusiasm that must dissipate all doubts about the success of the grand project which it was called to promote."[4]

While spirit and enthusiasm were not lacking, the need for financial backing was great. The management submitted a resolution to encourage investment: "that it is not only feasible, but may be constructed at an expense greatly below the average cost of railroads in New England—that such an investment promises a fair and an increasing remuneration to subscribers to the stock."[5]

Initial surveys were done, looking at two routes named "Western" and "Eastern." Although the Western route was estimated as a half mile longer and the expense was more, both routes were possible for construction.[6] The connection of the roads required more finances by the fall of 1846. The Portland, Saco and Portsmouth Railroad wanted to raise $100,000 in stock to connect with Kennebec. The news was encouraging: "The subscriptions in Augusta have more than doubled, and promise to become so in Hallowell and Gardiner. We shall obtain 400,000 dollars, at least, upon the Kennebec, and now have full confidence that the work will be commenced early in the spring."[7] The company appealed to all to take subscriptions (stock).

Meetings were held in January 1847 to raise further capital. The towns along the Kennebec road had obtained $500,000 and attempted to increase that amount to $800,000 in subscriptions. There were discussions of extending the road to Somerset and Penobscot Counties and obtain subscriptions to its stock by the citizens in those communities.[8] Now with the funding in place and the narrow and uniform gouge of the Western roads adopted by the Kennebec and Portland, it was time to move on to the next stage.

The 1870 publication on the History of Augusta states: "George S. Green[e] of Boston, as chief engineer, was engaged to locate the Kennebec road, and the first assessment [dividend] per stock was made March 1st, and on the first day of the following June the construction of the road was commenced, with some ceremony, by breaking ground at Bath."[9] The most likely reason for Greene's short time at Boston & Providence Railroad was the opportunity for advancement. He was contributing to the growth of the B&P, but with the Kennebec & Portland, it was Greene who was in control, consulting with other engineers in his field connecting other roads to build a great network in the state of Maine. He must have felt that the results of Western Maryland could be applied here.

Greene was already familiar with the area. It brought back the memories of George and Martha when they first met in Maine during a survey that George was doing for the railroad in 1836. Their family continued to grow with the arrival of James John Greene on September 4, 1847, but their joy and love for James turned to sorrow with his death in Brunswick in October 1848.[10] The cause of death was unknown, but this gave little comfort to the parents. They had each other and the other children to help them in keeping them busy and soothing the pain in their hearts. For George, he used the work on the Kennebec road as therapy. It was familiar territory for him.

For the Kennebec and Portland Railroad, Greene supervised the process of using for the track, longitudinal sleepers of hemlock. They were treated with coal tar to make them durable. The timber was removed and treated in a building in Augusta, near the dam, that used water power for the machinery. It framed the timber and then passed into a huge boiler to be treated.[11] The framed timber was laid on the grade with steel joints inserted on both ends. The hemlock was used then to keep them (the boards) in place. Finally, the track was laid down to finish the road. It was a time consuming and challenging job, but Greene was a professional and it did not faze him.

It was June 27, 1850 in Providence, Rhode Island that the Greene's became parents for the last time. They named their son, Francis Vinton (after George's second son by his first marriage).[12] The reason for being in Providence was to be with relatives and receive care for her and the other children. Martha may have had a difficult pregnancy because of her age (41) and with the recent loss of James, Greene wanted to prevent any concerns they may have discussed.

By the end of 1850, the President of the Kennebec & Portland, R. Williams was looking at estimates and overall financial operation to present a report to the stockholders. One of those engineers under Greene replied to Williams: "Agreeably to your request I saw Col. Nash at Brunswick and received the accompanying bill for extra work by the hand of his son, which he said embraced all demands they hold against the Co. for labor performed. I have examined this bill carefully and have made some deductions from items about which I knew."[13]

A final estimate of the work done on the first part of the railroad was sent to Williams. After a breakdown of numbers by sections, the amount of $112,549.99 1/2 was the total.[14] It had pleased Williams and as his office was looking at the figures for the change in the capacity of Deering's Mill Pond by the railroad, the faith in the stockholders was shown by keeping cost low.[15] Greene, as chief engineer, was showing the company, the stockholders, and townspeople that their faith and trust were not unfounded as it was nearing completion.

By the spring of 1852, the work for Greene on the Kennebec and Portland was finished. With the demand increased for engineers, Greene contributed his efforts to the Albany & Susquehanna Railroad in surveying its location that summer. It was more of being a consultant to the chief engineer, Martin B. Inches of Boston, and the other engineers for the new company (chartered in April 1851).[16] Greene returned to his home state of Rhode Island as an engineer on the Bristol and Providence Railroad from 1852 to 1856.[17] He sent the company his report on the survey from Bristol and Warren to Providence. While the route from Bristol to Warren was a clear choice, the company had to choose between two lines from Warren to Providence.

Greene stated, "one passing to the east of the village, and crossing the river above the bridge; the other passing along the shore of Warren Harbor, and through Water-street, west of the dwelling houses and east of the wharves, and crossing the river below the bridge. This last line will shorten the distance 1500feet."[18] He clearly favored the latter route for the following reasons, "the western route has the advantage of less land damages," and "the western route has also the advantage of best uniting with the most desirable route through Warren village."[19]

He gave an estimated cost of $292,039 dollars for everything involved for the road; its construction, land damages, fences, machinery and buildings.[20] Greene's contribution to the success of the Bristol & Providence Railroad brought his engineering skills to the attention of colleagues in New York for his next engineering project.

Before this took place in 1856, there were two events that dealt with Greene's past and his future. The first was Greene's father, Caleb Greene. The widowed 81 year old had died on December 4, 1853 in the house that he had built for his bride in 1795.[21] Caleb had been a loving father to George and his brothers and sisters. He was not the successful businessman after the War of 1812, but did manage his finances for the family. Greene saw his father's business applications in his own engineering skills. He received his support when he went into the world on his own (New York & West Point) and influence him in dealing with the loss of his family in 1832-33. The siblings erected a large granite stone to his memory and inscribed the genealogical record of the family.[22]

The second was his profession. Across the country, Civil Engineers were sought after for improvements to public works and expansion into underdeveloped areas. Their impact on those communities affected the economy. Seeing the need to organize, a letter was sent out in late October 1852, to practitioners of civil engineering around the New York City area.[23] George Sears Greene was one of the twelve respondents who met in the Croton Aqueduct Department office, Rotunda Park to draft and adopt a Constitution for the American Society of Civil Engineers and Architects.

He may have been in the city during this time conducting business for the railroad or personal reasons that are unknown when he received this letter. These men are known as the "Founders" of the ASCE, The other men were Alfred W. Craven, chief engineer of the Croton Aqueduct Department, Julius W. Adams, J.W. Ayres, Thomas A. Emmett, Edward Gardiner, Robert B. Gorsuch, James

Laurie, W.H. Morell, & W. H. Sidell from New York; S.S. Post of Oswego and W.H. Talcott of New Jersey.[24]

The knowledge and experiences these men brought to this new organization complimented the projects of the U.S. Army Corps of Engineers that helped local and state governments. As time went by, George Sears Greene became President of the Society in the later years after its reorganization.[25] He was not too busy to turn away smaller projects, like the new construction plans he had drawn for the new Presbyterian Church in Canton, Michigan in 1856 after being approached by the Trustees.[26] His reputation was gaining a national following upon his achievements. But now, Greene's focus was on his return to New York City and the growing tensions that was moving the country towards a Civil War.

Chapter Seven

New York and the Drift towards Civil War

The city of New York was no stranger to George Sears Greene. His time spent in the city in 1819 was the beginning of his pursuits for a better education (West Point) and the last visit in 1852 (creation of the ASCE) helped further Greene's career in the Civil Engineering field. Since those days back in 1852, Greene's name was remembered by one of his fellow engineers named Alfred Craven. He knew about Greene's education, the work with surveying and construction of the railroads, and being one of the founders of the American Society of Civil Engineers. These factors led Craven to recommend him to the Croton Aqueduct Department of NYC to help build the Central Park Reservoir.

With the growth of the city's (New York) population, water consumption increased, making it essential for expansion of the Croton Aqueduct. The land (106 acres) was purchased (to be known as Central Park) for a reservoir named Lake Manahatta by an act of the state legislature in June 1853.[1] Greene was in charge of the daily work (with Alfred Craven as Chief Engineer) and faced delays on the Central Park project from its beginning in 1856. The city gave Fairchild & Co. the job after a lawsuit had moved up to the Supreme Court brought by Dinsmore, Wood & Co., which had given a lower bid, but was rejected by the aqueduct board as inadequate. Also, while the case was being decided, work continued on clearing, grading and landscaping among the number of farms and squatters' shacks.[2]

The design and construction of this engineering project included the wrought-iron pipe on High Bridge across Harlem River, and cast-iron pipe across Manhattan Valley. This single pipe was 90 inches in diameter and was more than a quarter of a mile long, supported by saddles, laying on rollers. It had levitated the bottleneck on the Harlem River that supplied half of the water from two pipes before Greene's work had changed it for the better.

Greene took precautions against leakage and loss of water by founding the puddle walls in the surrounding embankments on concrete laid in trenches in the solid rock.[3] Using his skills and taking a novel approach, he used thin layers in building up the embankments that had been rolled with a grooved roller. The next step was the use of concrete.[4] Concrete was used in large masses and he used pipes joined by half-sleeves bolted together.[5]

Here again, Greene was experimenting because there was no model for engineers to use concrete in this way. In 1858, Greene was able to accomplish this with the invention of the stone cutter. This process helped to lower expenses and placing large unwrought stones thereby enlarging the specific gravity of the concrete mass.[6] This was a new process in using pipes and its effectiveness became a part of future engineering projects.

While these years of work on the biggest challenge of his professional career brought security and prestige, it also gave him joy to see his two oldest sons becoming men. In 1856, George Jr. attended Harvard College, but left in 1857 to study under his father's tutelage and become an assistant engineer on the Croton Aqueduct.[7] Since education was very important to Greene, he probably felt that his son could learn more with hands-on training in a field that he worked. Could there be a better teacher? With no records stating of problems at Harvard, George Jr. may have written home and asked to work with his Dad. If so, the father made sure he earned this degree in the workplace and not be coddled. Greene's faith and work ethic with George Jr. was rewarded as he became a well-respected civil engineer in New York City and other areas that he traveled.

His second son, Samuel Dana attended the Naval Academy at Annapolis and graduate in 1859.[8] He was on a ship in the Far East during the next two years. Greene could be proud of them and hoped the best for all of his children. He had other issues besides his son, George in 1857. There was a depression in the country that year. Because of the situation, finances from the city had a role in employing many of the laborers in the construction of the reservoir. From the time that ground was broken on April 17, 1858 until the reservoir was finished in August 1862, close to 2,000 men (many of those being immigrants) were used.[9]

The size of this project was a risk to the safety of the laborers and local population. A 10 year old named William Mealy drowned, as the New York Times reported in June 1861, while bathing in a water-filled trench dug for aqueduct piping.[10] The citizens in the community felt safe and did not feel routines should be changed around the construction area. Children had played and bathed in these water-filled trenches before and with recent rainfall in the area, the higher water level became a deathtrap for little William Mealy.

This was a terrible accident that the company and George Sears Greene did not want to be repeated. Whatever measures were taken to prevent another accident, it was accomplished. There were not further incidents reported by August 1862 with the completion of the reservoir.

During these years in New York City, Greene could not be immune to the events of the day. The nation had been growing more apart in the 1850's. Newspapers were sold by boys in the streets telling of the violence between anti-slavery and pro-slavery forces in Kansas. Southerners felt they were losing their rights to the North because of the slavery issue. The Dred Scot decision by the Supreme Court in 1857 (stating the negro was not a citizen) and John Brown's raid on Harper's Ferry in 1859 (to arm slaves and start a rebellion across the South) only enflamed the passions and mistrust on both sides of the Mason-Dixon line.

The talk of secession from the Union was gaining prominence in the land. Greene may have read in the newspapers about one of his Senators, Preston King of New York. Elected to the Senate in 1857, an unknown writer stated, "he had the high honor of speaking in the Senate of the United States the first plain words which told the Southern leaders that if they chose war, war they should have."[11] This Republican politician voiced his concerns to a friend during the 1860 election year and foretold the events to come:

"It seems to me the dispersion at Charleston must break up and destroy the organization of the Democratic Party. The cuses have been long at work and the differences of principles and interests are irreconcileable—and they cannot be compromised. The Slaveholders insist upon the extension of slavery, the Republicans will not consent to it-and upon this question there is no ground of compermise. It is a question that must be decided."[12]

With the election of the Republican candidate Abraham Lincoln in November 1860, South Carolina was the first of the Southern states to secede on December 20th. Only a few days later, Senator King conveyed his feelings about the administration and Secessionists: "Some of them talk of the secession as only a temporary thing-of making terms and of reunion. I do not think any compromise whatever practible. The secessionist require that Slaves shall be put upon the same footing as horses and that the owners shall have the rights in both-in other words to establish slavery by a provision of the constitution throughout the Union."[13] As more states in the South held conventions to vote for secession, the safety of Washington was a growing concern.[14] Both Greene and Senator Preston King developed a bond in their fight for justice in the upcoming struggle.

It is interesting to note that George Sears Greene did not consider politics as part of his character. Writing about his father in later years, Francis Vinton gave an insight on him and even his siblings, "his sympathies were with the Whig party."[15] This was valid because over the years of the Whig party, their main platform was for internal improvements. Greene loved this because it meant work for him as a civil engineer. While they dealt with other issues of the day, both the Western and Eastern states wanted improvements. Who could be against improving the quality of life? This almost non-political issue appealed to Greene's character. "He had no sympathy with abolition ideas, although some of his brothers and sisters were rabid abolitionists, but he has a profound respect for the law and legal authority and intense antipathy to rebellion or any defiance or evasion of the law."[16]

This is a profound statement of the man on the eve of Civil War. Greene was well traveled and he saw and shared those experiences with the people in the South, West, and East. To Greene, abolition was thinking of a closed mind (much like the Southern Fire-eater). There was no middle ground for discussion. You were either right or wrong. This may be the reason why Greene does not say anything about his brothers and sisters. How could they relate to their brother, George? There can be no doubt that any political discussions between the siblings could have produced bitter feelings. Greene's days at West Point, his service in the Army, and study for the law had defined who he was. When the Civil War did begin in April 1861 (with the firing of Ft. Sumter), George Sears Greene would offer his services to the War Department, not to get rid of slavery, but to save the Union.[17]

Chapter Eight

Save the Union

The Croton Aqueduct extension that Greene had worked so hard on was finished by the work crews and the company. His focus was to restore law and order to the nation and he waited to hear from the War department. Throughout the summer of 1861 and into the fall season, no solution was reached for a quick end to the Civil War either by one battle on the field or through political compromise. Yet, Greene was still waiting to be accepted by the government.

He had been looked at with skepticism by Governor Edwin Morgan of New York in many of the applicants papers that came across his desk. Despite his good health, a West Point education and a former army officer, there were disadvantages against Greene. He was over the age of sixty, he had been out of the army for twenty-five years (with no fighting experience that many had in the Mexican War of the mid-1840's or against the Seminole Indians in Florida), and had little political influence in the state, since he was considered a newcomer to New York.[1] As time went by, the Governor was presented with a problem that required the attention of a strong-willed, no-nonsense individual. That individual was George Sears Greene.

The men of the 60th New York regiment came primarily from St. Lawrence and Franklin counties in the northern part of the state. Many were farmers, hunters, and laborers in civilian life.[2] Like many of those across the North, the townspeople came out to support the men and their government to save the Union. Donald Brown, a recent immigrant from Scotland and member of Company

D, remembered those early days; "The same fall, the regiment was taken down the Hudson in a fine boat. We embarked at Albany, with light hearts-a thousand strong. Fathers, fond mothers, and sweethearts followed their loved ones thither, while banners waved, heavy drums rolled, and tears fell fast. As we sailed down the beautiful waters of the Hudson, the bands continued to play at intervals, and from every balcony of the mansions which top the Palisades, white handkerchiefs were waving."[3]

With their arrival in Maryland, the Rebels had to wait to fight them, as indicated in this 10th Maine soldier's diary entry of November 9th; "Toward night the Sixtieth New York Reg't came in and encamped next to us. It was raining hard and they pitched their tents in the muddiest spot there was. They are a pretty good looking set of men. The plain is for them to relieve us of our position and part of our duty. To guard the RR track from Relay to Baltimore."[4] Guard duty on the railroad out of Baltimore was not received with enthusiasm among the men. The companies were spread out among the depot, stations, and bridges with time spent in drilling.[5] After two days, John Gould's outlook of the New Yorkers started to change; "I was noticing the dress parade of the 60th New York today. I never saw such a piece of work. If they can't guard the RR better than they can drill and parade, the whole concern will go to pot in a weeks time."[6]

There was a growing dissatisfaction with Colonel Hayward and the men blamed him for the conditions they were subjected. It may have been too much responsibility for Hayward. Gould thought he was idiotic and singular in all of his movements (after his battle with the New Yorkers to get to the Relay House for the pay rolls).[7] He probably distanced himself and lost any remaining confidence as a leader. This is shown to the readers back home in a letter to the Ogdensburg Advance newspaper; "Lieut.-Col. Goodrich is becoming much liked by the entire regiment." "Major Brundage still maintains the high popular position he earned in our opinion. He is a military man and a gentleman; not in that distant and dignified sense which places a deep and vast abyss between him and those lower in office and station," (Adjutant

Gale)-"finding time to greet us with a hearty good day."[8] There would be no praise for Colonel Hayward.

In fact, the company commanders petitioned him to resign. The outbreak of measles and typhoid fever brought a number of deaths and a further decline in the regiment's morale.[9] One soldier felt Hayward made a good clerk rather than a colonel when commenting on the gift the regiment received on the news of Colonel William B. Hayward 's resignation on New Years day in 1862.[10] He told the chaplain, Richard Eddy, that his reasons were private, but it was clear to everyone that his spirit was broken and he let problems grow without taking measures to make things better.[11]

Here was the ugly situation that came to Governor Morgan's attention and believed that a West Point man was needed to change the outlook of the regiment's demise. Since many young men with a West Point background (and army service) had already been appointed in the summer and fall of 1861, it gave George Sears Greene the chance to serve his country and the 60th New York regiment shall be informed. "We hope yet to make our mark, and teach our Southern brothers that the sturdy sons of St. Lawrence will perish to a man or see the old time honored flag wave over their soil," writes a 60th New Yorker to reassure the homefolk as they await who will be their next commander.[12]

Before Greene's arrival, the shadow around the regiment continued with the accidental shooting by Private Simon Fishbeck of Company B of William Knight with the Patapsco Guards. Both men had been playing around with each other with jabbing bayonets as they had met for a salute in the middle of the bridge (due to changing of the guards every two hours), Knight was shot in the shoulder and died in a few minutes. Dr. McGlaughlin had saw what happened and tried to help Knight, crossing the bridge from Ellicotts Mills, but to no avail. This daytime incident was not only tragic, but showed the lack of discipline, since loaded guns were not allowed to be carried by the New Yorkers, and Fishbeck had claimed to have picked up the wrong gun.[13]

In a petition to Governor Morgan, William B. Goodrich was listed by the officers of the regiment to fill the vacancy of Colonel, and perhaps enhance their own chances for promotion. However, as they waited, Greene "the gray haired old regular, took down his grandpa's sword, a blade stained with the rust of Monmouth and Brandywine and Eutaw Springs, mounted his good steed and rode to Washington as leader of the Sixtieth New York Volunteers."[14]

During this time, Greene had been offered a colonel's appointment for a regiment by Governor Andrews of Massachusetts. Since he had been waiting to be accepted, Greene may have asked his wife's relatives to intervene with the governor. The Dana family was well known for their role in Massachusetts politics. Another alternative was the need for West Point men and raising regiments to fill the government's quota for each state. Regardless, Greene had made his decision.[15]

The chaplain, Richard Eddy commented, "It seems that [we] were too late I making our petition to Governor Morgan for our new colonel." He had no objections with Goodrich, but stated that "the position had already been tendered to a man of excellent qualifications." [16]

Since Morgan and the other governors were to discontinue recruiting volunteers by General Orders No. 105 (now to be handled by the War Department) in December 1861, this prevented Greene from recruiting his own regiment. Until the governors were able to have the order rescinded on April 3, 1862, the only way Greene could have been appointed was by death or resignation in an existing regiment.[17]

On January 27, 1862 the officers "were grievously disappointed, as we all were much surprised, by the arrival, of Colonel George Sears Greene, who produced a commission from Governor Morgan, authorizing and instructing him to be our commander."[18] Writing to the editor of the St. Lawrence Republican, the chaplain spoke in a cautious tone, "I hope that he is the man we need. If so, he will I am sure, gain the esteem confidence and affection of the entire regiment. If appearances should indicate that he is not, then I fear most unhappy results, both for him and ourselves."[19]

Greene observed the men as they were getting settled in their barracks (which were built during their time outdoors and the growing numbers of sick), which they called Camp Preston King, in honor of the New York Senator who the men held in esteem.[20] After telling the officers in his tent, who had been summoned to this meeting, what he expected, one observant remarked, "Colonel Green was greatly pleased with the appearance of our men, apprehending at once that the regiment was composed of most excellent material, and that, under favorable circumstances for discipline and drill, it would be equal to any in the service." [21]

This could be stated about the 60th NY officers (see note 8), even with a visit to a neighboring regiment (the 5th New York Volunteers) by Capt. John C. O. Redington, who asked his former student, Charles Brandegee about his scholars and expressed joy in seeing him.[22] The open communication between the officers and men was prevalent before Greene's arrival in camp. Could the men adjust to his style of command over time? Even as Greene planned to visit the scattered companies, a private in Company K cheated death, as described here.

"Walking on his guard beat, he noticed a train coming on the track where he stood, and immediately stepping off on another track to avoid danger, was struck by the locomotive of an Express train, coming from an opposite direction. He was violently thrown quite a distance, but providentially escaped with only a few flesh wounds, and a very severe shock to his nervous system."[23]

Despite the recent death of two soldiers from the same company (due to fever), improvements were being made in discipline and general welfare of the men. Drill was one method that Greene had stated to his officers, but a soldier could not be effective without his rifle. This was told by the regimental historian; "by his order the arms were subjected to a severe test, and Lieutenant Clark, a practical gunsmith, was charged with their through inspection. Until this time, the bayonets had not been fitted to the rifles; now the gun was either made complete in every respect, or wholly condemned."[24]

One of Greene's early days in his new command was described by E. L. Crane, who was unclear if the men liked their new Colonel, "the first time that he took command at Dress [Parade] the adjutant brought us to a present arms when the Col ordered us to shoulder arms or something else I don't know what and there was not one of the Reg that know what he ment he spoke so different that we could not understand him." [25]

When not drilling or performing their duties, Greene encouraged such activities as a Literary Society, prayer meetings, a Temperance organization and even found that a spelling school was formed by one company.[26] The men's prospects were improving in spirit, but there was still much work to do, and Greene was determined to make the 60th New York regiment a model for other Union regiments.

Commenting years later on his father's relationship with the 60th New York regiment, Francis Vinton Greene shows us his character in dealing with those in his civil engineering work had stayed the same; "He never understood nor sought to learn the arts of gaining popularity; and while he did whatever lay within his power to care for his men and to save them from unnecessary discomfort of hardship, yet he was a very strict disciplinarian, his manner was at times severe and even harsh, and he insisted upon the same unquestioning obedience of his orders that he himself rendered to the orders of his own superiors."[27] As time went by, Greene and his men developed confidence and respect for each other.

With his regiment beginning to take shape, Colonel Greene thought more about his family since his departure and wrote a letter to his youngest son; "I rec'd yr letter containing a description of the new Erickson steam battery 'Monitor' which I was very thankful for. I have not heard anything or the progress since she was launched. I hope Dana or you will write what is doing with her."[28] He was very interested in the design and work of this new ship (no surprise) and knowing his son, Samuel Dana, was assigned to the Monitor in January 1862 (when it was launched), Greene wanted to learn more from him. He referred to their upcoming silver anniversary and tried to obtain leave, and spoke about the capture of Fort Donelson.

He told Frank, "I paid [for] a beautiful pair of postols and a horse & have a saddle on the way and it has not arrived although it was sent on the 4th of this month. It was sent by some Railroad Agents and not by Express. I have written to Mr. Felton the President of the P.W. & Balt. RR to look it up for me," and the progress of the regiment, "We are having company drills every day when it does not rain & when it does rain we have a drill at the [moved] in quarters. We are going to fire with blank carritages this week & accustom the men to the drill of parade which they have not yet."[29]

While remembering friends at home, Greene told Frank, "I hope you are carefully attentive to your studies my dear son and do not give cause to your teachers to impose any extra tasks upon you by way of punishment," and expressed his love, "I am very glad my dear Frank to hear that you are a good boy and are kind & gentle to your mother. I hope I shall not be disappointed in seeing you all again before Dana goes to sea again."[30] He did obtain leave and left camp to see his loved ones.

The men were getting tired of guarding the railroad and wanted to fight the Rebels in battle, but enjoyed for now the drills each day of the drummers and fifers. It was the first time since leaving Washington they had been together. The are favorites among the men in camp.[31] There had been rumors of joining an expedition leaving from Annapolis, but were unfounded. They gave credit to the talk in camp that George S. Greene had accepted the commission of Colonel as a condition for removing the regiment from the railroad. In less than a month, one soldier said "he commands the respect of all."[32]

Returning to camp on February 22nd, Greene sat down and wrote his wife (after asking for items to send); "I hope my dear wife you will not pine on this disposition of providence which separates us but look forward to the days say when we shall be again reunited. God will prosper us as for as maybe our good & whatever may be our loss we know that it is the time for us."[33]

With a cold he was fighting, thinking of his age, the known diseases in the camps, and threat of a battle to come, it had been an emotional event for George and Martha celebrating their 25 years of marriage.

He tried to be reassuring to her and continued in the letter, "I hope the children will be dutiful and attentive to your comforts. I did not as I wished say much to Anna about her music I hope she practices & devotes herself to it as much as possible. God keep you & our darlings & have you all in his holy keeping prays yr affectionate devoted George."[34]

Like their Colonel, these young men had written home to family and friends. Lester Willson told his family about visiting Baltimore; "The Union people in the city are having good times though they cleaned out one Secesh paper yesterday, and imprisoned quite a number of persons. The faces of secesh are getting so long that the Barbers charge double & for shaving."[35] George E. Elderkin of Company C, although happy about the Union victories in the West, is concerned about finances as stated to his friend; "I must say that we have not drawed our pay yet, but I hope that you will go and see if my family stands in need of anything. If they do, I hope that you will not see them suffor for anything, and I will send money as soon as I get my pay, for I know that they must stand in need of all that I can send to them. We should have drawn our pay the first of March, and here it is the 25th of March and not got it yet, and the Captain told me this morning that we would get paid before the 10th of April. That seems very hard for our families, that are for from us. It is hard but we cannot help it. We expect our pay every two months, but there are three months pay behind now, or will be the first of April. The reason is there is no money in the Treasury now."[36]

Luther L. Gates of Company A revealed his love in a passionate manner; "What would you say if I should put my arms around you and press you to my bosome and kiss you two or three times & throw you on the bed and climb on _____ to the bed with you & one thing [and] another," and if he was tempted, he said, "there is a plenty of ladyes here but my love and my thoughts are at home with you."[37] Not everyone was behaved however, as Greene had followed through with orders for discipline.

For various crimes, such as disorder and mutinous conduct, and absent from guard duty without leave, a general court martial was conducted and the sentences handed out. In these cases, the problem was drinking rum.[38] Another issue was a petition from soldiers of Company C for Captain J.C.O. Redington's resignation. The word "mutiny" was used in descriptions given by Redington and the regimental historian over grievances that had existed. While acknowledging "a part only the company sent in a written complaint," (unknown since neither party gave an example) another document was signed by all "expressing regret for the first and asking permission to withdraw it."[39]

Greene was made aware of this possible discipline trouble and had a few soldiers put temporarily under arrest who signed the original petition. Greene did not want the positive steps taken by the regiment to suffer a setback. Was discipline breaking down? Greene felt otherwise since he released those arrested, but if those soldiers were correct about Redington having "greater interest elsewhere," then he was now under scrutiny and the Colonel would take action against him.[40]

One soldier told a comrade that he should "see the airs that the little man puts on," after Greene had drills performed. This Company C soldier did not express good feelings about his Colonel; "he has some of the foolishest orders that you ever heard. I could compare them to little children while at play."[41] As long as discipline was maintained, Greene knew he could expect results.

This distasteful duty was not shared by George Sears Greene to his son, Frank in replying to his letter about his studies: "Go on my dear son in the same course of excellence and you will give me great joy and prepare yourself to be useful to your family & your country."[42] He referred to his brother Dana; "We have seen the public's account of the fight of the Monitor but I have not had anything from Dana yet at which I am very much disappointed. Capt. Worden is in Washington and I shall try to go there tomorrow and try to see them. It is said he may recover his sight."[43] Greene had obtained leave to see Dana at Old Point, Virginia and was told of the Monitor's fight against the Rebel ship, CSS Virginia at Hampton Roads. Dana had taken command after Captain Worden's disability due to a rebel shell and defended the area and U.S. shipping. The Virginia withdrew and even though Dana followed orders and received praise from officials in Washington, there were some in naval circles that felt he should have pursued the Virginia.[44]

Worried that his son might be given undue criticism in the newspapers, George told Martha; "Whatever it is Dana wrote must be so far confidential that it must not go beyond the family or the Cravens. Charles must not publish anything which he sends home."[45]

Greene told Frank of the current military situation and his own frustration; "Col. Robinson who commanded the railroad brigade has gone with his regiment to Old Point and Col. Dixon S. Miles, an old school mate of West Point is in command of the brigade. The 10 companies of the regiment are here scattered along the road for 20 miles & we have only a guard at headquarters & I may as well be hurdling stone walls in recognition for all the soldiering I am doing. I do not know when I shall get out of this duty. All the troops at Washington have gone over the river & the enemy have gone. Several regiments have gone to Old Point in steamer from this place & there are a large number of boats now waiting for troops to go somewhere."[46]

Although Greene had seen his family and some friends since becoming the Colonel of the 60th New York, it was his first time meeting with an old schoolmate from West Point. Dixon S. Miles had entered West Point in 1819 with Greene, but was held back for one year, graduating in 1824. He had served in the Regular Army and had participated in the battle of Bull Run, amid accusations of being drunk. The sharing of memories of cadet days at West Point and other life experiences had brightened Greene's spirits. He related to Martha, "Col. Miles is a very pleasant old soldier. We get along very well."[47]

Greene's frustration is understandable because he shared his men's distaste for guarding railroads and felt the war was passing him by. The newspapers in the North were always encouraging the march to Richmond. He saw troop movements from Harper's Ferry of General Sedwicks division to the Potomac and the recent marching of Slocum's regiment. He told Martha what he believed it all meant:

"The indications are for a movement in force to some point down the Potomac River from Washington probably to Newport News or York River most likely a large force will be left on the lower Potomac, to protect the navigation, and also in part Washington. I think a large force will move up the neck-between York & James Rivers on Richmond taking the Rebellion or the Rappahannock & threatening Richmond, forcing the Rebels to fall back and fight in front of Richmond or leave. I look for the speedy fall of both Richmond & Jeff Davis."[48]

It is a remarkable observation into General McClellan's forthcoming Peninsular Campaign to take Richmond in 1862. This is why he offered his services to the government, to save the Union, not to guard railroads, but to fight. The rank and file in the 60th New York had improved itself and he felt it was time for them to be reassigned to other duties.

In the meantime, while they awaited for those orders, camp life continued on. From headquarters, the band arrived in Baltimore and delighted the people with their musical selections. [49] Luther Gates wrote home about the regiment getting new dress uniforms and the possibility of going to Fortress Monroe in Virginia. He had hoped to obtain a furlough and see the children; "tell Charles W bless his little boddy if I could get hold of him I would shake his little boots tell him pa has not forgotten him. I should like to come home and go on a farm and have my boys to help me our girl is rather small to make cheese but she will grow to it."[50]

Despite the activities in camp, the spring weather was an incentive to look for female companionship.

"There is some men here that have been to the hospital to be doctord for a disease that no lady in Baltimore can give me at the same time they would write to their wives they longed for the time to come when they could come home. If I had been in that fix I should not care about home," wrote one soldier.[51] The risk of being a casualty on the battlefield seemed remote when compared with a trip into the city for a good time. For the casualty was real and there was no badge of honor for this battlefield to show family and friends with pride.

In late April, another casualty had occurred in Company A, but this time it was an accident. Sitting in their bunk playing cards, Elderkin Rose and Wallace Smith were enjoying the game when Rose accused Smith of cheating. They resumed playing, but Smith had a revolver near the bunk that presumably was not loaded. When Rose made the accusation again, they both got hold of the revolver and it discharged. The ball struck Smith, entering his right breast and fell back saying "Oh, Rose" and died in less that five minutes.[52]

One of the hometown newspapers quoted a soldier about the great change in the regiment over the months and the respect for their Colonel. Speaking for the 60th New York, he said, "we like Col. Green[e] exceedingly well."[53] Colonel Miles helped Greene obtained leave to go to Washington for two days in mid-April. Perhaps this was to have him meet select members of the House or Senate to improve his chances of a promotion from Congress. The results were good because Greene left for six days (beginning April 21) to New York to share the news with his family and put in his order for a general's uniform.[54]

That same week on April 28, 1862 (and confirmed on May 1st by the Senate), Colonel George Sears Greene was appointed a brigadier general. William B. Goodrich, who had been the officers choice to be their colonel, now took the command. On leaving the 60th New York, Greene expressed "his pleasure at the improvement in the regiment during the time he had had command of it, and at the evident desire of officers and men to fit themselves for good service for their country in this its hour of greatest trial."[55]

The great disappointment that some of the officers had felt back in January with Greene's arrival had changed to respect. The letters turned over to General Greene "expressed their high regard for him, their appreciation of his ability, an acknowledgment of benefits received in the connection now about to be dissolved, and the good wishes with which they should follow him in his new position and honors." [56]

George Sears Greene had gained the respect of his peers in the military and politicians in New York and Washington. When his name was submitted to Congress on the promotion list, it most likely was attached with letters in his favor by Senator King, Governor Morgan, Col. Richardson, Col. Miles, prominent citizens of New York City, and friends. Improvement of the regiment had not been overlooked and even though they had not shared their trail by fire, the future dictated what lies ahead. For Greene, it meant a new command.

Chapter Nine

Greene Enters the War

Although Brigadier-General George Sears Greene had turned over the regiment on May 18, 1862 to Colonel Goodrich, his thoughts were still of his old regiment as he prepared to report to his new command. He went into the local office of the American Telegraph Company five days later and had a telegram sent to H. A. Whalen & Senator Preston King, requesting that the 60th New York regiment be put under his command. He stated their desire for active service.[1]

Due to a clerk's error, it was signed, "John S. Green" and passed on from the Senator to the War Department. The War Department had not questioned who was "John S. Green, Brigadier-General" (since Senator King left it uncorrected), but replied back to King, stating "that troop could not be transferred to any particular command except by the Commanding General of Departments."[2] He had to wonder if this was going to be a problem in being recognized with the growth of the Union armies and the politics from Washington.

Despite this setback, Greene brought two servants with him (adding a third on May 18th) that provided for his care. Regretfully there is little information on them. Their names are James (5'7, Dark), Ellen, and Bridget (both 5'2 & light complexion, which suggest they were mulatto).[3] It was a common sight to see runaway slaves or slaves freed from the plantation with the Union armies doing various jobs such as cooking, laundry work or digging ditches. Not only officers (who were required to show expenses), but some enlisted men had employed these poor lost souls. Many feared going back into slavery if they didn't stay with the Union army. Greene took care of them and saw that no harm from alleged slave owners could occur under his command.

He reported to the Army command in the Shenandoah Valley of Virginia. This was under the leader ship of General Nathaniel Banks. It was an awkward beginning for Greene since he was with Banks staff and had not been given a field command. It provided for him the outlook of how a battle is perceived from headquarters. During the attacks on Front Royal and Winchester in late May 1862 by Stonewall Jackson's Confederates, the Union army retreated through the town and surrounding area, stopping at Williamsport, Maryland upon crossing the Potomac River. In his report to the War Department, Banks stated that Greene gave "the most valuable assistance."[4]

What did he mean by valuable assistance? When panic or confusion reigns in a withdraw of an army, there are conflicting reports of enemy movements or strong moral leadership needed to reassure those in the lower ranks. Greene examined that information with Banks staff and had even gone to the area to evaluate the soldiers and look at the terrain for a possible defense. Unlike those in Banks Army who had been outmatched by Jackson's marching columns and fighting in the Valley Campaign of 1862, Greene believed discipline was needed where uncertainty reigned and given the chance, he could provide the moral leadership that his West Point years and Civil Engineering work had instilled in him for most of his life. Discipline was very important to General Jackson and came to battle Greene's soldiers in the following months to come.

The newspapers make no mention of Greene in the retreat at Winchester, but it was on Samuel Dana's mind when he wrote to his mother; "My last letter from you stated that father was about to join Bank's division. I hop he was not with him, if he was really defeated, for next to disgrace, I think a defeat most mortifying. If Banks was merely repulsed, I do not care."[5]

Samuel could see his father's good reputation smeared because of those who acted improperly. He shouldn't have worried because on May 28th, it was stated, "while at Williamsport a nice looking old gentleman in the uniform of a brigadier came to camp and presented instructions from the War Department placing him-General George S. Greene—in command of Gordan's Brigade."[6]

He was taking command of the Third Brigade of the First Division, which consisted of 2nd Massachusetts, 27th Indiana, 29th Pennsylvania, and 3rd Wisconsin.[7] The man Greene replaced was Colonel George H. Gordon of the 2nd Massachusetts, who was respected by all in the brigade and left for Washington to inquire about his promotion and retaining command of the brigade. Here again, like those days in his tenure with the 60th New York, Greene was looked at as an outsider with mixed emotions towards him. The difference here was their resentment towards Washington, the bond between them and Gordon for his actions at Winchester, and the frustration from their retreat out of the Valley.

How did the men get along with him? Could Greene gain their respect and bring discipline to the brigade? Alonzo Quint spoke about Greene, that "he was a good and brave soldier; but an angel-if a military angel exists-could not have satisfied the men, after their experiences of Colonel Gordon in retreat. A sense of injustice was prevalent."[8] One Massachusetts soldier's comments may have related to Greene in his new challenge at this time; "Nobody in this world who really deserves credit ever gets any & those who deserve none get all the praise."[9]

Their time in Williamsport was short as Greene had the brigade ready to move with Banks Army and follow Jackson's Confederates, withdrawing up the Shenandoah Valley. Richard Cary wrote home about their movements; "we struck camp & moved across the river to Falling Waters where we bivouacked in a driving rain storm, the next day we pushed on to Bunker Hill 18 miles where we camped & yesterday came here 20 miles; the roads were very bad owing to the previous rains but otherwise we got along very well. We marched through Winchester the band playing the John Brown Army Hymn, Dixie, Yankee Doodle & other appropriate airs, the town seemed much deserted by all except soldiers & negroes through one of two ladies displayed Union flags & gave other tokens of pleasure at seeing us back again."[10]

On the return to Winchester, the men of Greene's brigade were outspoken in threats to the citizens (including two regiments who spoke of burning houses) because of alleged firing from houses on their retreat and women hurling bedroom crockery. Greene could not let these feelings of revenge take effect as is related to us by William Fox, the historian of the Twelfth Corps:

"The wise old brigadier hear, but said nothing. Just before entering the town he issued orders that the troops should march through the streets in column of fours, and that no officer or man should leave the ranks for any reason whatever. As they entered the place the two disaffected regiments found themselves flanked y other troops closely on each side, and they were marched through Winchester without a halt, out into the fields beyond, feeling and looking more like a lot of captured prisoners than the gay, fighting fellows that they were. They cursed 'Old Greene' in muttered tones, but soon forgot it, guessed he was right, and in time cheered the general as nosily as any other regiments in the brigade."[11]

This potential destruction of Winchester was greater than previously known by the historian, as told by Charles F. Morse of the 2nd Massachusetts; "the night before we arrived in W. a guard on some government property was shot by a citizen, he died almost instantly, The citizen was rescued by the provost guard from the soldiers who would have torn him to pieces if they had been allowed. The private property adjacent to where the soldier was shot, including about twelve buildings was set fire to and destroyed by order of the provost marshal."[12] Greene knew his actions were subjected to criticism by the men, but in time they understood and respected him.

That was for the future, but the men won't see him as a good officer (perhaps of the pro-Gordon sentiment). "Genl. Greene (our Brigadier) is a finiking old Jackass: takes all day to do nothing & puts guards on all the houses to prevent the soldiers from doing any harm to the property of scoundrelly cut-throats of secessionists who inhabit this valley," stated one soldier.[13]

Another wrote, "our present Brig. Genl. Named Green[e] is a perfect old fool worse than ever Abercrombie was, he puts guards on rebel wheat fields, strawberry beds, clover fields, etc., etc., and probably when the season arrives will have us gather in the rebel crops and guard their barns."[14] Henry Comey told his sister about the General; "nobody likes Gen. Green[e]. He is so much like old Gen. Patterson. He will not let men get water on the march, and he takes on half the men to guard the citizens. Besides he is an old Beatty."[15]

An aide to Colonel Gordon, Henry Bruce Scott, had returned from Washington and expressed his feelings in a more forgiving manner; "Gen. Green[e], I parted with, with the best feelings. He is very kind and gentlemanly but not much of a military man. His knowledge is all theoretical, but the theory must be changed with great heat or wet, which he seems to forget. He puts a guard over every old secesher and if the men pull down rails to sit on when they halt, he makes them put them up and downs a great many little things which makes him unpopular."[16]

For discipline to take hold within the brigade, Greene needed the support of his officers. One night the men of the 29th Pennsylvania had torn down a fence and used it for firewood, which Greene discovered the next day and made them build a fence to replace it. Hearing of this, the boys of the 2nd Massachusetts avoided that problem and took firewood cut for home consumption out of a neighboring back yard.[17] Another incident involved an officer's refusal to put a guard on a house (despite the request of the owner) and let the men take onions and other items from the garden. He grabbed some lettuce for himself and ignored the threats of the owner![18] Luckily for the officer that Greene was not approached by the owner, because disciplinary measures were warranted.

The brigade left their camp at Newton on June 18th and marched twelve miles, first covered in dust and then with rain at intervals, bringing out a rainbow as they arrived near Front Royal.[19] Was this a good sign for the future for the men or Greene? They found out in a weeks time. Before the move to the Front Royal

area, Brigadier General George Sears Greene wrote to the Governor
of New York in relation to his family; "I am anxious of having my
son Charles T. Greene as my Aie[e] de Camp & with to have him
commissioned that he may be available for that duty. He is now in
Company G, 22 NY Militia Not. Grays in the service [west] of
Baltimore. He is 20 years of age, has been well drilled in the
company and is a steady, moral & reliable young man."[20]

Greene thought the Governor might give him the same chance
as he did with him earlier in the year; "I should be glad to have
him in the corps if possible as is expected that the Ajt. Of that
Regt [60th NY} will be made Asst Ajt. Gl. Which will make a
vacancy in their regt. If the Adjt. should be taken from the regt,.
But an appointment of 2 Lt. in any regiment will make him available
for my Aid[e]."[21]

Although Charles may have approached his father about joining
a regiment of volunteers, George S. Greene wanted to have him on
his staff so he could learn & grow with the service and be ready for
a command of his own. George also gave comfort to Martha by
having their son by his side and he needed men of his staff that did
not hold resentment towards him because of Gordon's departure.
While Greene found out that Charles was approved for a
commission and joined his father's staff, his tenure as commander
of the Third Brigade came to an end.

Returning from Washington with his promotion to Brigadier
General, George H. Gordon was given specific orders restoring
him to his old command. Greene turned over the command to
Gordon on June 26, 1862.[22] It was obvious to him that the men
favored Gordon and their feelings to some degree was expressed by
a 2nd Massachusetts soldier; "Gen'l Gordon is going to have
command of this brigade the difficulties in the way having been
smoothed over & all will be pleased with the change Gen'l Greene
being very unpopular on account of the extraordinary care he takes
to protect the property of the most rabid secessionists, a course
which I believe to be fraught with evil encouraging the rebels &
disappointing Union men."[23]

If the men were generally happy with the change, then how

did General Greene feel? He had every right to feel disappointment, but not for his actions with the brigade. Despite the recent promotion, Greene outranked Gordon by seniority and Gordon could have been reassigned. Greene had not received the support of his junior officers, since they shared the same feelings of the enlisted men in discipline and morale. Finally, because Greene's personality was looked at as rigid or stern in the short time together, they were reluctant to give him a fair chance (if that was possible for anyone taking over after the retreat). Only the advent of time can they realize what Greene tried to do for the Brigade and respected him for it.

Since no tears were being shed on Greene's departure, one soldier regretted the leaving of a friend; "I feel rather sorry for Charley Horton, he undoubtedly expected to be appointed by Gordon Adj. Gen. I imagine Charley was rather in politic in his course with the rest of Gordon's staff, bullying considerable while he held a position there. We all bade him goodbye the other night, and I doubt whether we ever see him again in the regiment, he went off with Genl. Greene to Washington."[24]

Charles P. Horton, born in Boston in 1837, had graduated from Harvard in 1857 (did he know George Jr. from those days?) and was a coal merchant at the outbreak of the war. At the time of Greene's command of the brigade, Horton was a 1st Lt. in Company K. He believed his best chance for promotion was to follow Greene and Greene needed a man capable of handling the responsibilities of staff work. It was a good match for both as Horton was promoted to Captain and Assistant Adjutant General on his staff and Greene had found a valuable officer during their service together.[25]

They went to Washington, with Brigadier General George Sears Greene reporting to General Pope.

Pope was made the commander of the Army of Virginia, which included Banks Corps (known as the Fifth Corps). This Corps was renamed the Second Corps, Army of Virginia, and Greene was ordered on July 9, 1862 to take command of the Third Brigade, Second (General Augur) Division of the Second Corps, which was located in Warrenton, Virginia.

Those regiments, close to 1,420 men under his command were the 60th New York, 78th New York, 3rd Delaware, 1st District of Columbia, and the Purnell Legion of Maryland.[26]

With this new assignment, Greene could be pleased that he had the 60th New York under his command and served as a role model for the other regiments. One 60th New Yorker called it, "the best and largest" and was glad to be under the General's command (despite some sickness in camp due to the summer heat).[27]

After a few days in camp, he returned to Washington to put in a request for additional staff members; "I believe that the law allowing extra aid[e] de camp is suspended but it is thought that it would not be required in lieu of the 300,000 men to be raised & if so there may be a chance of the appointment which we desire. Cannot you ask some member to look after it & see that the paper gets to the president."[28]

The time was getting closer for Greene's first battle as a leader, with General Pope moving the Union army to confront the Army of Northern Virginia. Getting his troops prepared, an old problem (typhoid fever) resurfaced that caused Greene to be concerned about the 60th New York; "On the 30th (July), fever raged like the plague. We had over two hundred cases. The Medical Director gave it as his opinion that the regiment would go to destruction, unless immediately withdrawn from the field' and Gen. Augur made application to Gen. Pope to send us either to some of the fortifications about Washington, or to Harper's Ferry. On the first of August the Corps was paraded to listen to the Order and Address with reference to the death of Ex-President (Martin) Van Buren. After the parade the troops were drilled by General Banks The Sixtieth numbered only about one hundred, and of these several were so debilitated that they fell out of the ranks before the drill was completed."[29]

It turned out that Greene had met Stonewall Jackson's soldiers about 8 miles southwest of Culpeper Court House, near Cedar Mountain. Because of detachment from his brigade, which numbered 457 men, including the Sixth Maine battery, Brigadier General George S. Greene was held in reserve.[30] General Banks had Augur's Division to the left of Orange Culpeper Road, comprising of Geary's Brigade, then Prince's Brigade, and Greene's Brigade on the extreme left. He was left with only two regiments, the 78th New York and 1st District of Columbia, making his brigade the smallest of the field. With the danger of being flanked by the Confederate infantry on Cedar Mountain, Greene's men (comprised of 372) supported the Federal guns near Mitchell's Station Road.[31] This road traveled south of Orange Culpeper Road and parallel to Cedar Mountain.

The Battle of Cedar Mountain on August 9, 1862 began with Banks artillery opening up on Jackson's troops, who were deployed, not knowing how large a force they faced. This was due to cover given to the Federals by the cornfield and the dense woods South and North of Orange Culpeper Road.[32] Supporting Captain Freeman McGilvery's Sixth Maine Battery, Greene watched the bombardment from the ridge of the Mitchell's Station Road against General Ewell (directly opposite) and General Winder (to Greene's right) on the Confederate right. The fighting commenced at 2 o'clock in the afternoon.

"We were posted on the extreme left of our line of battle and for three long hours we were subjected to a most cruel cross fire from the enemies Artillery. It was the most terrible fire I ever saw, but our boys stood nobly to their guns. Gen. Augur repeatedly sent us orders to hold our position at all hazards as we were preventing the enemy from effecting a flank movement," wrote a Maine gunner.[33]

It was a severe test of skill for the gunners of both armies. In his report after the battle, Greene stated the precision of the Confederate batteries, "their round shot striking the top of the ridge & falling among the men & horses of the command."[34] But the Confederates had casualties too and one of them was the death of General Winder, who had left the ambulance and was giving directions to his gunners when struck by a shell that plowed through his left arm and side. He fell straight back and his body quivered on the ground. Upon his removal from the front line, Winder had died within a few hours.[35]

The Federal troops launched their attack at 5:30 pm, making gains in the center and on the right. The Confederates were being pushed back, but reinforcements were being brought up and Stonewall Jackson rode up into the melee, brandishing his sword (with the scabbard still attached) above his head to rally his men. Due to casualties and lacking reserves to break Jackson's line, Banks saw his army stall and provided Jackson the opportunity to counterattack.[36]

Daylight remained and the Confederates advanced against these tired and disorganized soldiers. The Federals were pushed back on the right and the center. General Greene was now in command of Augur's division (center) as the fighting retreat left Gen. Augur wounded, along with his other brigade commanders incapacitated (Geary was wounded in arm and Prince captured) from rendering service. His actions in this crisis received praise from Generals Augur and Pope (who arrived on the field late that day).[37] He worked to stabilize his front line with the depleted ranks and have the artillery slow down the onrushing Confederates.

Wounded in the left arm during the retreat, Lt. Charles E. Jayne of Company C, 102nd New York Volunteers stated; "It was a terrible fight out of 16 of our company that went into the fight 3 only escaped without being killed or wounded. The old regiment that was in the fight say they never saw anything like it."[38]

Jackson wanted to continue the advance, as testified by Edward Wiggin Jr. of the Sixth Maine Battery; "Under cover of the darkness after the sun had been down sometime their infantry charged on us and were quite near us before we discovered them. We gave them a warm welcome with grape and canister but as all the rest of our forces had retired it was useless for us to stay longer. So we limbered up at the order from Gen. Green[e] and left the field amid a perfect shower of Minie balls. My gun was engaged during the whole time, fired about 150 rounds, and was the last gun to leave the field. There were five batteries engaged on our side and our loss was more than all the rest put together. So you may judge our position was rather a hard one for raw troops."[39]

With General Ewell's men tired after their pursuit, they came across in the night some of the Federal ammunition wagons, one gun, and other supplies. There were some casualties from intermitted firing and prisoners taken due to the close proximity of both sides. Greene's command (involved in the battle as observers on the left flank) of the 78th New York and 1st District of Columbia suffered the loss of three wounded and 24 prisoners at the end of the fighting.[40] Total casualties differ with one source estimating 1,276 for the Confederates in killed, wounded and captured to 2,381 for the Federals and another gave figures of 1,418 and 2,403 respectively.[41]

After a flag of truce to bury the dead and collect the wounded the next day, Jackson departed with his army August 11th southward and deceived Pope and Banks by having campfires along the line when it became night. There was no immediate pursuit.[42] Due to the losses of many officers in the battle, Brigadier General George Sears Greene remained in command of the division. He could be proud of his contributions to the battle.

Greene had secured the Army's left flank in the opening and closing part of the fighting. As he indicated in his report to Banks, the Rebel General Winder was killed by the Maine guns under his command, depriving Jackson of a valuable officer and hurting the Southerners in their future campaigns.[43] He moved from brigade to division command, taking control of the fluid situation on his front when the Confederates threatened to break through and the command structure was breaking down because of losses.

At this critical moment, discipline and firm leadership was needed. George Sears Greene provided that and with the aid of the fading daylight kept Stonewall Jackson from repeating his exploits of sending Banks in retreat as Greene had witnessed at Winchester. His attention was now concentrated in dealing with the movements of the troops in Northern Virginia, but while Greene had fought to preserve the U.S. Government on the battlefield, he was remembered on the home front in preserving life.

It was reported in the New York Times of the great event not related to war news, concerning the Croton Aqueduct. During the celebration of the new Reservoir at Central Park, the crowd listened to the speeches (amid the music playing & firing of cannon) of the day. Speaking on behalf of the contractors Fairchild, Walker, Coleman & Co., Mr. Luther R. Marsh spoke about those who were given the credit for the hard work put into this project. He said "We miss here now, one was with us then, the engineer in charge." He was speaking of General George S. Greene, and commented of his participation on the battle of Cedar Mountain.[44]

How ironic that he missed this crowning achievement in the civil engineering work of this life. Providing life to the citizens of New York for generations to come was a great advertisement for further financial gains in his advancing years. After all, he provided for Anna (daughter) and Francis who were with Martha at home. Some officers would have resigned to return to civilian life because of Finances or take part in upcoming elections for political office. Not Greene. As long as the war went on, George Sears Greene was determined to stay in the ranks and his services were needed even more with the upcoming Maryland Campaign.

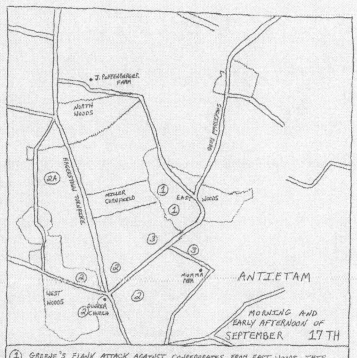

● J. POFFENBERGER
FARM

NORTH
WOODS

HAGERSTOWN TURNPIKE

2A

MILLER
CORNFIELD

1

EAST WOODS

1

3

SMOKETOWN ROAD

3

MUMMA
FARM

ANTIETAM

2

A

2

WEST
WOODS

DUNKER
CHURCH

2

MORNING AND
EARLY AFTERNOON OF
SEPTEMBER   17 TH

① GREENE'S FLANK ATTACK AGAINST CONFEDERATES FROM EAST WOODS. THIS
FIRST PHASE OF THE FIGHTING ENDED BEYOND MUMMA FARM AND NEAR DUNKER
CHURCH.

② GREENE HELD POSITION OUTSIDE OF WEST WOODS BY TURNING BACK TWO UNCOORDINATED
CONFEDERATE ATTACKS IN SECOND PHASE OF FIGHTING.

②A FORCED OUT OF NORTH WOODS AND TO THE WEST OF HAGERSTOWN TURNPIKE, THE CONFEDERATES
REGROUP AND SEND GREENE'S DETACHED BRIGADE (DOUBLEDAY'S DIVISION) IN RETREAT.

③ WITH REINFORCEMENTS, THE CONFEDERATES HIT BOTH OF GREENE'S FLANKS. UNABLE
TO HOLD, GREENE'S MEN FALL BACK UNTIL REINFORCEMENTS HALT THE CONFEDERATE ATTACK.

Chapter Ten

The Maryland Campaign

The late summer days approached the Virginian landscape with the armies of General Pope and General Lee maneuvering for advantage in the Second Manassas Campaign. But in the fighting that followed at the end of August 1862, Greene's division had not participated until it was too late. Casualties were relatively light during this battle because Banks Army was guarding supply trains (wagons) and covered the retreat of Pope's Army. In Greene's division (2nd), the number was 108, including 63 captured or missing from the Purnell Legion, Maryland.[1] Most likely these soldiers were stragglers that Jackson's Corps had caught on the field at Chantilly on September 2nd.

A Maine soldier voiced his frustrations of the retreat on Greene; "The 2nd Division in advance. Greene, the most contemptible old Beatty I ever saw is in command and manages or mismanages things were queerly. We kept on the same road, one running between the Old Pike and the RR and halted many times to allow the teams of Greene's division to move along."[2] Although Greene rode among his men and heard the grumbling and saw the fatigue in their eyes, he knew the discipline in the ranks was there. Morale was at a low ebb as the Army retreated into Maryland to the safety of the forts that surrounded Washington D.C.

With the removal of Pope and Banks, General McClellan was reinstated as commander of the Army of the Potomac. As part of that reorganization, Banks's Army was named the Twelfth Corps, with Joseph K. F. Mansfield as its commanding General.[3] General

Alpheus S. Williams took over temporary command until Mansfield's arrival.

Brigadier General George Sears Greene had three brigades in his 2nd Division to command. The regiments in those brigades are as follows: First Brigade-5th Ohio, 7th Ohio, 29th Ohio, 66th Ohio and 28th Pennsylvania; Second Brigade—3rd Maryland, 102nd New York, 109th Pennsylvania, and 111th Pennsylvania; and Third Brigade-3rd Delaware, Purnell Legion Maryland, 60th New York and 78th New York.[4] A notable exception is the 1st District of Columbia, formally a part of Greene's brigade at Cedar Mountain, was basically no longer an organized regiment due to a high number of desertion and sickness. It played no role in the Maryland Campaign.

As General Robert E. Lee had his Confederates cross the Potomac and move through Maryland, McClellan had restored morale in the Federal Army and had the soldiers marching out to find Lee's men. Writing home to his brother and sister from their camp near Poolesville, Maryland, Captain Merwin Eugene Cornell of Company D, 102nd New York was not worried about the Rebels; "I have gone through all safe and sound. Have had a good many balls pass very near me. Yet I don't think the ball is yet made that is agoing to take me down."[5] Cornell complained about taking on additional duties of his brother (Lt. Stephen S. Cornell) who went away on leave and felt he should resign because an officer should not leave his command during this time. Knowing that this battle could be his last, he said "I trust in God. If I should fall on the battlefield while *doing my duty*—I die happy."[6]

A corporal with the 28th Pennsylvania had looked forward to receiving new conscripts to replace their losses for their next fight. When none had arrived, he told his father "I think they are filling up Regiments that have a longer time to serve than ours," and believed the politicians had interfered with the Army's displacement of reinforcements.[7]

The Twelfth Corps reached Frederick, Maryland and set up camp on September 13th on the same site that Confederate troops had been only yesterday. Finding documents wrapped around cigars in the field, the men of the 27th Indiana turned them over to their commander. Deemed as genuine, it was a copy of Lee's Special Orders No. 191, that showed McClellan the routes of march and the timetable that the Southerners in their dispersed columns had followed. Presented with this new information, it was essential for McClellan to bring the Army of the Potomac upon Lee's scattered forces before they could reunite.[8]

McClellan had the Army move west, as one of Greene's men recalled, "As we marched along the dusty roads, many ladies came out to meet us bearing bowls of bread and milk. Now for a while we marched through fields of wheat to give the artillery a chance to catch up. All seemed in good spirits, eager to fight and put an end to the war. We have loaded ourselves with sacks of food in the towns through which we had passed, not knowing that we would not get time to eat it."[9]

The tiring march had brought them to South Mountain, but they were put in reserve for the September 14th battle. The division of Confederate General D. H. Hill had held the Federals, giving Lee time to consolidate his army. Hill retreated during the night and the next day, one of the Twelfth Corps saw "the road were strewn with broken wagons, cannons and tents containing wounded rebels" as they marched toward Keedysville.[10]

As both armies were near, on September 16th, McClellan hesitated to launch an all-out attack against Lee, who continued to bring his army together. Only a short distance from Antietam creek, a member of the 7th Ohio remembered the scene: "Everywhere the brigades and divisions of the other corps were going into position.

As far as the view extended were regiments, many of them closed en masse on close column by division that looked like solid squares with their colors in the center. It was a grand, a memorable sight."[11]

Towards the evening, "random gins ere fired and the sharpshooters continued to peck at each other," said a 60th New York soldier and General Alpheus Williams told his daughters that it was "so dark, so obscure, so mysterious, so uncertain: with the occasional rapid volleys of pickets and outposts, the low solemn sound of the command as troops came into position, and withal so sleepy that there was a half-dreamy sensation about it all."[12]

The men had bedded down, tired and anxious, but knew tomorrow they were going to fight a battle. It could decide the fate of the Union. The Twelfth Corps is 1/12 miles in the rear of General Hooker's First Corps, in a northeastern direction of the J. Poffenberger farm. The Battle of Antietam (named after the creek by Northerners) ran in a north-south direction of the battle lines. For Greene's division, they were posted on either side of the Smoketown Road. It runs north-east of the Hagerstown Turnpike. The area consisted of woods, a cornfield, ridges and farms. One building that became a focal point of the fighting was the Dunker Church, a plain white building jutting outside of the West Woods along the Hagerstown Turnpike.

The morning fog greeted the soldiers as they awakened and started fires to cook their breakfast, but many were unable to enjoy their hardtack or tin of sliced potatoes because of orders to fall in.[13] "At the first sound of cannon at daylight on the morning of the 17th instant, the command was put in movement, each regiment, by order of General Mansfield, marching in columns of companies, closed in mass." said General Williams.[14] The reports vary, but the time estimated of Greene's arrival was 6:30 AM.

General Greene's men deployed on a ridge to the left of Gordon's brigade (Williams division) at the Smoketown Road to the area north of Dunker Church. At this time, Greene had his Third Brigade taken from him, due to the request of reinforcements for General Doubleday's division. First Corps, on their right to stabilize their front.[15] This action proved to be a major factor in the outcome of Greene's portion of the battlefield. Greene reported that day that his division consisted of 2,504 men.[16] Those numbers were further reduced with the 29th Ohio and 109th Pennsylvania Infantry (along with the Third Brigade) on detached service, giving Greene close to 1,727 men.[17]

It is important to begin here with the Third Brigade because they had been forgotten in various studies of Antietam through the years and raised the question: Was this action necessary to help

the First Corps on the right or could they have remained with
Greene's division? As they marched on in silence, Donald Brown
of the 60th New York saw "the country was open and almost level
and the burning sun pored down on the dead and dying.

We were under fire now and marching along in the rear of the
first line of battle to take our place on the right wing.

Shot and shell were cracking through our ranks."[18]

Writing to the local paper back home, 2nd Lieutenant Stephen
H. Borgardus, Jr. of the Purnells Maryland Legion stated "About
7am. Our brigade was ordered forward as the first reserve. The
boys went willingly, although they had had nothing to eat since
the night before. In a little while we were ordered to advance and
enter into action."[19] As they approached Hooker's First Corps, the
soldiers saw a cornfield in their front and woods (West Woods) to
their right. When fire came in on their flank, Captain J.C.O.
Redington took his Company (C) and kept casualties down "with
admirable skill and effect" by clearing the enemy sharpshooters in
the woods.[20] However, many fell before they reached their place in
line, as one soldier had seen his comrade shot, cried out "Jesus, I
am shot" and fell dead to the ground.[21]

A soldier wrote "we were ordered to take the cornfield, and
support the 124th Pennsylvania Volunteers, a new regiment."
Another expressed his fears as if he was all alone, "I had experienced
a trembling sensation in watching those long lines of grey uniforms,
stretching far to the left, swaying restlessly to and fro, like the
waves of a swelling sea."[22]

Here was Colonel William B. Goodrich, Greene's successor of
the 60th New York, leading the Third Brigade in combat for the
first time. A lawyer from Canton & editor of a newspaper before
the war, Goodrich was a favorite among the New Yorkers. As the
Rebel lines moved forward, "our colonel was fifty feet in the rear of
the line of battle, his right hand resting on the neck of his little
black horse. Calm and brave he was, giving his command, "Steady!
Shoot low!"" remembered Donald Brown.[23]

This 60th New Yorker had turned around to view the solid
shot and shell fall into the timber behind them. As he did, Brown

saw Goodrich put his left hand to his heart. He had been killed by a sharpshooter (possibly up in a tree) from those woods to the right, giving cover fire to their advancing line.[24] While this was taking place, Williams (who took command of the Corps after General Mansfield was mortally wounded) wanted to see what happened to those men and to see about their return to Greene's command. He wrote "As I entered the narrow lane running to the right and front a battery opened a cross-fire and Pittman and myself had the excitement of riding a mile or so out and back under its severest salutations. We found Gen. Doubleday sheltered in a ravine and apparently in bland ignorance of what was doing on his front or what need he had of my troops, except to relieve his own."[25]

The battery that the Confederates had moved across the cornfield was causing problems on their flank, but General Williams had it silenced by placing one battery himself and got support from another in the rear.[26] Despite this success, the rebels had fixed bayonets and attacked, when their ranks began to give way. The mounting casualties and fatigue contributed to their right being turned, "we fell back in utter confusion, trying desperately to hold up the flag and assembling in groups which were shot down like cattle. Thought fire and smoke, I could see the mounted officers of the enemy, sword in hand, urging on their yelling ranks."[27]

One soldier recalled the cornfield "a horrible sight." He viewed dead rebels in different positions "Here, one shot through the heart; there one with his leg torn off; and still farther on, a trunk without a head."[28] A wounded rebel prisoner had cursed the Union soldier's Enfield Rifles, which accounted for 60 to 70 dead rebels found with head wounds in the cornfield.[29]

It slowed their advance, but the Confederates pushed on. Greene's men had given enough time for the army to bring up additional batteries on the ridge to their rear. Now the ranks of the advancing Confederates were met with solid shot and shell. As they closed ranks and moved toward the batteries, the artillerymen switched to loading grape and canister. These shotgun blast of flying metal was too much for the Rebels to overcome, as they left their dead and wounded at the farthest advance of the ridge.[30]

The fighting that had started early in the morning had by 12 noon saw both sides near the same lines, with the Confederates at the edge of the cornfield and in the woods (West Woods). The Third Brigade was kept in line, except for the Purnell Maryland Legion, which was sent to General Greene after repeated request for reinforcement during the fighting with his other brigades.

Brigadier-General George Sears Greene could not have imagined the horrors of the battlefield as the sun burned away the morning fog. For almost two hours, the fighting had gone back and forth through the East Woods, Miller's Cornfield and along the Hagerstown Turnpike.[31] Dead and wounded soldiers, horses, rifles, ammunition chests were some of the items that littered the ground. As Hood's Texans, Colquitt's Georgians, and McRae's North Carolinians were sending the remainder of Hooker's men back out of Miller's Cornfield, Greene reported "the division encountering the enemy in the first woods in our front drove them before it, and entering the open ground partly covered with corn, moved to the left and took position of the right of the post and rail fence inclosing the field on the right of the burned house (Poffeberger's)."[32]

The two brigades had deployed their troops, received some fire as they moved forward from the northeast, to hit the Confederates in their right flank. One of the first casualties came from the 102nd New York, as Captain M. Eugene Cornell, who had thought he could not be a casualty, was shot in the head and killed at the front of his command.[33] McRae's North Carolinians were the first ones to feel the momentum change as panic ensued when an officer of the 5th North Carolina saw Greene's soldiers coming towards them. Words of being flanked were shouted and "The most unutterable stampede occurred. It was one of those marvelous flights that beggar explanation or description," stated McRae.[34]

An Alabama officer in Hood's division did not panic, but said Greene achieved "a terrible and overwhelming attack on our front," with fire on three sides.[35] Moving forward, Greene's brigades went into the East Woods and fought tenaciously, which forced the

Confederates to retreat. A large number of prisoners are taken
including some officers.[36]

One of those officers may have been a North Carolinian office
who had been grabbed by a wounded Captain from the 5th Texas
Furious at the panic taking place, he had abruptly reversed a
order to fire on those retreating North Carolinians. The captai
shouted above the gunfire for the man's name and regimen
Thinking only of his safety, the officer said "I'll be damned if I wi
tell you!" and joined his comrades who continued on their way.

The 7th Ohio reached the crest of a hill in the East Woods ar
saw many of the rebels rallied behind a rail fence to stop Green
advance.[38] In front of the fence was a cornfield that the 5th & 7
Ohio regiments followed the rebels into. Major Collins report
"while in the corn our regiment engaged a Georgia regiment in
hand-to-hand combat, using clubbed guns, a portion of the m
having no bayonets."[39] The adjutant of the 7th Ohio used his sw
to make a Confederate officer surrender and the color-bearer lost
flag when it was ripped from its staff by a 7th Ohio soldier.[40]

Eugene Powell of the 66th Ohio had dissuaded Major Cra
of the 7th Ohio that those troops were Federals when they :
them at the rail fence. Supporting the 7th Ohio on their l
Powell gave the order to fire and stated in later years, "the sigh
the fence, where the enemy [Colquitt's men] was standing w
we gave our first fire, was beyond description." When the 2
Pennsylvania fired into the rear of the Georgians, after clearing
woods, "dead men were literally piled upon and across each othe

Overwhelmed and falling back in disorder, Private B.
Witcher of the 6th Georgia encouraged a soldier to stand fast
him, and pointed to the neatly aligned ranks still lying to
right and left. He yelled back to him those men are dead
showed him by firing a shot into a man a few yards away or
ground. The man did not move. This convinced Witcher to
the retreat.[42]

This created a opening in the Confederate line that Brig
General George S. Greene wanted to exploit and coordinate
attack before Robert E. Lee sent reinforcements to plug tha

in the line. In taking prisoners during this short fight, a soldier of the 28th Pennsylvania saw no guards on the Rebels as "whom we had simply ordered to go to the rear," so they could continue their advance.[43] One soldier unable to follow was John P. Murphy. A private with the 5th Ohio Infantry, this Irish immigrant in fighting Law's brigade of Hood's division, captured the flag of the 13th Alabama Infantry and was wounded in the left leg by a minie ball. For his actions that day, John P. Murphy received his new country's highest award, the Congressional Medal of Honor.[44]

It was fortunate for the 111th Pennsylvania because they had met heavy resistance as they reached the edge of the East Woods. "Our men were dropping very fast, and we could not see the effect of our fire," wrote one soldier.[45] The smoke on the field may have given some protection at that moment for the Confederates. Cheers were heard in the woods as the 111th Pennsylvania followed the retreating troops. Among the prisoners taken to the rear by Peter Fraley of Company I was an Ass't. Adj't. General belonging to D. H. Hill's division, Longstreet's Corps.[46]

Due to the smoke or poor communication, Major Walker had moved the 111th Pennsylvania to the right, connecting with the 28th Pennsylvania to pour a crossfire into the retreating Rebels. The rest of the Second Brigade had wheeled to the left, which created an opportunity for the Confederates to push reinforcements through this gap.

Lieut. Col. James C. Lane of the 102nd New York reported of their advance to the left near the burning building in the field. This was the Mumma farm, which was torched by General D. H. Hill's orders so Federal sharpshooters could not use them. Lane wrote, "From this building our men pursued the enemy to the corn-field in advance, where the One hundred and second halted and commenced firing at a battery, which was playing on the right of the brigade, just beyond the cornfield. This battery retired immediately after our opening fire upon it."[47]

The opportunity passed and the brigade came together again as they moved to the right. The Ohioans had knocked down the fence rails, passing the enemy dead and recalled one 7th Ohio

soldier, "we pusued them like hounds after the frightened deer."[48] Greene's division approached the Dunker Church, near the Hagerstown Pike with huzzahs and "for a few minutes the air was blue with expletives" from Sergeant Jere G. Chafflin because a rebel bullet hit him on the shin.[49]

Near the church, Private Cornet remembered "we discovered a very large body of troops were advancing up the slope towards us." After they began firing on the 28th Pennsylvania, the regiment rose up as one man and poured in another tremendous volley at point blank range. Casualties had mounted on both sides.[50]

General George Sears Greene was told by his commanders they were low on ammunition and they stayed behind a low ridge across the Hagerstown Turnpike. However, Greene had seen the 102nd New York regiment advance, which exposed their flanks to Confederate fire. He rode ahead of them, putting himself in the line of fire and shouted for the regiment to halt. "You are bully boys, but don't go any further! Halt where you are! I will have a battery here to help you," Greene yelled over the roar of the battlefield.[51]

Besides replenishing their cartridge boxes, the brigades also needed artillery support. Greene had seen that the woods (West Woods) had many Rebels and a battery had received casualties because of their advance beyond infantry support (one gun was brought back by volunteers from Greene's men).[52] The 5th & 7th Ohio regiments had fixed bayonets behind Monroe's battery to hold their position, and waited for the ammunition to be brought up.[53] The fire along the line grew and the colors of the 5th Ohio was seen by the soldiers to fall as a shell exploded among the color guard. Perhaps looking as a critical moment, the Confederates of Joseph Kershaw's South Carolina brigade moved out of the woods, past the Dunker Church to attack.[54]

It was a sight to behold for the Ohio troops when they saw General Greene personally escorting a six-gun Rhode Island Battery to the left of the brigade, under the direction of Captain John A. Tompkins. They cheered Greene, looking "so heroic and knightly," and he acknowledged his men amid the roar of the battle, by rising up in the stirrups and lifting his hat to them. "Hold your place there, boys" said one of the Rhode Islanders, "we will stand by you while there is a shot in the locker!" [55]

Laying down of the ridge, with fixed bayonets and resupplied with ammunition, the oncoming troops of Kershaw's South Carolina Brigade were allowed to approach at close range (the estimates vary from 25 yards to 70 yards). They rose up, took aim and fired.[56] Samuel Rowan of the 2nd South Carolina fell while holding the colors with a wound in the right arm. Lieutenant William Darby, who only 12 days earlier expressed his desire in a letter to live and come home, was killed. Lieutenant Solomon Lorick moved to the front, called to his men to follow, waved his sword, and fell badly wounded in the face.[57]

The South Carolinians had many killed and wounded, trying to return fire, but as Major Walker of the 111th Pennsylvania stated "we rushed forward to the mouths of the cannon, handsomely repulsing their charge."[58]

Robert Shand of the 2nd South Carolina spoke for both sides saying, "Men were falling all around me, and I could see numbers of the enemy falling in my front." One of those Pennsylvania soldiers came in Shand's view "I aimed at the one who stood third from the color bearer in my from and pulled trigger. He threw up his arms and fell to the ground."[59]

From the cornfield down to the Dunker Church, Greene's men moved forward, with the Confederates having retreated into the West Woods. In a short time, a second brigade joined Kershaw's men in attacking Greene's men. The Confederate attacks were uncoordinated, which hampered their efforts to defeat Greene's advance. Lt. Colonel Powell of the 66th Ohio remembered, "when they were within close range our men gave them a volley so destructive that the enemy again broke for the shelter of the woods. The artillery fire again slackened and another line of the enemy moved out from the woods about the church."[60]

The Rhode Island Batteries of Monroe and Tompkins were the main targets of Kershaw's men, but they were repulsed, leaving many dead soldiers of the 3rd and 7th South Carolina in their area.[61] One Southerner felt it was the worse fire of cannons he had seen with cannonballs "dancing over the ground" during the entire war. Two of those shells shattered the formation of Company B in the 3rd South Carolina, killing and wounding nine men.[62]

During the advance of Greene's men against the retreating Rebels into the West Woods (for a second time), a 28th Pennsylvania soldier named Jacob George Orth in Company D came across the color guard of the 7th South Carolina. In a hand-to-hand encounter, although he was wounded in the shoulder, Orth captured their flag and is awarded the Medal of Honor for his actions. A messmate of Orth's, Corporal Henry Hayward wrote home that George "shot the traitor that held it and took it from him," and each man tore off a piece of the flag before it was turned over to headquarters.[63]

They had taken the high ground east of the Dunker Church and crossed the Hagerstown Turnpike and into the West Woods. Greene knew the men were fatigued and ran low of ammunition again due to the severity of the fighting. Asking for reinforcements, General Williams saw the opportunity Greene presented for the Army of the Potomac in splitting Robert E. Lee's line and could destroy their chance of retreat. Because the Confederates were still in the woods along Greene's position, Williams sent a communication to General McClellan that stated "We hold the field at present. Please give us all the aid you can." As the time approached 10 am, there was a lull on the field and the soldiers looked on with uneasiness from both sides.[64]

Did Greene take the proper action by remaining or continued to advance? Since this was his first attack as a divisional commander, coordinating the movement was essential to bring maximum firepower and prevent gaps in the line that the Confederates could exploit and hit them on either flank. This had happened with the advance to the Mumma Farm, created a gap of almost half a mile and only because General Sedgwick moved up into this gap (as the rest of the Third Brigade moved to the right), it prevented the attack.[65]

Also, the Confederates were in broken fragments and could not take advantage without reinforcements. There were Confederates still in the West Woods and possible reinforcements close by and if

Greene had advanced, without reinforcements of his own or support on his flanks, it could have been a severe loss in men and jeopardize the Union's battle line. George S. Greene needed to consolidate his position, give his men the rest they needed and ammunition that was running low, and artillery support for the continued advance.[66]

This gave Colonel S. D. Lee, whose artillery had lost one gun to the 28th Pennsylvania and suffered heavy losses of men and horses, relief because he worried about the collapse of the Confederate left. Colonel Lee was told after delivering a message from General Hood that reinforcements were approaching and to hold his ground.[67]

The 28th Pennsylvania in Colonel Tyndale's brigade had given Colonel Lee a valid reason to worry by the heroic example of the color bearer, Lieutenant Joseph A. Moore related, "As we advanced towards the Dunker Church a rebel shell struck our flag bearer under the arms and cut him in two. I barely escaped it, being first by his side. Another of the color guard picked up the flag and had not proceeded twenty steps till he was shot, and a third man grasped the old flag carrying it to the fort but was also shot as we advanced steadily driving the rebels back. The fourth color bearer stood bravely through the terrible hail of shell and musketry until we had moved well down the open field facing the Sharpsburg Pike and opposite the old Church."[68]

The Confederates had better luck on Tyndale's right by pushing those troops back and wounded the Lt. Colonel of the 66th Ohio who had been sent by the Colonel to rally those unidentified troops.[69] Colonel Hector Tyndale, saw an opportunity to hit the Rebels in the flank as his troops were resupplied with ammunition, took off his hat and shouted loud over the field, "Boys, you have fought nobly; and by the Great God who looks down on me, you shall have your reward! What the Ohio and Pennsylvania boys can't do nobody can!"[70]

The plateau gave Tyndale the element of surprise as the Rebels were suddenly faced with Greene's men at the top of the hill and "poured into their advancing columns volley after volley." "So terrific was the fire of our men that the enemy fell like grass before the mower," said Major Crane of the 7th Ohio. For the next thirty minutes, the Confederates tried to maintain the ground they had taken, but fell back after Colonel Tyndale ordered the advance.

"We were cheered by the Ohio boys," remembered a 28th Pennsylvania soldier as they surged forward to prevent the enemy from regrouping. Many of the rebels captured, including some officers had feared being shot in the back because of the close quarter fighting. One soldier of the 7th Ohio, Edward Atwater of Company C, had captured a Lt. Col., pursuing him into the West Woods. Because of little ammunition and reinforcements, Greene had to withdraw the brigade, since his position on both flanks was unsecure.[71]

The artillery support arrived with a section of Knap's Pennsylvania Battery ordered to the left. Greene reported "the ground on our left and front was broken and wooded, an concealed the movements of the enemy. I placed the division in line, with the right thrown back, and sent forward skirmishers and sought re-inforcements from General Williams."[72]

Leaving for the battlefront at 10 o'clock, they assisted two other batteries that were engaged on the left and found themselves under fire from a Rebel battery. By 12 noon, one section of Knap's battery had been ordered to assist Tyndale's 28th Pennsylvania at a clump of woods, which was the advance of Greene's line.[73]

Sgt. David Nichol of Knap's Battery described what took place they received cheers from the 28th, "Her Col. Tingdale took out his spy glass & was showing McGill where a body of Rebels was. We thought that they must be some distance off. When they were through, McGill ordered us to the edge of the woods to unlimber & get in Battery. While in the act, a Rebel Brigade rose right up out of a cornfield, about 500 yards off, and poured a deadly volley into us."[74]

Because of their exposed position, despite infantry support, the battery was ordered back to their original position after suffering casualties from this surprise attack. "We had a good many horses killed and lost Number 2 gun," wrote one artillerymen and told his homefolk "James Marshall was shot in the side, he affected a piercing shriek and fell dead, Wm Anderson was shot in the elbo and make a narrow escape. Saml. Clark was also shot in arm, ball still in shoulder, Sergeant Shaw, wounded in side. John Lewis wounded in three places, very severe."[75] If General Greene was to continue the advance, it had to be soon or he may be forced back.

General Sumner, whose troops had been repulsed and saw Tyndale hit the Confederates in the flank, thought along with Greene in their situation. He wanted to continue the attack south toward Sharpsburg, since the Confederate guns were removed west of Hagertown Turnpike.

"Sumner would use the troops lying down on the eastern slope of the ridge, those he had seen enter the woods in the vicinity of the white building [both are Greene's men], and those that Gordon had passed as he entered the western woodlot."[76]

At this critical moment for their forces to regain the offensive, Greene searched for General Hancock for assistance as General Williams had told him that Hancock was only a few minutes away from his headquarters. Being unable to secure his support, "I had been absent but a few minutes," stated Greene as he rode back to his division's front and witnessed the fighting begin again.[77]

Sumner wanted to coordinate the advance and sent aides to tell General Greene to be ready to move.

However, the Confederates had launched their own attack that was done on both of Greene's flanks (1:30-2pm) separately and ended up as a coordinated assault. General Williams had received no reinforcements from McClellan, but had been able to send the Purnell Maryland Legion from the Third Brigade and General Gordan sent the 13th New Jersey Regiment to Greene. They were placed on Greene's right flank. Another regiment, the 27th Indiana was sent to Greene's command, but had exhausted their ammunition and forced to retire.[78]

The brigades of Ransom, McRae and two regiments (3rd Arkansas & 27th North Carolina) of John R. Cooke hit Greene on the right first and then left flank respectfully, pushing those troops back with superior numbers.[79] General Greene had placed the 13th

New Jersey himself on the extreme right of the brigade, in the woods on the left side of the Dunker Church. Through the trees was an open field and orders were given to fire at the unseen enemy. James Smith of the 13th New Jersey remembered, "with the first volley my comrade on the right, James Taylor, threw up his hands and fell forward, the blood spurting from his forehead in a thick stream."[80]

After fighting for an hour, orders were issued to stop firing as the smoke cleared showing the Confederates at the edge of the woods. The next event that took place was not mentioned by Greene, Col. Ezra Carman of the 13th NJ or the Confederates in the Official Records. The Confederates were seen moving towards them with their guns down, pretending to surrender and out of ammunition and held up a flag. The adjutant, Charles Hopkins tied a white handkerchief on a sword and went with another officer to meet them between the lines.

They came closer to the Union line and when the two stopped, the Confederates brought their arms up and fired a volley. The 13th New Jersey had hesitated, because of hitting their men caught in the open, but the firing resumed and all agreed it was a miracle when they returned to their ranks unharmed.[81]

These green troops in their first battle could not be blamed for this ruse, which gave the Rebels an advantage in making this flank attack. A Purnell Maryland Legion soldier, wounded and carried to the rear, had experienced a similar incident. "I was hit by a musket ball coming from a party of rebels carrying our flag. This was the second time I saw the same treachery during the battle."[82] They caused Greene's right flank to collapse.

At the same time, General Longstreet had ordered an attack to prevent his flank from being threatened in the center of the Confederate line. The men of Greene's division had started to withdraw to deal with their right when this attack was launched.

Brigadier-General John G. Walker reported "Battery after battery, regiment after regiment opened their fire upon them" and despite the heroic attempts of Greene's troops to rally and stop the onslaught "three times the enemy broke and fled before their impetuos charge."[83] The casualties and the retreat of Greene's soldiers gave one 102nd New Yorker the impression that "it seemed as if whole companies were wiped out of existence."

[84]Again, ammunition was running low and General Greene had given orders for the 28th Pennsylvania to withdraw from the woods and avoid being surrounded. Both Greene and Colonel Tyndale showed their bravery under fire.

The admiration for General Greene is related here by J. Addison More during the retreat:

"The writer was standing close to General Greene who was dismounted from his horse and holding the rein while directing the fighting. The fire of the enemy was terrific at this moment, when a ball struck his horse dead at his feet. The General without the least perturbation, and with the utmost coolness, deliberately took off the bridle and saddle and carried them in his arms. The enemy closed in on both flanks of the now depleted division and compelled it to fall back on the main line of battle. The General saved his saddle and bridle, and carried them back to his new battle line."[85]

Colonel Hector Tyndale was not so fortunate. As he moved along the line and encouraged the men from his horse, Tyndale had a ball strike him in the head, fracturing his skull. Since it hit a depression point in Tyndale's skull, the ball traveled down to the upper side of his neck, resting between the jaw and an artery.[86]

Lt. Barbridge and Corporal Hayward had seen their commander fall to the ground and brought him off the field, narrowly avoiding being hit from Confederate fire. "A ball knocked of[f] my cap and nearly took me from my feet," recalled one of Tyndale's rescuer's, but smiled after putting his hand to his head and saw there was no blood.[87] The wound was thought to be mortal, but he survived and had suffered from its effects until his death in 1880.

The area became like a hornet's nest with minie balls all around. One Pennsylvania soldier said "the rebels made their appearance on both our flanks, and in front, and opened fire on us. We fell back as rapidly as we could and narrowly escaped capture, and much slaughter." Seeing the Rebels setting up rails in a pile for a defense (they came from a fence), this soldier ran for his life and saw "the rebel balls zipped thick and fast about me and struck the ground as rapidly as hail."[88] The retreat came to an end with the Federal guns stabilizing the front lines.

General Williams told his daughters, "I was near one of our brass twelve-pound Napoleon gun batteries and seeing the Rebel colors appearing over the rolling ground I directed the two left pieces charged with canister to be turned on the point. In the moment the Rebel line appeared and both guns were discharged at short range.

Each canister contains several hundred balls. They fell in the very front of the line and all along it apparently, stirring up a dust like a thick cloud. When the dust blew away no regiment and not a living man was to be seen"[89]

A Georgian rebel had felt he could walk across the area of Greene's last stand and not touch the ground because it looked like a sea of blue.[90] Greene's men were ordered back to rest, to enjoy a drink of water for parched throats and clean their guns after fighting for almost seven hours. It was late afternoon that a commotion was heard along the line and the rider that approached Greene's soldiers was General McClellan. One 7th Ohio soldier felt "every soldier in the army has the utmost confidence in 'Little Mac!'" The division was ordered at 5:30 pm to be in position behind General William B. Franklin's Corps as a reserve, which ended the division's part in the battle and slept through the night.[91]

The see-saw battle of September 17th wasn't continued next day, both sides sent out burial details and helped the wounded. Their defensive postures changed on the 19th as Lee took his army back into Virginia and the Army of the Potomac contented to stay on the battlefield. Brigadier General George Sears Greene was proud of his division's actions on the field, "so many acted with distinguished gallantry," and with pride reported his son, Lieutenant Charles T. Greene "displayed great coolness under the most trying circumstances, and rendered most efficient service."[92]

Charles wrote to his sister, Susan about their experience that day:

"We were immediately drawn up in a line of battle and commenced driving the rebels through the woods and through a cornfield. When we got to the cornfield, Father sent me back to bring up the ammunition wagons, which I did as soon as I could, and joined him soon again. The rebels soon after, charged on a battery which we were supporting, but we repulsed them. Again they charged on the right of the battery so as to be out of range of the guns, when we repulsed them and drove them through a piece of woods.

In the first part of the engagement, the 3rd brigade was detached from us and at this time our force has gotten so scattered that it was reduced very much and I was sent for reinforcements. I got the 27th Indiana (infantry) but when it fired its 40 rounds it retired and I got the 13th New Jersey. These run and our small force had to retire. Just before this I was sent back for the Ammunition train, and, when I got up I found our force had retired. I was by father's side most of the time, and the only aid (sic) he had the greater part of the time. Mr. Shipman [an aid] was hit by a piece of shell before we had been on the field 5 minutes. Captain Horton had his horse shot."[93]

All that remained was to bury the dead, and take care of the wounded and prisoners. Major Pardee of the 28th Pennsylvania sent home a battle flag of the 8th South Carolina and some of those prisoners were friends from his school days. He said of Kershaw's brigade, "the regts. named suffered terribly under our fire. The ground was litterly covered with their killed and wounded."[94] Joseph Diltz of the 66th Ohio spoke of the dead like they were hogs, "the rebels was laying over the field bloated up as big as a horse and as black as a negro and the boys run over them and serch their pockets as unconcerned." He had done the same with "a big grayback as black as the ase of spade," but moved on in a happy mood.[95]

Another 66th Ohio man, William Sayre, told his father about how a shell had tore into some of the men and what remained of them lay exposed on a steep hill.[96] Donald Brown of the 60th New York ate his breakfast from the food of the dead of both armies.

While many wounded begged for water or shelter from the sun, others attempted to dress their own wounds.

Of those Confederates that Brown saw lying dead on the field, "a stark dead rebel remained, rifle in hand, one eye closed and the other wide open, shot in the act of taking aim." [97] Two days after the battle, Edward Wiggin, Jr. of the 6th Maine Battery (who had been with Greene at Cedar Mountain) came upon those Rebels that had fought Greene, "they lay in all positions just as they fell. One had his thumb and finger in his cartridge box, another had a cartridge in his teeth just ready to tear it."[98]

One moment on the battlefield stood out as a testimony to the soldiers of both armies. At the barn where the hospital was near the 13th New Jersey Regiment, a rebel soldier was seen carrying on his shoulders a wounded Yank. The group outside the barn cheered these men and brought them to the surgeons to be cared for immediately. The rebel had been directed to the area by the Yank because he was blind due to a minie ball that passed directly across both eyes. It never was forgotten by the soldiers.[99]

George Sears Greene had given McClellan his best opportunity to defeat Lee at Antietam and possibly decide the outcome of the war. The element of surprise enabled Greene to drive a wedge in the flank of the Rebels. First there had been confusion & then uncoordinated attacks by the Confederates which brought heavy casualties and an unstable front. Ammunition and reinforcements were problems that Greene had made efforts to solve.

The ammunition crisis was rectified twice, but found lacking when they were forced to retreat. Despite the cover of woods and cornfields, Greene could have overcome these obstacles if General McClellan had released troops to reinforce Greene as he and General Williams had requested. Even the return of the Third Brigade (800 men) that Williams had requested may have been enough to make McClellan commit his reserves to split Lee's Army.

Greene had brought 2,504 soldiers onto the field and suffered a total of 651 killed, wounded, and missing.[100] The Brigadier General's disciplinary methods & bravery on the field of battle proved their test of faith with the men of the division. Greene told the Adjutant General for McClellan that "those men would do as much service as the same number of men from any division of the service could do." Before Antietam, they "hooted and hissed" at Greene. After Antietam, they "got up three cheers for him."[101]

Chapter Eleven

Expeditions in Virginia

Brigadier General George Sears Greene had shown his superiors that he had earned a divisional command (not on a temporary basis because of officer casualties at Cedar Mountain) and perhaps a promotion to Major General for his actions at Antietam. Greene remembered two regiments in particular among his brave troopers who served the Union on that terrible day. The one was Purnell Maryland Legion, which had fought with the Third Brigade, and then conducted a fighting retreat on Greene's right in the afternoon. With 27 casualties out of 193 men in battle, stated one historian "they were complimented by Gen. Greene for their gallant conduct on the field."[1]

The other regiment was the 111th Pennsylvania, which had been on Greene's left and taken Kershaw's South Carolinians in the flank during their first sortie out of the West Woods. Greene praised their actions publicly and witnessed Colonel Stainrook present the depleted regiment an elegantly finished flag.

Starting with 220 men, only 105 men came out unharmed.[2] He recognized them in a letter to the Governor of Pennsylvania, Andrew Curtain, in a cordial tone of pride "The One Hundred and Eleventh Regiment behaved gallantly at the battle of Antietam, where I was witness to its good conduct."[3] It was time to move from the area and take stock in what was the Army's next move.

Greene's division marched with the 12th Corps towards Harper's Ferry, had crossed the pontoon bridge set up by engineers near the ruins of the bridge that stood as a testament to the earlier battle that month.

Government buildings of brick and stone were damaged also for the newcomers to see.[4] One soldier reflected more on the scenery of nature around Harper's Ferry, "the trees were in autumnal foliage, the current of the river was stiff and the water foaming," and felt the surrounding beauty left a person in awe by day or watched it by moonlight.[5]

The soldiers were sent out to the surrounding heights of Harper's Ferry to cut down timber and build fortifications to defend against the Rebels. Some timber was not good enough for soldiers as doors, boards, or bricks were used to fix up their living quarters. Despite their creative artistry, it could not keep out the large spotted adders that slithered into their tents and caused a ruckus of fear and laughter among the men.[6]

They had their spirits lifted on September 30, 1862 by General Greene, who issued a special order, so the troops could be mustered for pay. Many families suffered with a limited income and needed the pay from their loved ones. Since they had not received it a month ago because of their quick marching, Greene saw their encampment at Loudon Heights (near Harper's Ferry) as the first opportunity to relieve their anxieties and prevent desertions that may arise from hardships at home.[7]

Since Harper's Ferry was fortified, it had been vulnerable to attack due to the four heights that encompassed the town. Greene didn't want to be caught surrounded with rebel infantry and artillery on the heights like his old West Point cadet Colonel Miles, who surrendered the town and was killed there only days before Antietam. He sent out a reconnaissance to gather information on October 4, 1862, led by Lieutenant Wesley McGregor of the 78th New York Infantry. After being reinforced, he returned to Loudon Heights after three days and reported to Greene of rebel cavalry gathering cattle and bringing in conscripts. McGregor felt the out-lying towns could be held with a minimal force of cavalry or infantry if cavalry was not available.[8]

Greene could not take these measures in McGregor's report due to a change in command and was granted a leave of absence. Catching up to the 12th Corps, Brigadier General John White

Geary took over command of the 2nd Division from Greene at Loudon Heights. It could have wounded George Sears Greene's pride to have this volunteer officer, with only 3 days seniority replace him. Why replace a former regular army officer, who had commanded a brigade, and division, and was highly praised from senior officers for his performance at Cedar Mountain and Antietam? The reason was politics. Geary had been wounded at Cedar Mountain in the arm and felt while he recovered that he could lose his command.

Having been in politics before the war, Geary had friends in Pennsylvania and Washington D.C. and he looked for his advancement in the army to lead him into a political office either during or after the war. Geary hinted about this, in talking about a Congressman that could help him, and told his wife about "ulterior designs" and delayed a trip to Harrisburg.[9]

Had Geary blocked Greene's promotion? While Greene received no praise from General McClellan (because it would show his error in handling the battle) at Antietam, he hadn't actively campaigned for a promotion like Geary. Geary however, discussed his plans for a Major General's command, and insisted, "if I am no promoted it shall not be because I did no deserve to be."[10] One described him in simple terms, "John White was a self promoter and took care to present himself as the star."[11]

Greene went on his leave of absence, but Geary revealed he was physically limited to return to the field. From his first letter to his wife, Mary on taking command ("My arm does not improve," "painful & sore") to his astonishing admission on November 11, 1862 of his weakened state, "I hope it will soon gain strength as my necessities require two good arms" was something he may not have shared with the army surgeons. Geary could have been relieved and prevented to hold a field command in the Army. So keeping quiet had blocked Greene's promotion.[12]

In an odd twist of fate, Greene had been granted a leave of absence for "the benefit of his good health" by Special Orders No. 276 on October 10,1862 on General McClellan's approval for twenty days.[13] Since his request had gone through channels (which took time), it is possible he took ill when Geary arrived in camp. One possible explanation was given by General O.O. Howard in referring to Antietam, "It was hard to bury the dead and to get rid of the stench from the large number of horses which were killed in the battle. There was not breeze enough to carry off the poisonous gases and infected air, so that many of our best officers became ill before or soon after reaching Harper's Ferry".[14]

The time away had restored his health and upon his return to Harper's Ferry, Greene wrote to Governor Morgan of New York about the 60th New York regiment. Because of death and ill health among the field officers, a colonel was needed for the regiment. Greene recommended the Chaplain Richard Eddy for the position. They had known each other since January 1862 when Greene arrived in the camp as the 60th New York's new colonel.

He described Eddy to the Governor, to be promoted, "by his education, intelligence, industry and devotion to the service I believe he will fully justify the confidence I ask you to repose in him."[15] Although Eddy was passed over by the Governor, it was a remarkable statement made by Greene showing he believed that discipline and leadership were qualities that the Chaplain could instill within the regiment.

The Chaplain was not the only subject related to the Governor.

"After my return to duty from a short sick leave" wrote Greene, "regret to find that the 60th Regt. Has been transferred from my command. I have in my {3rd} Brigade now the 78, 102, 137 & 149 N.Y. Vols & 2 Regts {109th & 111th} from Pennsylvania."[16] The 60th New York was now in the 2nd Brigade and returned to command of a brigade, Greene regretted the loss of this well-trained regiment of his past association. While the other regiments he was familiar with, the 137th and 149th New York were new regiments that had arrived from western New York and had never been in a battle. He worked hard to discipline and drill the men to get them ready when the next battle arose.

An officer with the 149th New York spoke about Greene and his conduct for all of his comrades, "he was a West Point graduate, about sixty years old [61 1/2], thick set, five feet ten inches high, dark complexioned, iron-gray hair, full graybeard and mustache, gruff in manner and stern in appearance, but with all an excellent officer, and under a rough exterior possessing a kind heart. In the end the men learned to love and respect him as much as in the beginning they feared him, and this was saying a good deal on the subject. He know how to drill, how to command, and in the hour of peril how to care for his command, and the men respected him accordingly."[17]

Greene moved the brigade to Bolivar Heights and remained there until December 10th. Since this ground had been occupied by McClellan's troops previously, they cleaned up the filth and refuse and cut down trees to build huts for comfortable quarters. Some of Greene's men had to deal with body lice from the refuse (one was seen running in a soldier's clothing joked the boys), and some members of the 137th New York had strayed beyond the line of picket duty which resulted in their capture by rebel cavalry scouts.[18]

Picket duty at Bolivar Heights had men from both sides alert as they attempted to gather information on the enemy or exchanging items such as newspapers or tobacco.[19] Geary had himself tried to obtain information on the enemy's location by ascending in one of Professor Thaddeus Lowe's balloons. This aerial reconnaissance did not scare him, he told his wife "I experienced no sensations of giddiness, and upon the whole if it had not been quite so windy, my aerial voyage would have been rather a pleasant one, as it was I could not complain of it."[20]

Greene moved out with his brigade on November 9th as they participated in the march through Halltown and arrived at Charlestown, where John Brown was tried and executed for capturing Harper's Ferry and encouraging a slave rebellion in 1859. The rebel cavalry had retreated through the streets and set their light artillery in position outside Charlestown. Amid the exchange of artillery fire, the men loaded their weapons and some were nervous from Greene's new regiments as they took their place behind the artillery to give support.[21]

The men advanced with the forward movement of the artillery, but they did not fire at the rebels because they withdrew and after moving some four miles beyond Charlestown the advance was halted. They had captured a few prisoners and saw the campfires burning where the rebels had been. In their hurried retreat, they left behind their cattle.[22] General Greene was not one to look the other way on matters of unauthorized foraging.

He saw his new regiments (137th &149th NY) undisciplined as described by the Surgeon John Farmington, "all would have gone on well had not General Greene, unfortunately for us, ridden back along the line and discovered the horned recruits to his command." He continued, "Mortified and indignant at our action he ordered the animals liberated, much to the regret of the boys, who already were enjoying beefsteak in anticipation."[23]

Not all the cattle went free as the next morning hides were seen lying in the camp. Others chose to rummage through a store in Charlestown and carried away hats, coats and other articles remembered one soldier.[24] Writing home to his parents, Oliver Ormsby of the 149th New York was distraught over the lack of music, "we haven't got a drum or fife in the whole outfit. The drums all got broken and the only good fifer in the whole regiment died just before we got into Virginia. The rest of the musicians that havn't run away have gone into the ranks." Even the company drummer had ran away![25] The reconnaissance was a success and the men returned to Bolivar Heights.

The men were put back to building fortification, like they had at Loudon Heights, but it did have its risks as Charles Engle attested to, "there was one man got both his legs broke and another his arm and one is hurt in the back so that he can't walk."[26] While getting food to the troops helped to keep them healthy (Ex. soft bread, potatoes), Greene was faced with an old adversary that was more dangerous than the Rebels.

"There was one man died out of our company this weak. He had the Tiefoid fever. There is from ten to fifteen dies every day in the hospittle at the Ferry," wrote a soldier from the 137th New York.[27] In a report by the surgeon for November 10th to December 10th 1862, there were about 400 cases of typhoid fever with the most urgent cases sent to the general hospital.[28]

Like a ghost from the past, disease in the campsites had been with Greene when he joined the 60th New York in January that year and had raised its ugly head again in the summer before Cedar Mountain. He believed then and continued to believe that one way to combat it was to strengthen the body by drilling and performing outdoor activities (Ex. Chopping wood). Besides a good diet, this kept illness from being a common dilemma, lowered the death rate, and made them better soldiers on the march. Greene had been a good role model for a man his age. The next movement from camp was a challenge for General Greene in terms of evaluating his men and the conduct of an Army officer.

Just after two o'clock in the morning of December 2nd, the 2nd division moved from their camp and marched towards Halltown. They marched 20 miles and passed through Charlestown as they dealt with cavalry again like their first expedition. The Rebels were seen carrying off some of their wounded from being shelled by Union artillery. Guerillas had fired upon the rear guard on several occasions, but no one was injured. They took the road the next day in the direction of Berryville.[29]

The December days grew cold as the men tried to keep warm in the camp at night by using fence rails from the property of farmers to build their fires. Although sympathetic to the men's needs, General Greene could not tolerate destruction of property and stationed guards at the farms to curtail this activity.

Greene didn't win this battle as the soldiers kept warm and burned the fence rails on the fires. They also enjoyed a full stomach on Southern pork, poultry, and beef cattle. Years later, Captain George K. Collins in his regimental history of the 149th New York, wrote of that expedition "Gen. Greene was credited with making the remark that he believed the 149th would yet steal the Southern Confederacy poor and take the shoes from off Gen. Lee's charger."[30]

At Berryville, the rebel cavalry charged the lead column and retreated after they received a few shells from pieces of artillery brought up. This "cat and mouse" game showed the Confederates lacked sufficient numbers to turn back any Union columns like

Geary's division. But Geary took a cautious approach as they marched to Winchester, sending out skirmishers on both flanks and some of his artillery led the advance on the highway,. Cavalry scouts were sent out on the countryside to search for any concealed battcries or forces in the area. Geary's fear of walking into a Rebel trap was unfounded.[31]

"We was drawn in line of battle 2 miles this sied of Winchester and General Geary sent a flag of truce to tel the women and children to leave and the news came back that they had moved from there," recalled the 137th New Yorker Charles Engle.[32] A white flag was seen flying from a large building and the soldiers were marched into town with drums beating and flags flying. The town carried the scars of previous fighting with the destruction of the railroad and its adjoining buildings in ruins. They were greeted with laughter and joy by many slaves and welcomed by citizens who had been in hiding to escape conscription. Some of these contrabands followed the soldiers as they commenced their march back to Bolivar Heights.[33]

Greene's soldiers rested on the Martinsburg pike on their march northward when firing was heard in the rear. A soldier in Greene's command saw their cavalry being driven in "as fast as the horses could run but we had one canon with us and they shot twice amonst them and it made them scedadel but they come close enough so that their bulits whired over our heads and would hit some of us but we was in a hollow in the woods."[34] The next day their march was resumed towards Bunker Hill which contained grist-mills that had wagons full of flour that the men liberated from their Southern citizens. Pancakes were made from the graham flour providing a welcomed meal since supplies were became scant.[35]

Leaving Mill Creek, where they had bivouacked that night, on December 5th Oliver Ormsby (who had one time guarded Greene's headquarters) wrote in his diary "started at 7 am and marched 12 miles at double quick. General Geary gave General Green[e] a blowing up for marching us so fast. Started snowing so we encamped."[36] They had made camp in a section of woods just four miles south of Charlestown after a "disagreeable and laborious" march during the day and evening.[37]

Why did Geary react to Greene in that manner? Was there straggling in the ranks? Was Geary fatigued himself and took out his frustration on Greene, thinking about what could happen if they were suddenly attacked? Regretfully, Geary made no mention of the incident in his letters and Greene remained silent on the issue.

The regular army officer from West Point being upbraided by a young politician / turned volunteer in front of his men for keeping the columns together and evaluating the troops for the drilling they had worked together to be ready for battle was too much for Greene. He had not received the respect that was important in his life. Greene looked out for the welfare of his men, while Geary did also, but had the hidden agenda that the soldier was a vote and represented his future. Before the month was over, Greene had his army command looked at by others to rectify this situation.

By December 6th the troops had returned to Bolivar Heights after trudging through deep snow, which prevented straggling, and enjoyed a few days in camp before they moved out again.[38] The movement began on December 10th for the Twelfth Corps, under command of Major General Henry W. Slocum. They had marched to the support of General Burnside, who was gathering the Army of the Potomac to attack the Confederates at Fredericksburg.

It was difficult to travel on the dirt roads as they passed through Leesburg (which had a deserted Rebel fort nearby) and Gum Springs because of snow drifts in some places or the sun in the afternoon created mud and slushy conditions.[39] Lysander Welman described the area in his diary, "the farms are verry large and poorly cultivated. The houses are generally of an ungainly state and about them there is a slovenly look that you do not see in our farming district."[40]

With the rainfall during their march to Fairfax Court House, the men were covered in mud and slowed their movement. As they moved out the next day, December 14th, they traveled on a corduroy (built of logs)road for four miles to Fairfax Station. This method was used to prevent artillery and wagons from getting stuck in the mud.[41] The rain fell as they continued the march back on the muddy road reaching Dumfries.

The sounds of artillery from Fredericksburg had ended upon their arrival at Dumfries on December 16th. They were about 40 miles away from Burnside and the army, but the battle was over and they now received orders to countermarch back to Fairfax Station, leaving the 1st Brigade of the 2nd Division to hold the town.[42] To the soldiers of the Twelfth Corps, it was more depressing to march back over the wet and muddy roads, than missing a battle. Attempts were made during the afternoon to dry out their clothes, which included their socks and shoes by the fire. Sometimes a soldier fell in a water-filled hole or rut along the way.[43]

Brigadier General George Sears Greene shared with his men the hardships on the march. He went one step further at Dumfries along the Ocoquan River "as we were crossing a little stream we met a few regts on the advance guarding supplies as the boys were anxious to get along and did not halt to let us cross on the narrow bridge," wrote one of Greene's men.[44]

These soldiers were from the 66th Ohio regiment that had been under Greene's command at Antietam. They did not listen to Greene, despite his order repeatedly to stop, as they continued to cross. One New Yorker soldier stated "Green[e] saw that there was some obstruction & rode back and ordered the to halt but they did not obey. So he made a pitch for one lanky fellow who dodged him and got on the bridge before Green[e] could reach him and in his eagerness he rode to near the edge & in he went horse and all."[45]

Apparently the bank had given way from erosion and the combined weight of Greene and his horse.

Fortunately, the General was not hurt and received help from the 66th soldiers in getting out of the creek, while the rest of their regiment continued over the bridge. The boys roared with laughter and perhaps to recover his pride and discipline within the ranks, he made the rest of the brigade ford the creek.[46]

With their return to Fairfax Station, another expedition was to begin for Greene but of a different forum. Richard Eddy, chaplain of the 60th New York, had become a supporter of Greene's treatment of the boys and a friend and confidant during their service together. He had even been recommended by Greene for promotion to be the colonel of his old regiment. Now it was the Chaplain who wanted to return the favor. It is likely that the story of Geary's remarks against Greene on December 5th had reached Eddy's attention, either by Greene or through gossip in the ranks of the Twelfth Corps.

He wrote a letter to the friend of the 60th New York, Senator Preston King, recommending Greene for promotion to Major General.

Among his kind words, Eddy felt Greene was unjustly removed from division command. He thought "Geary having 3 days seniority over Greene" and "believed he had been given command because of wound in action" presented the error of what was done to a proven officer on the battlefield.[47] The same day, General Williams from the 1st Division in the 12th Corps, had wrote a letter to the Secretary of War Edwin Stanton, and said Greene was "a gallant officer of military experience & education" and reinforced Greene's action at Antietam.[48]

Further support came from E.D. Morgan, the Governor of New York and Senator Preston King. Morgan thought Greene was "fairly entitled" to be a Major General and "abundantly competent to discharge" those duties.[49] Greene told the Senator "it would have been more in concurrance with my feelings to have had the initiative in the matter, rather by others, but as this is not the usual practice it is necessary to fall into the customary routine."[50] While King was reluctant to interfere in the process of promoting Generals, he passed on these letters to Stanton because he respected Greene and feared he could impede his chances due to a prejudice act on his part.[51]

On the surface, it seemed that Richard Eddy was the person who organized this effort for Greene. Besides his sincere feelings for Greene, another benefit of his promotion was the return of the 60th New York to his (division) command. Greene had never been given a reason for their removal to the 2nd Brigade and asked to have them returned. If Greene knew about Eddy's involvement, like Senator King, he won't interfere with it.

In fact, Greene told his son Francis he was the one who sent the originals (letters) to the Senator, but said "I do not think that will amount to much unless it is followed up by some of our friends."[52] What friends did he mean? He asked King to show the letter (which one?) to Mr. Wheeler of the House and the Senator of Rhode Island "Reps Anthony & Arnold who are our cousins, of the blood of the Greenes all of Rhode Islanders." He felt they "will be glad to do anything for me which shall not interfere with their other interest or desires." There was discussions in Washington about passing a law to increase the number of Major Generals.[53]

Greene was learning about the politics in the Union army. He could look back at his removal of June 1862 and October 1862 from brigade and division command as politics. Lesser men of military experience had been promoted or took credit for events that were unfounded. This was Geary in the fall of 1862 as Greene read the newspapers and saw the correspondents lavish praise on Geary (which he did have contacts).[54]

Unless he resigned or asked for a transfer, which Greene cannot accept, because he believed it displayed a sign of weakness, politics remained his only option. If that was true, then Geary was Greene's superior in this arena. He could have informed his friends in Washington to block his nomination and this prevented Geary to give up his division command or be transferred. Greene's political battle was lost, but the battle against the Confederacy was ongoing.

The men battled the elements more than the Rebels these days. Such items as blankets, gloves, and stockings were requested in the newspapers of the homefolks to send them.[55] The sick were attended to as one soldier, sent to a hospital in Washington D.C., had pleurisy and typhoid fever met the poet Walt Whitman, who wrote the boy's mother and left him fruit to enjoy.[56] Despite the tents and the timber for fires in camp, a soldier complained about one cold night and stated the "water froze hard enough to burst some of our canteens."[57] They remained for the week as orders came for a reconnaissance on December 27th.

Greene took his command to Dumfries and the next day reached the Ocoquan River, skirmishing with the Rebel cavalry. They crossed the river and halted for dinner after a march of three to four miles. General Slocum rode by with his body guard, and after he spoke with the 137th New York's colonel, was given three cheers by the men as they rose to their feet. The General raised his hat and the group rode out of sight only to return quickly, attacked by Rebel cavalry. The soldiers went into the line of battle and the artillery followed and sent the Rebels in retreat through the woods.[58] It was a decoy by Stuart's cavalry as they went on a bigger raid and Greene returned to his brigade to Fairfax Station on December 30th.

General Greene rode up to Colonel Ireland the next day after their performance against Stuart's cavalry, and witnessed by the surgeon of the 137th, took him by the hand saying "Colonel your regiment did splendidly yesterday."[59] He thanked him and the drilling and discipline had promising results for Greene. The soldiers used the nick name "Pap" or "Pop" and spoke of their General as a son to his father. The days of hearing "old Beatty" by disgruntled soldiers last summer were behind him.

After having a early morning inspection and review for General Slocum on January 5, 1863 (which had gone well), Greene wrote home and told everyone of hearing about Dana's safety. Samuel Dana Greene's ship, the USS Monitor, had capsized during a storm off the North Carolina coast in December 1862. He told his son Francis, "we first heard of his shipwreck on Sunday about noon in the Washington paper." Regretting that Dana hadn't come to visit him, he figured Dana had nothing to wear and his tone was one of relief. "How grateful we ought to be for his safe return to us after so great peril."[60]

Greene spoke of the Navy's reaction to Dana's conduct and looked at the Monitor from an engineer's standpoint, "We today have left Bankheads report in which he speaks of Dana in times of praise for his gallant bravery & good conduct. I am not disappointed in the fate of the Monitor & the cause of her loss undoubtedly was from the square angle, if that space had been filled in that she would have been comparatively safe. She was one of its amonged craft in everything but the turrent which is a capital idea well carried out."[61]

Since there was a few lives lost at sea and Dana had some in naval areas that frowned upon his handling of the Monitor-Virginia fight in March 1862, George Sears Greene wanted his son to get a fair review if there should be an investigation. There was no reprimand against Samuel Dana Greene and he was reassigned to another ship.

Greene's soldiers were issued rations and new clothing as they were prepared to march out from Fairfax Station on General Burnside's orders. Some thought they were returning to Harper's Ferry or perhaps going on transports to North Carolina.[62] Greene's brigade was now all New York regiments as he welcomed back his old regiment, the 60th New York, and the two Pennsylvania regiments were relocated to other brigades in the 12th Corps.

They left their camp with clear skies that morning on January 19th and reached the outskirts of Dumfries by crossing the Ocoquan River the next day. That night, as the men made their camp among an old rebel campsite, the heavy rains came down. The rebel huts, which had been burned, could have provided better cover, for their shelter tents were not sufficient.

"The rain drove through them drenching one to the skin," remembered Lysnader Welman. Men woke up feeling damp and seeing a stream of water running through their tents.[63] Two soldiers for the 149th New York tried to prevent sleeping in the standing water from the rainfall by putting their tents on a hillside with a log held in place by stakes. They slept this way until morning (in a standing position) before sliding down the hill and their feet over the log.[64]

A sea of mud and rain became a nightmare for the Union Army. Wagons were stuck, with supplies thrown out of hardtack and pork to make the trains lighter, but to no avail. Horses and mules were found dead along the sides of the road of march. Others were literally buried in the mud with their harness still on them. Mud of 3 inches to 12 inches in depth had prevented Ambrose

Burnside's movement across the Rappahannock to meet General Lee's Army in battle, and was named Burnside's Mud March.[65]

After marching two miles without a break, Dr. Taylor Elmore of the 137th New York wrote in his diary, "I wonder if General Green[e] intends to kill them all today."[66] General Greene found himself, like the teamsters with their trains, having difficulties with the terrain. After leaving Dumfries on January 21st, the men had to look for another area to cross the Quantico creek, which was swollen due to the heavy rains.

The Chaplain of the 60th New York stated what happened next, "I remember that General Greene, having a short-legged horse, thought to keep dry by accepting the use of another, but accidentally hitting the beast with his spurs, as he raised his feet that they might clear the water, the horse made such haste to cross that he struck into the deepest places, and the General got an extraordinary dose of that which he had hope to escape."[67]

By the time they arrived at Aquia Landing, along the Potomac and railroad that brought in supplies from the docks, the march was over for the 12th Corps. This was on January 26th and the memories of those dark days of suffering remained with the soldiers. Ironically, one man from Greene's command saw a view that held him in awe, "I ascended to a hill above our camp and took a look at the long white line of wagons with here and there the dark blue uniforms of the infantry who are guarding them. It was a picturesque sight."[68] The soldiers relocated a half mile to Acquia Creek on February 7th and here Greene's men settled in for the next seven weeks.[69] The men and General Greene were brought together due to hardships they faced. It was time to rest and prepare themselves for the spring campaign.

Chapter Twelve

"Winter Quarters"

A change from campaigning to settle down into their winter quarters was welcomed news to the Army of the Potomac. Except for missing the battle at Fredericksburg in December 1862, Greene's soldiers had marched and skirmished with the Confederates almost on a regular basis since November of last year. Another change was the removal of General Burnside on January 25, 1863 by Lincoln and General Joseph Hooker became the new commander. Hooker attempted to improve morale, provided supplies to the army, cut down the desertion rate, and get the soldiers prepared for the upcoming spring campaign.

Stationed around the vicinity of Aquia creek, the area was described as having "immense poverty, the poorness of its soil, the meanness of its inhabitants, and the scarcity of provisions."[1] Log huts were built and the roofs were covered by their shelter tents. Their comfort was enhanced by fireplaces, but it couldn't keep out the snow and rain. Told about this recent storm, a soldier commented "it was hard for us to lay on the ground, the water run[s] down under our beds and you can judge how we soldiers get along."[2] Being homesick, Charles Engle told his wife "the money is what ceeps this war agoing. The officers don't do their duties. They all want to get rich and we have got to suffer and die for it."[3]

The daily routine of drill and inspection became the life of the camp. Hooker tried to reduce the desertion rate that prevailed in the Army. He began by ordering the soldiers to be paid and furloughs to be granted. Many regiments had gone for months without pay and some of the deserters brought back into camp used this reason for their departure. Their families at home depended on this money, yet there were other regiments that had gone longer without pay and did not have that problem.[4]

One soldier made his feelings very clear, "I am here and I won't desert for I would rather be shot then to desert."[5] A furlough, granting ten days leave, was given to one man from each company in a regiment and repeated over again with his return to camp.[6] For those soldiers, who returned from their time at home, they had renewed confidence that General Hooker was the right person to lead the Union Army.

Another measure to instill pride was the creation of badges for identification. For the 12th Corps, a star symbol was chosen and the color was white for Geary's 2nd Division. The men were proud of its status and others saw the white star on their hats, knowing from their first battle to the end of the war, that they were to be respected.[7] Greene could see the effect it had on his men and appreciated its symbolic gesture it put on his own efforts to have the drills and discipline make them better soldiers. If Greene could not get the recognition in Washington, his soldiers could get the Rebels to see the white stars on the field of battle.

Improvements were made in the food with beef, pork, potatoes and onions (to prevent scurvy) with soft bread and hardtack to compliment their meals. Other items issued by the government were knapsacks (thrown away on the last march), shoes, and shirts. Many of the men had extra shirts now since they had brought some from home. A 149th New Yorker joked "if you know of anyone in need of shirts send them down here because they can get then dirt cheap."[8]

A fort was completed near the railroad mounting 11 guns by Greene's men to protect supplies. Despite their labor and better food to keep themselves healthy, many were ill ranging from colds to typhoid fever. One soldier felt it was due to the changes in the weather, but sanitary conditions in camp was more of a factor. "All I ask for is good health," said one man and "I will risk the bullets."[9]

General Greene may have been intrigued by a 78th New York soldier's commentary on the war, "I think there has been a great deal of mismanagement with our Generals since the war commenced." He believed "the northern states are making a great fuss about the Conscript law," and felt that "in some states there are so many opposed to it that I am afraid they will have Civil War amongst themselves if they undertake to force the men in the army."[10] Those northerners who had southern sympathies were resented by the fighting men and were called Copperheads. It was always on their minds when they received news from the home front.

When the Emancipation Proclamation freed slaves in those areas held under rebellion on January 1, 1863, the men from Greene's brigade had not placed much importance in Lincoln's draft. There was little revealed in their diaries or letters. However, there was no doubt how this soldier felt about the issue "I don't approve of having the negroes free but Lincoln saw fit to free them and so we must submit to it." To preserve the union was forgotten as "a great many say we are fighting for the niger. I think myself the niger is the cause of the war."[11]

Besides the lowered rate of desertions and the conscript law, the ranks had to be filled to replace those who were killed, or still in the hospitals. Recruiting officers, such as Lieutenant Gleason of the 60th New York, were sent north to help enlist men, gave them clothing and after meeting at a pre-designated spot were sent to their new regiments in Virginia.[12] Government officials made inspections at this time of the 324 regiments in the Army of the Potomac. The 60th New York was granted a second inspection, because the first was of a short duration due to the inclement weather. John C. O. Redington of the 60th New York felt they had been hurt despite the favorable second report because it was a part of the record.

General Greene may have felt the same way for General Orders No. 18 was issued by the government on March 30, 1863 granting extended furloughs and other benefits to the top 11 regiments in the army.[14]

None of his New York regiments were included, but he could take pride knowing the 111th Pennsylvania which was under his command for a time had been chosen. The 60th New York men were also preoccupied at their inspection since they were informed by the Governor of New York that all flags and banners worn too much for further service were to be sent to Albany. While the heart of a command was its leader, its soul was enshrined in the flag of a regiment. The officers expressed their regret of this decree.[15]

An old friend came to the campgrounds of the 60th New York and met Greene during this time. With his term in the Senate over in early March 1863, Preston King had visited the men, gave encouragement to all and wanted to help their families back home.[16] Another reason may have been to tell Greene in person that his promotion to Major General was no longer considered in Washington. Greene respected the integrity of King's character and knew people like him were essential if they were to win the war.

The major event that announced the beginning of the spring campaign was the review of the troops by President Lincoln and General Hooker. This was the first time that Greene met the President, at a lunch arranged by Hooker.[17] The review was near Stafford Court House and "Uncle Abe" (as he was called by the soldiers) rode "with his hat off and looked real natural."[18] They rode around (the generals) with his guard in front of 12 to 15 thousand men. The President's wife (Mary Todd Lincoln) was in a carriage drawn by four magnificent horses dressed in black. The rumor was going around that this was for her brother killed in the rebel army. The boats blew their whistles as the President returned to the docks at Aquia Landing.[19]

The commander-in-chief gave Hooker his approval, but not all the men felt he was qualified or fit to lead the army. One sergeant told his captain that he saw Hooker as they were reviewed and commented, "I think he drink his Rations at least from the looks of his continence."[20] He was ready to put his Army on the roads with the warm weather was approaching for the spring campaign and Hooker felt those improvements made in recent months had prepared them for battle.

Rations were issued and the men knew the winter quarters were now part of the past. Hooker knew Lee's Army was near and orders were sent out to move. Greene's drilling and discipline had showed itself in reviews, including the last with President Lincoln, that his soldiers looked sharp and they needed to give their best. Not since Antietam had they been in a major battle and this was to be their first battle as a brigade against Lee's Confederates. Even the newer regiments were anxious to prove themselves to their General and the folks back home. General Greene did all that he could for his boys and it was time to get on with the job at hand.

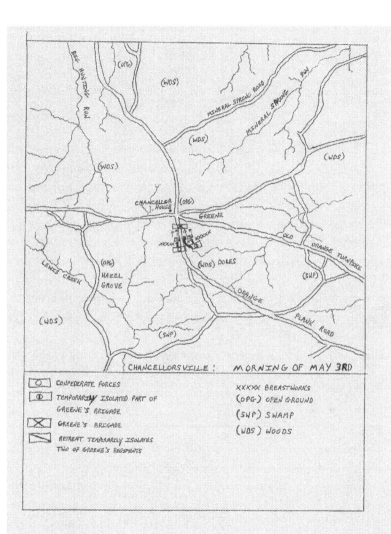

CHANCELLORSVILLE: MORNING OF MAY 3RD

	CONFEDERATE FORCES	XXXXX BREASTWORKS
	TEMPORARILY ISOLATED PART OF GREENE'S BRIGADE	(OPG) OPEN GROUND
	GREENE'S BRIGADE	(SWP) SWAMP
	RETREAT TEMPORARILY ISOLATES TWO OF GREENE'S REGIMENTS	(WDS) WOODS

Chapter Thirteen

Chancellorsville

The men of Greene's brigade awoke in good spirits on the morning of April 27, 1863 as the sounds of camp came alive that morning. One of the boys from the 60th New York amused his comrades by slapping his thighs, threw back his head and crowed like a rooster, that brought smiles or chuckling as they enjoyed breakfast.[1] After they were supplied with eight day rations and checked their rifles, Greene's soldiers fell in behind General Williams's First Division at Stafford Court House.

Starting at 7 am, they moved out in a southwest direction, marching on the Telegraph Road and reached Hartwood Church on the Warrenton Post Road. The brigade had marched eight miles, and bedded down for the night.[2] The outlook was bleak that first day since the roads in the area had recent rainfall. "Terrible," was how General Williams described it to his daughters, "my pioneer corps was busily at work cutting new roads all through the pines."[3]

Their approach (northwest) on the Warrenton Post Road took them to Grove Church and Crittenden Mills and brought them to the Rappahannock River. The 12th Corps followed behind the wagon trains of the 11th Corps and it caused General Joseph Hooker, who came down the road, to view Geary's 2nd Division not closed up and reprimand the general in front of his men.[4] If General Greene saw this or heard about it, those feelings ran the gauntlet from satisfaction to sympathy because of the unwarranted criticism back in December 1862. Hooker wanted to get his army around Lee's Confederates and get him to come out from his defenses and fight in the open field. Lee could either be overwhelmed by superior numbers or forced to retreat, which left Richmond open to attack. So far, the Federals were not detected and Hooker wanted no delays in the march.

General Greene wrote that "crossing the Rappahannock at Kelly's Ford, we pressed on, one division of our corps wading, at Germania Ford, water to the armpits and capturing a company of rebel soldiers, who were quietly rebuilding the bridge."[5] On April 29th, they captured about 50 or 60 prisoners, and 125 Rebels caught by the rest of the 12th Corps. Greene's men had formed on the side of the road that evening, with huge fires built on both sides of the Rapidan River. Greene looked on as the 11th Corps passed his men. "I shall never forget the scene," he said as they moved across the hastily constructed foot-bridge. "Long lines of glistening bayonets wound down to the stream, and the air was filled with the songs of the Fatherland. Above and below, horsemen stemmed the current and emerged, dripping, upon the opposite shore."[6]

The next morning, April 30th, Greene's brigade took the advance at 7:30 am in an easterly direction towards Chancellorsville. Skirmishers were thrown out in the sunny warm weather, the side of the road was littered with overcoats and woolen blankets. This was a familiar sight along the march, but one soldier remembered that death awaited them on that road as a Union soldier, dead and partially consumed by hogs, laid by the side of the road as a warning to others.[7]

Greene's brigade arrived at Chancellorsville and were put in a line of battle that ran across the Orange Plank Road among the dense woods on the ridge. This position was a half mile in front of the Chancellor House, a large brick house where General Hooker established his headquarters.[8] The soldiers fought in terrain that varied from being open and cultivated to thick woods with swamp and covered in short scrubby evergreens. General Greene felt they were in a good position and the next day, May 1st, they marched in a southeastern direction on the Plank road two lines were formed. Skirmishers had been and it was hard for the men to stay in line because of the evergreens. The advance came to a halt on an open piece of ground.[9]

Just as Greene's brigade formed their line, the boom of cannons were heard from the woods. There in the distance, rebel batteries had spotted their movement and as Oliver Ormsby recalled "we all lay tight to the ground."[10] "We dident go far before the shells began to come," remembered one of Greene's men and "our battery opend and they had quite an artillery fight."[11] After a time difference of 15 minutes to a half hour, orders were received to fall back and return to their original line. No one was hurt, but most of the shells fired by the Rebels had cut off the limbs of the trees which fell among the men.[12]

From the time they had left camp on April 27, 1863 until the order was received to fall back to original line outside the Chancellor House, the movement was approved to trap Lee's Army. Greene questioned this change from a offensive to defensive posture. He said "with all deference to the ability of the engineer officer who superintended the lines, it is difficult to understand why we were ordered back from the fine, high open country that we then traversed, into the lower brushwood officially assigned us."[13]

They had no contact with infantry and the advance cavalry pickets reported no rebel cavalry or infantry in the area. If Hooker was concerned about Lee's Confederates attacking his forces here, Greene saw with an engineer's eye and an artillery officer's knowledge of the area how to prevent it. "A field piled with cordwood seemed to invite us to intrench ourselves, and guns there placed in position could have swept an advancing column," said Greene, but he followed orders and soon the Rebels occupied this ground that he had been reluctant to give away without a fight.[14]

Greene's men returned to campground late in the afternoon on May 1st and were exalted for their action that day by General John Geary, their division commander. He reported, "the conduct of Greene's brigade was admirable at this juncture. Although exposed for quite a length of time to the fire of the enemy in a position where they could neither shelter nor defend themselves, nor return the assault, they bore themselves with the calmness and discipline of veterans, emulating the example given them by their brigade commander."[15]

Praise for his men at this juncture was less important to Greene than saving the lives of his soldiers.

Knowing the higher command had made a mistake (and he had obeyed the order), he attempted to corrected it by protecting his men from the expected assaults. Later that night, they had their supper and skirmishers sent out as pickets, Greene's men "dug rifle pits all night using their bayonets and tin plates," wrote one New Yorker to his parents.[16]

Some of the men referred to them as breastworks. Donald Brown of the 60th New York said they had to use tin plates and bayonets since there were no picks or shovels to use.[17] Colonel James C. Lane of the 102nd New York called them "rife-pits of logs, with abates in front, and filled in outside with the dirt from the trenches."[18] The men cleared the trees with their axes 200 feet in the front of the brigade, with the branches (abates) forward toward the Rebels. Logs and tree trunks were piled behind them.[19]

In his report, General Greene wrote, "in the evening and night we formed an abates and breastwork of logs and earth with a trench in the rear, making a good defensive work."[20] This innovative action by Greene taught his men that if Lee attacked them either by frontal or flank assaults in great strength in the woods, this could be minimized by an unbroken front line (with a trench in the rear), giving maximum protection to his men.

The lessons of Antietam in the fight at Dunker Church and the retreat from his right flank that day back in September 1862 had remained with Greene. With the 11th Corps on their right flank (of the 12th Corps) and the 3rd Corps on their left flank, Greene's actions presented the brigade with a solid front in case of retreat or a temporary staging area to advance against Lee's Army.

The sounds of cannon fire in the distance and the thuds of minie balls from the enemy sharpshooters awoke Greene's soldiers that morning of May 2nd. Picket duty became more tedious, not knowing where the rebels were in the area. "We were posted in the woods and bushes," said one 149th New Yorker and "you could hardly see a man a rod away."[21] While Greene waited for orders into the early afternoon, he took out his frustration by cursing the whippoorwills, calling them "wretched birds." Their singing for the last two days Greene had referred to as "shrill cries" that were "ominous as the croakings of ravens."[22] Many years after the war, the bird's tones were called the "voice of conscience" to the wounded and dying by an old veteran.[23]

Reports that morning came in of the Confederates marching to the right along the 3rd and 12th Corps front by some of the skirmishers in the woods. Hooker believed Lee began to retreat and had sent out a reconnaissance with a part of the 12th Corps to confirm it. Greene's brigade was kept out of it, and began to march out on the Plank Road that afternoon, but was ordered back to their old position.[24] The reconnaissance had captured some prisoners and wagons, but was halted because of the collapsing right flank of the Union Army.

Stonewall Jackson had marched his men, under the eyes of the Union front lines, around the 11th Corps unprotected right flank and attacked late in the day. That night was filled with hissing sounds of the shells bursting among the retreating troops. Flashes of musketry lit up the area like fireflies with officers giving commands and trying to reestablish a defense line. Because the 11th Corps broke "they took one of our batteries and they got in the rear of us," wrote a 137th New York soldier.[25]

Greene reported that night "straggler came in from the Eleventh Corps, with three regimental flags, and were arrested by the command."[26] A second line of breast works was built to the right and rear on the edge of the woods in the direction where the retreating troops had come during the night. "We were ordered to shoot any man who tried to pass us," but this was difficult, said one soldier since he saw a few "bleeding without their arms."[27]

It wasn't a restful night because Greene's men know May 3rd had to restart the confederate offensive. At early sunrise, the Rebels commenced throwing shells and grape and canister, knocking down trees and bushes as the men hugged the entrenchments. Some of these found Greene's men. "He was about six feet from me," was Dudley Messereau of the 137th New York when his comrade saw him hit with a shell, "it went though his head" and killed him.[28] The 29th Ohio was sent over to Greene as a reserve as the officers attempted to bring in the pickets to the reserve position. Not everyone got the word or were too late when Rebel yells signaled the infantry attack.

Oliver Ormsby of the 149th New York related what happened to him at that moment, "We came up on a regiment of Rebs that were lying on the ground in the thick bushes. We got to within two rods from them when we saw them. They jumped up, leveled their guns at us and told us to surrender. As there were only 10 of us we had to give up. Our forces had already fallen back on the right of us which gave the Rebs a chance to move into the rear of us without our knowledge."[29]

Supporting Greene's brigade, Caius C. Lord of Co. I, 29th Ohio was struck lying on the ground from a piece of shell, tearing into his shoulder belt and produced a severe bruise, a lump about the size of a walnut.[30] "The firing on some parts of our line was very destructive," reported Colonel Lane of the 102nd New York, "bur the men generally kept well in the trenches."[31]

The Rebels had put batteries on the high ground around Hazel Grove, that Hooker's men had occupied at one time, which gave them an excellent field of fire. This caused a serious problem for the whole 2nd Division. The initial assault by the rebels was pushed back. "Down fell our poor crowing comrade, shot through the head" of the 60th New York from that day in camp back in April. Another man was nearly cut in two by a rebel shell.[32] This could not unnerve some as Colonel David Ireland stated, "the men were perfectly cool, and some of them threw shells over the entrenchments where they exploded."[33]

There were so many fragments of shells that a person in the area could have filled their pockets.[34] This fighting of rolling artillery fire and infantry attacks reached a climax at 8 am that morning, after it had commenced at 5:30 am. Greene's soldiers had given a good account of themselves in holding their front, but they were in danger of being surrounded as the Confederates were discovered moving past their right flank.

Greene was ordered to pull back, but when the regiments were informed of the orders, there was two regiments that were unaware of the withdrawal.[35] The 60th New York and 102nd New York were fighting the Rebels, and thought they were supported, when they were actually covering the ordered retreat. Lt. Col. John C. Redington of the 60th New York said of both regiments that their fire and charge over the breastworks was made "with unflinching valor and terrible effect"[36]

After the division command was given temporarily to General Greene because General Geary lost his voice shouting over the crashing burst of shells, it seemed like everyone was a target. "They fired on us from one way and their battery from the other," relayed one soldier to the homefolk.[37] As the line gave way, Samuel R. Lusk from the 137th New York saw "men with part of their head blowed off trying to get off the field. Some with their legs partly shot off hobbling along to get out of reach of the enemy." For this soldier, there was no end to the human suffering.[38]

The aide Greene had sent to the 60th New York and 102nd New York could not get the new orders heard over the battle or was not able to reach them. Stragglers (probably from the 11th Corps) had been ordered to stop and when they had charged the Rebel line, one or two men of the 60th New York had been shot by these men and continued their retreat.[39]

"We were entirely unsupported," remarked the Lieut. Col. of the 60th New York. Just then, one of their own batteries open up on them, and believed they were Rebels. Four shells came thundering in and the color guard risked his life by going out in the open and displayed the colors. Yet they continued firing (believed it to be a trick by the Confederates) and killed and wounded some of those in the ranks. A case shot struck the steel scabbard of the Adjutant's sword which left him doubled up, but not seriously hurt.[40]

They gave the rebels volleys of musketry, which allowed Greene's other regiments to withdraw, but the 102nd New York, formed at right angles became separated from the 60th New York. The 102nd 's colonel described what happened next, "after they had passed, rebels came in on both sides, left and right, saying we were surrounded and must surrender, but instead of doing so we disarmed 2 commissioned officers, 1 flag sergeant, and 20 privates, taking the flag, and bringing our prisoners safe to the rear. The battle-flag and prisoners were from the Twelfth Georgia Volunteers."[41]

Those troops of Stonewall Jackson were Doles's Georgians, who sensed that a breakthrough was near. Amid shouts of surrender, both sides passed the wounded with outstretched hands to not leave them behind. Some of the 60th New York men fell back due to the heavy enfilading fire from the right flank (which was now between both of Greene's regiments).[42]

While trying to stem the growing numbers of Confederates firing from different directions, Oliver Buckley of the 60th New York never saw the Rebel that took aim at him as he was killed and fell at the feet of his buddy. He remembered seeing among the chaos, "a riderless horse was going like the wind over the dead and dying, wheeling around and dashing off in another direction whenever a shell would burst in front of them."[43] Knowing the Rebels were "surrounding us on three sides" with a force several times our own number," Lt. Col. Redington gave the order to fall back towards the Plank Road.[44]

General Greene felt the officers of these regiments had performed with "great gallantry" in covering the rest of the brigade (although he insisted the order to move had been given to them).[45] The enemy tried to prevent Greene's men from reaching the Orange Plank Road. "As we retreated the enemy pursued us clostly," Samuel Lusk stated, "as we passed our batteries they fired on the Rebs which were following us in mass & mowed them down." Casualties didn't seem to slow them down as "they must have lost three to our one," claimed one soldier.[46] Some of the 137th New Yorkers tried to quench their thirst by making coffee in a hallow in the woods, but the rebels had seen their smoke (thinking it was a battery), and broke up the gathering with a hail storm of grape, shells, and canister.[47]

The Chancellor House became the focal point to establish a defensive line and many of the walking wounded and stragglers came to the brick house, which was used as a hospital. The division was ordered by General Slocum to the rear of the house with the 60th & 102nd New York regiments detached to the left to support the batteries. After those regiments gave their support against the rebel attack, they rejoined the brigade stationed on the road a few miles from United States Ford.[48].

With the Rebel artillery crashing into the woods around the Chancellor House and upon it as the batteries moved up, it was time to evacuate the wounded. By the time they were safely removed down the road, the building was consumed by flames. They were the lucky ones as related by General Alpheus S. Williams, "not so fortunate were the poor fellows lying wounded in the woods, which, taking fire during the battle, burned fiercely in all directions, covering the country for miles with dense smoke and flames."[49]

The horror of that type of death was only surpassed in many soldier's minds of the carnage seen at the hospitals on the field. A soldier of the 149th New York saw the field surgeons working under a tree at an operating table, "near this was a pile of arms, legs, and feet, and about the table the grass was trampled down and covered with human blood. The scene was sickening."[50]

The dawn of May 4th had General Greene turn over command of the division to General Geary, who had sufficiently recovered. Explosions greeted the men that morning as shells came close to hitting the ammunition wagons that were parked by the hospital tents. Teamsters tried to hitch the frightened animals to the wagons and others ran to take cover. The wounded laid vulnerable in the tents and wondered if they could be killed by Rebel shells or the frightened animals passing by. In a short time, their guns were silenced by one of the batteries attached to Geary's division.[51]

Greene's men moved that evening towards Williams's division and commenced building entrenchments through the night and continued to work on them the next day.[52] The anticipated assault by the Confederates did not occur as Greene received orders the night of May 5th to recross the Rappahannock River. The regiments formed in close column as they marched to United States Ford and arrived at the pontoon bridges, where some of the wounded had been previously evacuated the last two days.[53] Even though the Confederates no longer pursued them, the other enemy, death followed as "a wind bearing a stench from the battlefield," wrote one soldier it was "so vile as to be almost unbearable."[54]

The brigade crossed the river on May 6, 1863 and reached the Acquia Creek in two days before setting up camp at the landing on May 9th where they were at the start of the campaign. Along the way, articles that had been thrown away by the soldiers were discovered in a farmer's barn and reissued to those in the ranks.[55]

Why did General Hooker, who had threatened Lee's left flank with three Corps across the Rappahannock River almost undetected go from an offensive operation to a defensive posture? General Greene saw the mistake of Hooker's decision on May 1st and related to his Twelfth Corps commander's feelings that day. General Henry W. Slocum had cried out to W.A. Roebling, dispatched to deliver the order falling back to the previous night's position, "Roebling, you are a damned liar! Nobody but a crazy man would give such an order when we have victory in sight!"[56] Despite the collapse of May 3rd on the Eleventh Corps right flank, Greene's men gave a good account of themselves and slowed the Confederates down in their attacks inflicting heavy casualties. No one in the ranks thought they should discontinue the battle. A 137th New York soldier thought the rebels had fought so hard because "they are all drunk on whisky and gunpowder and they don't fear enything."[57] Maybe Joe Hooker could have used some of that because he lost his nerve and let the reputation of General Robert E. Lee decide the battle when the battle's outcome was in doubt. Although the Union high command had failed, General George Sears Greene and his brigade learned valuable lessons in their first battle together.

One of those lessons was for better communications with the picket line and coordination among the regiments during a battle. A number of the prisoners captured from Greene's brigade were those pickets in the woods and evergreens on the morning of May 3rd. Although he criticized the Dutchmen of the 11th Corps for running "like a pack of cowards," Oliver Ormbsy of the 149th New York did not blame them entirely for his capture. He blamed their Major who told them to stay at their posts that afternoon on May 2nd and never came back to order their withdraw.[58]

A serious mistake was averted during the brigade's ordered retreat on May 3rd only because of the determined fight of the 60th & 102nd New York regiments. Greene stated that he was assured that the orders were issued to retire after he was told by the 60th's Lt. Colonel that he received no such order. It is interesting to note that Captain William H. Randall, of the 78th New York reported that "no order has reached us to retire," and they saw the pullback of their line and followed on their own losing 30 of their own that became prisoners.[60]

Was this aide, who either never reached those regiments or expected Colonel Lane of the 102nd New York to inform the 60th New York of their movement, Charles T. Greene of the General's staff? It was possible that he was unable to get through because of the rebel penetration and went back to Colonel Lane to see if he could have a runner pass on the order in case he could not find those regiments on the way back to his father's headquarters.

Greene made no mention of who he gave the order or who told him the orders were sent in the report.

Yet he believed Redington of the 60th New York should have "ascertained the nature of the movement" that took place and Lane should have contacted Redington about the orders.[61] No mention was made of Captain Randall's statement for the 78th New York of orders not received. If General Greene knew the aide he sent out to deliver that fateful order of May 3rd, he chose to omit him from his report to protect him.

Previously unknown to historians, new documentation sheds light for Greene's and Redington's conflicting reports on the May 3rd order to fall back. In June 1864, Redington had expressed outrage at Eddy's regimental history of the 60th New York which claimed he was missing at the Battle of Chancellorsville.

He wrote that "several officers will testify" that he was in "place at the center of the line," the rebels sent a heavy force on his right flank after sending a lieutenant back for orders. To avoid capture, Redington ordered his men to the rear (claiming to be the only Field Officer present) and "receive the orders he had sent for as to the next position to be taken."[62]

The chaplain wrote to his former regiment located near Marietta, Georgia that June with General Sherman's army. Asking for clarification of Lt. Col. Redington's absence and the order to fall back on May 3rd, six officers had responded in fact that Redington could not be found (believed killed or wounded) until the regiment was moved to the rear and he made his appearance known and took over command of their line reestablished. While these officers agreed that both Captains Thomas Elliot (Adjutant) and Hugh Smith were in command before Redington's mysterious return, they also agreed that the regiments was placed in a new position from Captain Forbes of General Geary's staff.[63] Because the Rebels tried to turn both flanks, I believe the 60th New York had temporarily split into two groups of companies, with Elliot/Smith in charge on the left and Redington on the right. "The left did not fall back first," stated those officers, but Redington had ordered his men back on the right after losing contact with the 102nd New York to keep the enemy in front. Yet from the time they began their withdraw until they moved towards the Chancellor House, it is clear that there was a breakdown in communication over the front line and Greene may have referred to Captain Forbes as the one who delivered the orders when they had already fell back without getting them earlier.[64]

The last lesson was building trenches or breastworks General Greene saw how his line had been pushed back at Antietam on the right flank from the Rebel attack out of the woods. When Hooker had ordered them to fall back, Greene used his engineering skills to prevent a flank attack and give the soldiers more protection by ordering them to use their bayonets and tin plates to build breastworks. Using the logs and branches for additional cover, the men realized Greene had found another way to fight the Confederates. Greene's men approved of this life-saving technique and no one approved of it more than Joshua Comfort, who told his parents of the bursting shells all around him as he laid down in the trenches and came out safe without a scratch.[65]

Without the breastworks, the casualties could have been more than the 528 of the 2,032 soldiers that were lost to Greene's brigade.[66] The results of the drill and discipline for his soldiers over the winter gave General Greene faith that his brigade could face any situation that arose on the battlefield. He spoke of their conduct at Chancellorsville, "the officers and men of my command have behaved with great coolness and gallantry whenever they have been under fire, and have displayed great patience and endurance under the severe labor and watching in trenches to which they have been subjected."[67]

Once again, George Sears Greene had proven himself in a brigade and a temporary division leadership role. Greene and his brigade used all the skills and lessons they learned for the next battle that many considered to be the turning point of the war.

Chapter Fourteen

Papa make them trot again

General George Sears Greene gave his men that firm leadership that could defeat the enemy on the field or compensate for mistakes by others during a crisis. Despite his personal bravery under fire, Greene felt irritated by Geary's indecision when the Rebels were hitting the division's flanks and said in front of his men to General Darius N. Couch, "My division can't hold its place; what shall I do?" "Fight it out," was Couch's reply which Greene would have concurred.[1] To Greene, this display of weakness undermined the morale of the troops and any doubts about orders (like Hooker's "hold at all hazards") should not be questioned in the open. Chancellorsville was a lesson for both men.

The next month was filled with the routines of camp life. In the first week after Chancellorsville, some prisoners and those wounded left behind were paroled and came into the Union lines, while others were brought back over the Rappahannock in ambulances from permission of Confederate authorities due to lack of medical supplies.[2] Not all the prisoners were so fortunate as some died from their grievous wounds and others like Sullivan F. McArthur of the 78th New York was captured on May 3rd and suffered the scenes of horror in Libby Prison until his exchange at the end of the year.[3] One soldier in a sarcastic tone told friend at home you could see more old maids at home if you came into the Army of the Potomac and a fellow soldier wrote to President Lincoln "to discontinue with this rebellion if conveniant."[4]

While General Greene put his men through drill practice, the resumption of mail service in camp was an outlet to tell about the war news and find out about life at home. Some paroled prisoner's mail arrived in camp and messages were relayed back to their loved ones. Not all the fighting at Vicksburg and Charleston by the Union fleet in the newspapers were topics of conversation, "I heard today that the state of Georgia had laid down their arms and come back in the Union as they were," Charles Engle had told his wife.[5] President Lincoln may have been pleased if this rumor was true if only the state wanted to have peace on their terms.

Towards the end of May 1863, Greene's men were ordered to build a fort, as they chopped down the surrounding woods. Surrounded by a ditch 12 feet deep, it measured about 300 feet long and 500 feet wide and the men wanted the rebels to fight them on their side of the river.[6] "We expect the rebels will try to get into Maryland again this summer," wrote a 78th New Yorker, "and we are preparing for it. I think that if they undertake it, they will find Old Joe around here . . . ."[7] The drum corps interrupted their work on June 2nd as the death march was played, with the chaplain and flag-covered corpse behind. They were followed by 12 men with muskets and the rest of the soldier's regiment. This man between fifty and sixty didn't have to fight, but the dignified funeral and sacrifice made the soldiers yearn for home.[8]

A common practice in the Army of the Potomac among the officers was to invite family members or friends to the campsites, which took place in times of inactivity. Since Greene's last visit home to his family was in late April 1862 (he had seen Dana after the Monitor's loss at sea), it was decided to get together at Acquia Landing with a few friends. Among Greene's family who came to see him was his wife Martha, his daughter Anna, and youngest son, Francis Vinton (or Frank). On their arrival, they took a ride towards Falmouth to view the war and received a report of rebel cavalry that fell back and artillery fire heard in the distance.[9]

This little theatric display brought responses among them and they enjoyed later their dinner "a pound-cake, carefully brought from home, was supplemented by some wild strawberries and a glass of excellent sherry," as General Greene remembered it.[10] It was a happy reunion for George Sr. and his son Charles to be together as a family. Their conversations varied from health to schooling and current events with friends and what took place in New York City. Papa found out soon enough that his visitors left their own memories that became part of the history of the 12th Corps.

On this hot day, June 4th, a review of the division was conducted by General Greene, his family was also in attendance. The double quick movements were performed by the men and tired out some of them. They felt displeased that they drilled only for the General's benefit.

"General Green[e]'s daughter," [Anna] recalled a 147th Pennsylvania soldier, "was sitting in a barouche and enjoying the movements of the troops. She said to the General: Papa make them trot again. I like to see them trot."[11]

Another soldier remembered it as "Papa, can't you trot them around again? It looks so funny," and her father replied "Of course I can; ain't I General?" The men repeated Anna's words to the General during their marches afterwards and they were not disciplined for it.[12] Since Greene was a disciplinarian, he felt the boys were entitled since they made that day a special moment for him.

The 137th New York didn't feel good that day because an order was read that night that reported their arms were found dirty, no furloughs could be issued until they were cleaned.[13] The division was commended by Generals Slocum, Geary, Greene and Thomas Kane for their fine appearance on their next review on June 10th. Some of Greene's men used their free time to explore the area, as related by the historian of the 149th New York:

"Among the curious objects which attracted attention of members of the regiment at this time was a bed of fossils at U-Be-Dam. They consisted of long spiral stones shaped like a cork-screw, and in some instances as long as a man's finger. The soft rock was filled with them, and the men gathered large quantities to send as souvenirs to their friends. These curious formations were the result of clay turned to stone inside of shells similar in character to those known to sailors as Marlinspikes. About this time the soldiers made their first acquaintance with the curious little insect know as the glow-worm, and many were boxed and shipped to the young folks at home."[14]

The day after the review, General Greene sat down at his desk in his tent and wrote a letter of recommendation for Colonel Joseph C. Lane to be appointed Colonel of the 15th Regiment of New York Volunteers. Noting his service with the 102nd New York and giving credit to himself and his command, Greene called him "a good officer" and hoped that Colonel Lane "will be successful in seeking a more extended field of operation."[15] Like Greene, Lane was a Civil Engineer and he had received recommendations from Generals Benham, Slocum, Hooker's Chief of Staff General Daniel Butterfield, and Joseph Hooker himself.

What made Colonel Lane request a transfer from Greene's brigade? General Benham stated in his letter that the 15th regiment was less three companies due to expire on June 17th and those remaining were to be in service for three years.[16] Usually a transfer indicated a promotion or a problem. Sometimes an officer wanted to go into another branch of the service. It is likely that Colonel Joseph C. Lane was hurt by Greene's remark in his report of Chancellorsville, which suggested his failure to communicate with the 60th New York on their orders to retire.[17] He may have asked Greene to delete that remark and when it remained, Lane carried a wounded pride and took the first opportunity that came his way. Whatever the reason, Colonel Lane remained with the 102nd New York and General Greene needed this valuable officer in the upcoming campaign.

Another campaign on Greene's mind was a solution to the Rebel Torpedoes that was giving problems for the U.S. Navy. He may have been asked by his son, Dana, or by another naval officer through private correspondence how to defeat this weapon. The engineer went into great detail to outfit a ship and how it could remove the threat to navigation:

It is proposed to fit up on a vessel of the Monitor class, a pneumatic chamber by which communication can readily be had from the interior of the vessel with the water in which she floats below the surface, for the purpose of placing mines (powder or other explosives) on the surface of the bottom of the sea; and then retiring the vessel & having a connection with the mines from the vessel by galvanic conductors, by which the mines can be fired without injuring the vessel, destroying torpedoes [mines] or obstructions in the vicinity of the spot where the mine was deposited, again advancing over the space last mined, depositing a new mine, & repeating the operation until the channel is cleared.[18]

The Navy received his proposal, but nothing came of it for use during the Civil War. Clearing underwater mines continued to be a problem into the wars of the 20th Century and Greene's concept of a minesweeper in 1863 was used by the naval authorities years later.

With General Lee's Confederates on the move through Northern Virginia and their destination unknown to Joe Hooker, he sent out orders to put his army on the march. His objective was to have defend Washington D.C. and follow after Lee's Army. As General Greene said his goodbyes to Martha, Anna and his friends, orders were received to march on June 13th, his son, Francis Vinton remained with him.

Greene obtained a pass for him and assured Martha of his safety to calm any fears. With father and Charles watching him, Frank could enjoy and see what the soldiers did on the march.

Frank began his diary on June 13th, "Left Aquia Landing at 7:30 am marched six miles to Potomac creek intending to do Picket duty. The General was riding all the morning finding where his picket line was to be. As I was with him & rode some twenty miles I was completely played out & could hardly stand up."[19]

They had marched along the railroad and telegraph line with the day hot and dry. Spencer H. Jasen of Company K, 137th New York felt the heat and complained "it made me sweat to carry my Knapsack."[20]

General Alpheus Williams wrote home about that first day, "The day was hot and we were busy moving the regiments from sunrise taking up a line from Aquia Creek some four miles long toward Potomac Creek and in establishing in front a long line of pickets. It was a hard job in a country so densely covered by thickets and broken by deepest ravines."[21]

After a delay in marching when new orders directed the 12th Corps toward Dumfries (due to a battery blocking the road), there was a report of rebels in the area. "We started [June 14th] in a drizzling rainstorm & marched till 4 1/2 am when we halted at Stafford for the men to get breakfast & the artillery to pass," recorded Francis Vinton in his diary.[22] Skirmishers were thrown out in the front and in the rear of the column in groups of three or four men so they could detect any rebel cavalry nearby.[23] Young Greene added to his diary, "it was very dark & 5 or 6 wagons were lost from tumbling into the ditch on the side of the road."[24]

Greene's brigade resumed their march, crossing Quantico creek, and set up camp at Dumfries in the afternoon. A march of 17 miles had a trail of debris, but no one bothered to collect any supplies due to exhaustion. General Greene's sons, Charles & Francis had Lt. Cantine come along with them to cool off by bathing in the Quantico.[25] The rest of the division crossed the pontoon bridge and began June 15th, a march that became the most difficult for those veterans of the 12th Corps. "The long march form Dumfries to Fairfax on the fifteenth," wrote the historian of the 12th Corps, "was a memorable one on account of the intense heat, several of the men falling in the road from exhaustion or smitten with sunstroke."[26]

Charles Engle struggled along and another soldier carried his knapsack, "I had all I could do to ceep up as it was." Arriving that night he continued "such stragling never wasd done. There was never troops marched so fast when it was so hot. There was a good meney sunstruck and some died on the road."[27]

Greene's son, Francis, could sympathize with his father's men "the heat was excessive [with] a great many falling out although we halted very often."[28]

One of Greene's men remembered that "we were marched to Fairfax Court House in such a hurried manner that nearly one-half of the men fell out from exhaustion, and sixteen were so seriously prostrated it became necessary to send them to general hospital at

Washington."[29] This march was made with hardly a cloud in sight, Steuben H. Coon of the 60th New York told his father. "It was one of the hottest days . . . I do not that there was any urgent necessity for our going so far that day." He stated the division of some 2500 men had between 15 and 20 soldiers put in the ambulances and died.[30] A 7th Ohio soldier, who had been with General Greene at Antietam, believed Geary's division had lost 15 men to the march.[31]

There was an urgency because they needed to keep pace with Lee's Confederates who kept advancing north and had stolen a march on Joe Hooker, a reversal of Hooker's advance over Lee those first few days towards Chancellorsville. Since their departure from Acquia Landing, the black plumes of smoke rose from the dock and government supplies that were torched to keep out of the rebels possession, to their fatigued arrival at Fairfax Court House, Greene's men had covered 50 miles.[32]

As the sun went down and the tents were fixed in place for Greene's brigade to rest that night, the air was filled "with enthusiastic cheers, and other demonstrations of applause." This was for Colonel Abel Goddard who rode into camp as the new commander of the 60th New York. He was respected by the men and had been with them since their original inception. Due to an error, Goddard was commissioned earlier but didn't get notified. For the moment they were no longer exhausted and their spirits rejuvenated.[33]

Rumors passed among the regiments of where the 12th Corps was headed. "I think we will go to Washington to do provost duty," said one of Greene's men.[34] Others believed it could be Alexandria or Winchester (where the Rebel forces had defeated Milroy's Union troops on June 13th).[35] Francis Vinton Greene and a companion went into the village on June 16, 1863 and thought the court house was in bad shape. "It is now used by the government as a sort of magazine. The only stores open were sutlers' which were jambed although they asked the most outrageous prices." He thought of going into his own business.[36]

They left camp on June 17th and General Greene didn't want his men to suffer in this hot weather like they did two days ago.

For 10 minutes of every hour they rested, but despite the pleasant morning, it difficult due to a mist that rose from the ground. After they marched 9 miles, Greene's brigade crossed Difficult Creek and Leesburg and Alexandria Railroad and set up their camp 2 miles south of Drainsville.[37] General Williams of the 1st Division was thankful for the short march because the heat was made worse for the dry old grass and woods caught fire due to the weather.[38].

Years later, a soldier of the 149th New York remembered about that part of their march on June 18th towards Leesburg, "the farms were comparatively small, under fair cultivation, and similar in appearance to those in Loudon and Shenandoah Valleys. The land was rolling, the timber hard wood, mostly oak, chestnut and walnut, and the general appearance of the country attractive."[39] The air was cool from a shower that opened upon the troops later in the day. They were pelted with "hailstones as large as walnuts," recalled a 60th New Yorker. He saw a number of the teams from the train attempt to take shelter in the woods. The results were "some of the mules got entangled, while others upset the wagons."[40]

With 12 miles covered that day the division arrived at Goose Creek. Greene's brigade had remained on the south side and the other two brigades crossed over a bridge made out of logs and fence rails. Placed on the stone piers of a destroyed stone and iron bridge, the rains and darkness made it dangerous to cross "the water was then up to the horses' backs and nearly to the top of the limber and caisson boxes carrying the ammunition." General Greene had placed two pieces of artillery in position at the ford in case of attack before the men settled in for the night.[41]

Captain Collins was detailed with the brigade pickets and in rain and mud had arrived within a mile of Leesburg. They attempted to dry their clothes by the kitchen fire (in the house where the hostess pre- pared a meal) and bedded down in their tents that were in the door yard.[42]

General Greene brought in his pickets and the pioneers under his direction built a new bridge since they awoke to the other one carried away by the rising waters. The ford became impassable for the mule trains, but with its completion by 2 pm, the rest of

Greene's brigade marched over on June 19th, arrived at Fort Evans near Leesburg and set up camp.[43]

It was here that Greene's men were ordered with the rest of the 12th Corps to witness the execution of three deserters from the 1st Division. Formed in a square with one side open, they stood in front of the new graves with coffins beside them. After the order to fire by the Provost-Marshal was carried out by the squad, the soldiers were marched past them as a reminder that deserters are punished.[44] It was said by General Slocum, commander of the 12th Corps, that it was a necessity to quickly carry out the execution because of an increase in desertions and the strong possibility of President Abraham Lincoln issuing pardons for these men. He felt an example needed to be made for the discipline of the army.[45]

Those next few days Greene's brigade worked on the earthwork referred to as Fort Evans, an abandoned rebel fort that had seen an earlier battle back in October 1861.[46] General Slocum deems its reconstruction and the building of a pontoon bridge as vital to the pursuit of General Lee's Confederates, "my command occupies three redoubts, constructed by the enemy. I consider the position a strong one, and am making it still stronger. One of the redoubts covers the approaches to Edwards Ferry. A bridge at that point would be valuable for obtaining supplies, in case of a movement of this wing of the army across the Potomac. The passage of the trains would be covered by the works at this place."[47]

The Army of the Potomac began concentrating their forces towards Edward Ferry. From this high ground, if General Greene had taken in the view from there, a person could see Maryland and Loudon Heights to the west, to the northeast was Sugar Loaf Mountain, and other points east in Maryland and Virginia toward Washington.[48] When Greene's men were not working on the fort, many of them visited Ball's Bluff (the battlefield of October 1861), outside of the town of Leesburg. The soldiers had conversed with some of the inhabitants about that terrible fight. "Above the Bluff, in a retired place in the woods" writes a 149th New Yorker years later, "were three or four trenches thirty or forty feet long in which were buried the Union dead. The sight of these trenches impressed the beholder with an indescribable dread of the fate of those known as the 'Unknown Dead'."[49]

In contrast, the surgeons from the 137th New York had visited Leesburg on June 23rd and saw a beautiful cemetery. Looking upon the 170 Confederate soldiers buried there, the head surgeon stated, "the head boards were painted white and appeared like marble and the graves covered with flowers by the people of Leesburg. Most of the dead were members of Mississippi regiments, some from Alabama, South Carolina and Virginia."[50] The assistant surgeon, Taylor Elmore, was thankful to be still with the living, his companions Lieutenant Biecher and the chaplain "went across Goose creek this afternoon [June 22nd] and had a narrow escape from six rebels, we having no arms."[51]

One of Greene's men on guard at the bridge saw Confederates approach him, but they had no weapons, he wrote home "they come with 15 prisoners this morning. They took them acrosed thense to Washington. They look so mean I would like to shoot every one of them."[52] Foragers collected supplies from the civilians which made their stay a pleasant one as one soldier related, "I went once and helped kill a hog that would weighed 250 and once we kicked a two year old steere and we got milk and all the cheeries we could eat." Besides food and drink, fresh horses and information from slaves could be obtained.[53].

The 11th Corps had crossed over the bridge followed by the 1st Corps and then the 3rd Corps in the mid afternoon of June 25th.[54] With Lee's Army in Maryland and Pennsylvania, it became more imperative to locate his forces and bring them to battle. General Greene prepared his brigade to move out on June 26, 1863 and followed behind the 3rd Corps. They moved out from camp at 5 am and crossed the pontoon bridge as the 50th New York Engineers looked on as they marched along their handiwork. "It was interesting to see the long line of troops, artillery and wagons crossing these bridges of boats, which seemed altogether too frail to bear the enormous weight, for they were crowded full from side to side."[55]

General Greene's brigade was now in Maryland, moving westward along the Chesapeake and Ohio Canal and bypassed

Poolesville. The 6th Corps had followed behind and the 5th Corps crossed the bridge at the end of the day. After Greene's men had marched 10 miles that day, the soldiers set up camp and started out early next morning.[56]

A 137th New York soldier, Corporal James S. Hyde of Company E recorded in his diary what transpired, "we crossed the river and were again in Maryland. We paused by 'Poolsville' in the morning.

It rained a little all the forenoon which made the rodes very muddy. We passed some very large fields of wheat, and corn, and as we went by the houses the folks were out to see us. Men were not afraid to show themselves here as they were in Virginia. We camped at the junction of the Monocacy with the Potomac. After I got my tent set, I went out to a house and got all the cherries I could eat. Cherries were very thick all along the road."[57]

June 27th began for Greene's men as they crossed the Monacacy that morning on the stone aqueduct with few halts until they were 2 miles from Point of Rocks. This was due to the 3rd Corps not moving ahead (they had been there all night). General Hooker had passed by the 12th Corps and received no cheers from the soldiers. Was this an omen to come? After the delay, the troops reached Point of Rocks in the afternoon by 1 pm, passed through a culvert with bowed heads and stepped out of the gap in the Catocin Mountains.[58]

As the men passed through the village of Peterville, cheers rang out when two flags of old glory were seen flying in the breeze and moved along in the warm weather, just about a mile from Knoxville and bivouaced there for the night after a march of 20-22 miles.[59] The men began the day, June 28th, not going to Harper's Ferry as some expected, but marched back to Peterville and through Jefferson by 11 am. During their 10 minute halt (on the hour) outside Jefferson, General Slocum rode down the column and spread the news that General Joe Hooker had been relieved and the new army commander was General George Gordon Meade.

There were some misgivings about this change because this former 5th Corps commander was unknown to them. Greene's brigade had crossed the Monacacy and camped outside in the woods from Frederick, finishing a 21 mile march.[60]

Orders were given on short notice to march on June 29th. Upon General Greene's departure, arrangements were made for his son, Francis, to be left behind in Frederick because of the upcoming battle to take place somewhere in Pennsylvania.[61] As the 12th Corps entered Frederick, "Greene ordered his troops to take the cadence step, and his well drilled regiments swing along through the streets of the city. The White Stars were greeted with cheers and cries of admiration from the throngs that lined the sidewalks."[62]

One enlisted man was more interested in the pretty girls amid the sounds of the band and drum corps playing with the flags flying in this atmosphere of a parade. Going through the town, they "passed some Union families and one woman gave to the soldiers all she had to eat." James S. Hyde enjoyed sweet milk, while others were greeted with pails of water and food to those on the roadway.[63]

Despite the delay caused by the baggage wagons, they passed through Walkersville and Woodburn (Woodsboro) and stopped to pitch their tents having marched 20 miles in the area of Taneytown near the Maryland-Pennsylvania state line.[64] Greene's soldiers awoke June 30th early in the morning and went through Taneytown, crossed into Pennsylvania and marched to Littlestown. The impression that Greene's men had of their new surroundings was told by a veteran years later:

"The country about Littlestown and Southern Pennsylvania through which the army passed is populated by Germans or people of German descent, and has the usual Dutch characteristics; Barns better than the houses and horses better kept than the women and children. It had a thrifty and prosperous look, but the people were more given to money-getting than aesthetic indulgences; life was a matter of business and not of of pleasure."[65]

The men were in good spirits as joyful citizens greeted them and offered refreshments. "I generally took a drink if the lady was handsome," stated the 137th New Yorker James S. Hyde. Having an eye for the ladies, from his experience in Frederick, Hyde continued, "one young lady saved a piece of bread for me by refusing several others ahead. 'Who wouldn't be a soldier!'"[66] By mid afternoon cavalry was observed from the sounds of cannon fire that approached them as they came closer to the conflict. As General Greene deployed his brigade, the two sides had broken off the fight. They ended their 12 mile march and rested a mile outside Littlestown.[67]

July 1, 1863 filled with tension for Greene's men because the rebel cavalry was nearby and they knew Lee's Army could not be far behind. Their march took them back to Littlestown and then moved north on the Baltimore Pike, reaching Two Taverns in the afternoon.

Sounds of artillery fire was heard in the distance while the men tried to sit and boil their coffee in an open field.[68] Was this another cavalry skirmish or did the Army of the Potomac find General Lee?

A staff officer of General Greene, Captain Charles Piltortan, wrote after the war for July 1st that "as the afternoon wore on, the increasing rapidity of the artillery fire and heavy musketry fire, now becoming audible, showed that a large force must be engaged, and that the action was more serious than we had supposed."[69] Greene had his men march with the rest of the 12th Corps to reinforce the army fighting at a town called Gettysburg.

On the way there, a number of wounded soldiers and rebel prisoners were seen for the first time.

Now artillery and stragglers occupied the road as they drew closer to thundering noise of shot and shell.

Civilians evacuated the town to look for a safe place.[70]. By early evening General Greene's brigade arrived on the outskirts of the borough of Gettysburg and the soldiers placed on the right side of Little Round Top in front of the Taneytown Road.[71]

"We halt in a wheatfield and lay on our arms during the night," wrote Sergeant Henry Rudy of Company I, 137th New York Regiment.

But not everyone had that in mind. As a member of the 147th Pennsylvania (deployed next to Greene's brigade) recalled, "on our front in the ravine General Green[e] was posting the pickets. The writer with a number of canteens was out searching for water and, it being moonlight, he saw a house in the distance for which he started. He passed General Green[e] who asked, 'Where are you going?' I replied 'Over to that house for water.' The General said 'You get back, for if you go that house for water, you will go to Richmond as the rebels are in that yard."[72]

Two members of the 137th New York enjoyed a good supper of sweet bread and milk at a nearby farm house that night. They were mesmerized by a pretty girl named Hannah. With the rebels near, "the old folks were nearly scared to death, [but] Hannah was brave as a lion."[73] Lucky for them that Greene didn't find them or they could have been put under arrest.

General George Sears Greene had seen the end of July 1, 1863 on the left side of the Union line south of the town of Gettysburg. The brigade had endured hot weather, exhaustive marches, and renewed enthusiasm after Chancellorsville as they meet grateful civilians, going through Virginia, Maryland and southern Pennsylvania. Greene had enjoyed the reunion of family members and friends for a time and had his youngest son, Francis, with him on part of the march (even celebrated Francis Vinton's birthday on June 27th).

Could the next day decide the battle that began with Confederate success? It was reported before the battle that General Robert E. Lee said of the new commander of the Army of the Potomac, "General Meade will commit no blunder in my front, and if I make one he will make haste to take advantage of it."[74]

But Meade did blunder on Lee's front, and it took General George Sears Greene and his soldiers to defend the area known as Culp's Hill and possibly decided the outcome of the war.

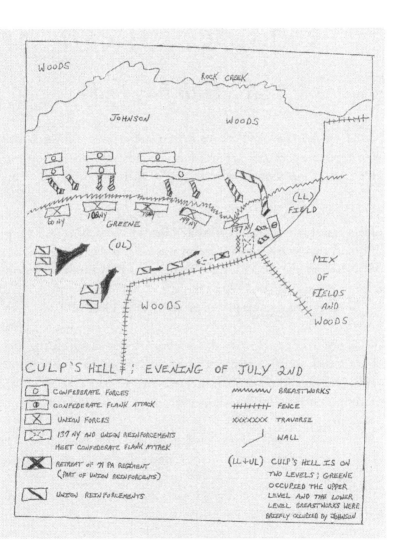

WOODS

ROCK CREEK

JOHNSON   WOODS

(LL.)
FIELD

60 NY   102 NY   149 NY
         GREENE

(UL)

MIX
OF
FIELDS
AND
WOODS

137 NY

WOODS

CULP'S HILL; EVENING OF JULY 2ND

▢	CONFEDERATE FORCES	⩘⩘⩘⩘ BREASTWORKS
▣	CONFEDERATE FLANK ATTACK	++++++++ FENCE
⊠	UNION FORCES	XXXXXX TRAVERSE
⊠	137 NY AND UNION REINFORCEMENTS	⌐ WALL
	MEET CONFEDERATE FLANK ATTACK	
◼	RETREAT OF 71 PA REGIMENT	(LL+UL) CULP'S HILL IS ON
	(PART OF UNION REINFORCEMENTS)	TWO LEVELS; GREENE
		OCCUPIED THE UPPER
◣	UNION REINFORCEMENTS	LEVEL AND THE LOWER
		LEVEL BREASTWORKS WERE
		BRIEFLY OCCUPIED BY JOHNSON

Chapter Fifteen

Culp's Hill: July 2nd

The Army of the Potomac's commander, General Meade rode next to General Henry J. Hunt (artillery advisor) along the Culp's Hill area on a reconnaissance for deployment of both artillery and infantry.

The division had cooked their breakfast while they awaited orders that early morning. Greene's Brigade, which moved (5 am to 6 am) out with Geary's division was relieved by General Sickles 3rd Corps to the Union's right flank, crossed Baltimore Pike and arrived at the crest of Culp's Hill.[1]

Greene's brigade was placed on the right of General Wadsworth's First Corps line their left formed a right angle and moved down the slope.[2] After they arrived, General Greene surveyed the area, "Rock Creek running past our front at the distance of 200 to 400 yards. Our position and the front were covered with a heavy growth of timber, free from undergrowth, with large ledges of rock projecting above the surface.

These rocks and trees offered good cover for marksmen. The surface was very steep on our left, diminishing to a gentle slope on our right."[3]

His regiments were aligned with the 60th New York on the left, followed by the 102nd, 149th, and 137th New York facing towards the east and the 78th New York in front of brigade as a skirmish line. The Second Brigade (General Kane) connected with Greene's men on the right and the First Brigade (Colonel Candy) was posted behind Greene's Brigade as a reserve.[4]

Colonel Lewis Stegman of the 102nd New York stated that

"immediately on its arrival, by order of General Greene, who personally superintended the work, the men commenced to construct earthworks, if they may be so called, composed of logs, cordwood, stones and earth, about breast high, a good protection against ordinary musketry."[5] Some were eager to get to it as "all instinctively felt that a life-and- death struggle was impending," related Captain Jesse H. Jones of the 60th New York. During those morning hours on the "right and left the men felled the trees, and blocked them up into a close rail fence.

Piles of cordwood which lay nearby were quickly appropriated. The sticks, set slanting on end against the outer face of the logs made excellent battening." [6]

How did these preparations come about at Culp's Hill? Did General Greene or individual officers in both divisions of the 12th Corps have discretion to entrench themselves since they received no orders from Generals Meade or Slocum? While the ordinary soldier in the ranks could see from the past battles that improved armaments in rifle fire and artillery were changing tactics on the field, some officers were resistant to this notion. As pointed out by one historian, soldiers did make use of walls and fences, but these were fixed emplacements that had existed before the battle to be used for protection.[7]

General Geary had called a conference of his brigade commanders to discuss the validity of building breastworks. Here was the defining moment that explained the mind of the volunteer / politician and the military / engineer. Giving his officers the choice to entrench themselves, Geary was against it because it unfitted men for fighting without them.

This brief experience at Chancellorsville of the rebel attacks on Geary's flanks was not a fair judgment to this new form of fighting. General Greene saw the effects of fighting behind breastworks at Chancellorsville and the morale it gave his men against a large force and better protection. He felt that saving lives was a priority over any theories and the men can have breastworks, provided they are given the time.[8]

Some men, like William C. Lewis of the 60th New York,

may have agreed with Greene, but were tired of building them because over time since Harper's Ferry, they were not used and moved to another location.[9] All along the line of the 12th Corps, the work was finished by noon. All his skills of engineering, West Point training, and battlefield experience showed Greene that Culp's Hill was a defensive redoubt to be the anchor for General Meade's fishhook line of defense. Ironically, Meade had thought of an offensive operation between 9:30 am and 10:00 am with the 12th Corps and 5th Corps, but after further examination and told it was not practical, the Culp's Hill offensive was cancelled.[10]

Greene's men had completed their work in two to three hours.

Some of the trees chopped down were used as a head log along a part of the line. This provided a soldier more protection from the upper chest to the head while he fired the musket through the opening below.[11] Under Greene's direction, the line ran the course of the ridge at right angles, that connected his right across a hollow which made a traverse. This engineering method played a vital role later in the day.[12]

He was curious why (with relief) the Confederates didn't attack that morning, since they could hear (if not see) the Union soldiers, as they fortified their position beyond their lines northeast of Rock Creek. It was quiet along their line, except for a rebel battery that fired a shell now and again. The 66th Ohio from Greene's command at Antietam had Sergeant Tallman seated next to another soldier under a tree when a shell burst among them that caused a slight wound to that soldier and missed Tallman.[13]

With the 12th Corps hospital established about two miles in the rear of their lines, by early afternoon the 137th New York surgeon, John Farmington had approached the town and rode his horse as one of the men walked beside him during this calm before the storm. He wrote, "I rode along our line as far as the Baltimore Pike where it goes over Cemetery Ridge to Gettysburg. The town was in possession of the rebels and they had sharpshooters stationed at various points. I was ignorant of that fact however and as soon as I came in view of the village a Minnie ball whizzed by my ear and

I told my companion I had seen enough, and retired a short distance down the Baltimore Pike."[14]

By four in the afternoon the long awaited assault by Lee's army came on the Union left. It sounded like a thunderstorm across the land as Greene's brigade looked toward their front. At Benner's Hill, located across Rock Creek, Major Joseph W. Latimer opened up with his artillery battalion on Geary's Division with 14 guns and two 20-pounder Parrotts.[15]

After a half hour artillery fire between Latimer's battalion (which was exposed on the knoll) and a section of both Knap's Independent Pennsylvania Battery and Company K, 5th U.S. Artillery, Latimer was mortally wounded and the battalion withdrawn.[16] General Greene and the men looked for the Rebel advance line but they saw no movement and the 12th Corps were affected by General Meade's decision later on the battlefield.

Skirmishers took an advanced position early that morning and afternoon by General Greene's order, Lieutenant Colonel John C. Redington was put in command. "We relieved about 8 a.m. two companies of the Seventh Indiana, of the First Corps, my force consisting of 7 officers and 170 men, with which I covered the entire front of the Second Division. We advanced beyond the brook, and held our line until the advance of the line of battle of the enemy, about 7 pm."[17] The 78th New York deployed as skirmishers later in the day from their position on the left to reinforce Redington's force.[18] He provided cover for the soldiers to dig entrenchments and found out where Rock Creek was shallow for men to cross to concentrate his force, thus he held up the advance of the enemy, and Redington made the Division's line a stronger obstacle to the Confederates.[19]

While some of the men had stacked their arms and others rested, feeling safe from the little activity around them, Captain Collins of the 149th observed that "some of the officers went down to the skirmish line in front of Wadsworth's Division [on Greene's left] and saw the enemy's troops forming in line in the suburbs of Gettysburg."[20] Orders were sent from headquarters to move out for the 12th Corps. The attack on the Union left by General

Longstreet had wrecked the 3rd Corps, pushed those divisions into the 5th and 2nd Corps regiments and moved towards Cemetery Ridge.[21]

Looking for reinforcements, General Meade had taken troops from other Corps and looked at Culp's Hill since there was no enemy advance that July 2nd morning and afternoon. While it is debated about what forces should remain behind at Culp's Hill, General Alpheus S. Williams wrote that Meade had asked for General Slocum to give him all the troops he could spare.[22] Because of Meade's poor judgment to strip his right flank in order to stop Longstreet's attack on his left flank, he seriously compromised the standing of the Union Army's battle line.

One soldier in the 102nd New York felt Meade's actions was a near disaster and suicidal move that warm July day.[23] For the Confederates planned to support Longstreet's attack with an attack of their own to capture Culp's Hill. This was to be conducted by Major General Edward "Old Allegheny" Johnson's division of Lt. General Richard S. Ewell's 2nd Corps. He advanced with 4,745 men from three brigades against the Culp's Hill breastworks.[24]

Johnson had altered the planned attack because his fourth brigade, under Brigadier General James Walker, was kept out of the fight and protected the far left from Union forces that could fire into the rear of the division.[25] This was a loss of 1,323 men that could be a factor in the fight.[26]

Towards 6:30 pm in the evening, Greene saw the First Division leave their entrenchments and march towards the Union left and Geary's Second Division to follow. Slocum had sent his assistant general, Colonel Hiram C. Rodgers to Meade's headquarters to amend his orders for a division to be kept in place. Because Meade felt the "point of real danger" was the Union left he rejected Slocum's request but since he deemed it "absolutely essential," Meade allowed Slocum, with misgivings, to keep one brigade. He chose General George Sears Greene and his 1,424 New Yorkers to guard and defend that area that two full divisions had covered on Culp's Hill.[27]

The skirmishers had traded shot with their rebel counterparts during the day, but now as the sun began to descend in the west late that day, an officer among Greene's skirmishers saw regiments of infantry come in his view. Admiring the movements and pageantry of the enemy officers he stated, "an officer and staff rode along the front line, and must have made some remarks to the men, as I distinctly saw a flutter of battle flags and hats waving in the air."[28]

Their line of march saw the first lines of Confederates removing the rail fences in their front to clear the way for the rest of Johnson's Division. Redington positioned his men at those most likely areas of Rock Creek where it was shallow, "I desired to hold a line about 100 yards this side of the brook and sweep them as they crossed the brook."[29] Sounds of gunfire broke out as Geary had called in his skirmishers to move out, but despite Slocum's order to keep Greene's Brigade on the line, a member of Greene's staff wrote of that critical moment "we received orders to move out of our works and reinforce the line on our left."

Because Greene received a report about the large force approaching from his skirmishers, he disobeyed the standing order to move and stopped the brigade. He sent out reinforcements to the skirmishers and informed Geary of his action. "Gen. Geary on receiving the report," stated Greene's staff officer "declined to confirm Gen. Greene's advice and ordered the Brigade to follow," but Greene's defiant course of action against Geary was upheld as Slocum's staff member Lt. Col. Rodgers met the officer with Geary's orders to leave General Greene at his place on the 12th Corps line.[30]

With orders from Slocum to occupy the line, Greene wrote "I immediately extended my men to the right of comply with the order as far as possible."[31] Steuben H. Coon of the 60th New York remembered what Greene did as he "came riding up and ordered every regiment except the 60th to fall into line. He told our Colonel that the other regiments were needed in another place and that he must put the men in single rank and far enough apart so to cover the ground before occupied by the whole brigade."[32] As he turned away and lead his horse to the right of the line to make sure of the proper alignments to contain the Rebel advance, Greene expressed his concern. "We must hold the position for everything depended on our keeping the enemy back."[33]

Sgt. Henry Rudy of Company I, 137th New York put in his diary, "we double quick to the right and take to thetrenches." These trenches are the ones vacated by General Thomas Kane's Second Brigade of Geary's Division that Greene had them holding the right flank, The traverse was behind them to aid in their protection.[34] The men from Company H were seen running back to the 137th New York from the line of skirmishers. Other men drifted back, firing at the rebels covered behind trees and rocks as they advanced. With the bugle sounds heard over the Rebel yell and the noise of battle told them where to come in, it became a race for survival to find safety behind the breastworks.[35]

The fading light was a concern as Redington stated in his report, "the darkness was so great in this part of the woods that we could not see the enemy, and we fired at the flashes of their guns. They were so lose to us that we took 12 prisoners. When within 50 yards of the works, I ordered the line to fall back into the earthworks."[36] They could have been captured or killed if not for the 200 men from Col. Herbert von Hammerstein's 78th New York that Greene sent out to help them as they retreated to their lines.[37]

They came into the line and told their comrades of the large number of rebels and bullets were buzzing like bees among the regiments. Their patience was tested at the breastworks, rifles kept under control, because of the danger of firing and hitting their own men. Some were killed on their approach and cries of desperation rang out as darkness made it harder to distinguish friend or foe.

Perry Norton of the 149th New York had been shot in the leg on his return to the breastworks. He wrote his father, "it is not the Rebs that done it-it was our own men. They took us to be Rebs and they fired tremendous volleys in our own men." One New Yorker put it bluntly, "we expected to be overpowered in a short time." The officers restrained the men as all the skirmishers who were not killed or wounded made it into the line as the rebel fire got closer and grew in volume.[38]

These men took their place among Greene's thin, stretched-out line.[39] The three brigades of Johnson's Division attacked Greene's troops were from right to left; Brigadier General John M. Jones of the 21st, 25th, 42, 44th, 48th, and 50th Virginia regiments, in the center was the 1st, 2nd, 10th, 14th, and 15th Louisiana regiments under Colonel Jesse M. Williams and on the left was Brigadier General George H. Steuart, consisting of the 1st Maryland Battalion, 1st and 3rd North Carolina, and the 10th, 23rd and 37th Virginia regiments.[40]

By now the Confederate attack, had crossed Rock Creek after 7 pm and reached the slopes of Culp's Hill where the heavy fire opened alongside Greene's brigade. The nature of the ground limited the visibility of artillery support, but some Rebels could be seen crossing from patches in the woods on East Cemetery Hill. General Wadsworth had approached Colonel Charles S. Wainwright's guns to fire those guns on the woods. The colonel felt it was their own lines, since he was in that area earlier in the day. He had been correct as stated in his diary, "we had not fired half a dozen shots when a major of the Twelfth Corps came over and said that we were dropping every shot directly into their line, and already disabled half a dozen men."[41]

Those troops were the 60th New York and some of General Jones Virginians were forced to move toward the left to avoid those shells. "I glanced up, and to the left of the curtain of trees in front of our position the Confederates were coming out from the cover of woods," recalled one 60th New Yorker. As they charged up the hill, "volley after volley we poured into their staggering ranks," remembered another. How anyone could live bewildered one 60th soldier since the Rebels were met with a long sheet of flames from their entrenchments.[42]

It was a rugged climb as more of the fighting grew from sighting the flashes in the dark. "The works in front of our lines were of a formidable character," the 44th Virginia captain observed, "and in some places they could scarcely be surmounted without scaling-ladders."[43] Directing fire on those Rebels behind a small tree in the rear of his Company I, Captain Jesse H. Jones was not protected by the works or the tree. Wearing beneath his blouse a pair of steel breastplates that he found, the 60th New Yorker was struck by a minie ball, hitting the edge of one plate at the area where they overlapped and bent it, causing it to make a dent in the other plate. The captain later wrote of his bruise, "God's hand to me reached down out of Heaven to save my life."[44]

Casualties increased as both Rebel and Yank continued to load and fire. The rebels were too close for Private Brown as "I feared for a time in spite of the good start we had made that the enemy would succeed in driving us back."[45] But this proved to be difficult as a 44th Virginia private saw only "a ditch filled with men firing down or our heads," while "the light from the muzzle blast" stated one 60th New Yorker, "lit the woods like day revealing Johnson's Confederates massed below."[46]

"The rebels yelled like wild Indians and charged upon us on a double quick," Steuben Coon told his father back home, "but very few got within 2 rods of us."[47] Their fire at close range caused a "terrible effect" on the rebel troops reported Colonel Abel Goddard of the 60th New York.[48]

This accurate fire had disrupted the Rebel chain of command as General Jones was hit in the thigh, causing him to lose more blood than initially realized from his wound and turned command over after 8:00 pm to Lt. Col. Robert H. Duncan, the senior brigade officer.[49]

Some of the 42nd Virginia soldiers had come within 30 paces of the works and the 50th Virginia could advance no further from a few feet of Greene's breastworks due to the heavy rifle fire.

Duncan's 48th Virginia had been ordered back 200 yards due to the severe fire after holding their place of 10 paces beyond the breastworks.[50] Their support from the Louisiana Brigade on their left had become bogged down due to meeting heavy resistance from Greene's men. Seeing the Rebels fall back on their part of the line, George F. Ryan of Company C, 60th New York stated that "two color-bearers of a [48th] Virginia regiment of the 'Stonewall' Brigade were killed about 20 feet in front of our regiment," as a number of the men were ordered over the works and took prisoners.[51]

John Wesley Hill of the 50th Virginia was determined Greene's men could not take him prisoner as he retreated behind a tree at the bottom of the cliff (slope) and continued to fire up at the Union works while his ammunition lasted.[52] But others were too close to the breastworks and gave themselves up as those wounded either walked into Greene's line or were helped in after crying for help.[53] It was believed that 56 prisoners were taken along with 7 officers and 89 Confederates killed during the engagement with 255 men of the 60th New York regiment.[54]

The 102nd New York had contributed to their fire next to them and also had help from the 78th New Yorkers that returned from skirmishing with the advancing Louisiana Brigade in the center. The 149th New York on their right added their firepower to the frontal assault. As it became dark, the Rebel Yell and the flash from their muskets as they advanced came through the developing gunsmoke on the field.[55]

Referring to that night as "hellish," one of the 149th New Yorkers said "the discharge of musketry was continued with great rapidity," against the brave Lousianians.[56]

Some of them from the 1st and 14th Louisiana are believed to have gotten over the breastworks, but were forced to withdraw or were captured, including one of the color-bearers who hid the flag from Greene's men.[57] Colonel Williams and his men were stopped within 100 yards and could not get support from Jones' Brigade on their right.[58] One of Greene's New Yorkers, Henry Moore of Company H, 149th New York had helped to slow down the oncoming Louisianans when they had pushed back the skirmishers and fell wounded in the shoulder (he died upon reaching the hospital).[59] Another 149th soldier couldn't get the breastworks to protect him as he was struck in the head and left eye.[60]

The resolve of his men in the 102nd New York was encouraged by Colonel James C. Lane, as he went back and forth along the line, exposed himself with this sword drawn high.[61] He believed that intervals between his men in compensating for the missing 12th Corps soldiers sent to the Union left required the officer to prove himself to General Greene.

Unlike Chancellorsville, there was no retreat. Near 9:00 pm, Colonel Lane was shot in the right arm while moving from one company to another and turned over the command to Captain Lewis R. Stegman.[62] Years later, Stegman was amazed how desperate the Confederates had fought, "they built breastworks of their own dead on this brigade front, so merciless was the Union fire; and the men who so used their comrades bodies were killed behind them."[63]

Each assault had been driven back and Williams' Brigade resorted to fire behind the boulders and trees realizing no more could be done to gain the works from Greene's troops. The timing was fortunate because the 149th New York fell back due to an unexplained order, which was countermanded by Lieutenant Colonel Randall.[64] This may have come about because some of the companies were soldiers moving on their right behind them. Was it the enemy or had reinforcements arrived? With their ammunition exhausted and not sure of what was happening on their right, the 149th's Colonel Henry A. Barnum reported, "we held the position with the bayonet and such limited firing as could be made with the ammunition of the killed and wounded."[65]

Reinforcements were on their way as the battle began as Greene had requested when the Rebels attacked that evening. He knew the topography of the deep slopes on his left and center could make it more difficult for the Confederates, but he was more concerned for this right flank since this section of Culp's Hill was closer to the enemy's line with only a slight incline. The 137th New York had moved into the entrenchments vacated by General Kane's Second Brigade, and stood alone to prevent them from turning their flank if the Rebels discovered their predicament.[66] For Greene, the battle's outcome and perhaps the war was decided by those next few hours.

Greene had sent members of this staff to ask Brigadier General James S. Wadsworth, commanding a division of the First Corps, and Major General Oliver O. Howard of the Eleventh Corps on the left of his line for assistance. The regiments Greene received were the 6th Wisconsin, 14th Brooklyn (also known as the 84th New York), 147th New York from the First Corps, and the 82nd

Illinois, 45th New York, 61st Ohio, 157th New York from the Eleventh Corps.[67] This additional reserve of 755 soldiers were placed within Greene's line as the battlefield was in near darkness, with only a bright moon as their guide.

While a staff officer from the 1st Corps brought the 157th New York and 61st Ohio to Greene's front, Major General Carl Schurz's division chief-of-staff, Lt. Col. August Otto had charge of the 82nd Illinois and 45th New York. [68] Knowing of the severe fighting on Greene's front, General Howard was moved by this young officer "I remember well when Otto promptly volunteered to guide these troops into position. Somehow it always affected me strongly to behold a hearty and fearless young man, after receiving an order, set forth without reluctance to execute it under such circumstances that there were few chances of ever seeing him again."[69]

Despite the confusion of orders from other staff officers as they marched to the right, those regiments were placed behind Greene's left and center part of the brigade line. The 157th New York's color-bearer was one of the few casualties and his flag was taken by a member of General Steuart's brigade, which suggested that they were near Greene's right flank.[70] However, the other regiments were directed towards Greene's right amid the smoke and firestorm of lead from the Confederates.

General George H. Steuart's Brigade had moved through the woods and reached a cornfield before they crossed Rock Creek and received fire from Greene's skirmishers. They took casualties in their exchange of fire which reduced the ranks of Company B, 1st Maryland Battalion with four soldiers wounded.[71] It was waist deep in some places remembered some veterans of the 2nd Maryland Infantry and were met with a heavy musketry fire as they moved up Culp's Hill from their southwestern advance.[72]

The 149th New York commenced fire on the 137th New York's left when the 3rd North Carolina and 1st Maryland Battalion came into view as they attempted to keep on the right and conform with Williams' Brigade. They advanced steadily toward Greene's breastworks, but General Steuart was concerned because the 137th

New York had opened up their fire against the 3rd North Carolina, which caused those troops many casualties from both flanks until they received some relief when fire was directed into the ranks of the 137th New York by the 1st Maryland Battalion.[73]

This initial fighting by the 137th New York was fortunate because they created this crossfire while Steuart's other regiments became separated, and the darkness, added to the difficulties of communication during the battle, which made their attack uncoordinated. "An angle in the enemy's works, not 100 yards to our right, exposed us to a severe flank fire," recalled those Maryland troops lying down for protection and saw "the Federals rise and fire at us" amid the drifting smoke.[74]

It felt like a thunderstorm with its deadly bolts of lightning crashing among them all that summer night. Greene's men continued to keep these Southerners pinned down as command of the Maryland troops went to Major William W. Goldsborough because Lt. Col. James R. Herbert was incapacitated by three wounds in leading his men.[75] Despite the lack of support on their left, the Maryland and North Carolina soldiers got some of the pressure taken off from them as time passed and the three Virginia regiments advanced against the 137th New York's right flank.[76]

Calling it "the hardest fighting he had been through, Corporal Hudson Jennings of Company K, 137th New York told his sister that "through some mistake, the line at the right of our Regiment was left unprotected, and the enemy came unrestricted into our works, and poured a heavy fire into the right flank and rear of our Regiment, and we were obliged to move to the left."[77] Because of the darkness, it was difficult for Steuart's three Virginia regiments to know if they had friendly troops in front or if they had marched to the top of the lower hill on Greene's right flank.[78] The 23rd Virginia's Lt. Col. Simeon Walton had the men hold their fire while Lt. Charles A. Raines (who volunteered) went forward to see if they were Yankees.[79]

Sergeant William Cresson thought reinforcements had come up and believed they fired in error into the 137th New York. He approached and saluted an officer. "What in h__l are you doing!

Don't you see you are firing into our line, and will hurt someone?" The officer asked who he belonged to and Cresson replied "137th New York! What troops are you?" The reply "Ewell's Command" sent Cresson jumping behind a rock, avoiding a pistol bullet sent in his direction as the officer ran backward to his command.[80]

With this information, the three Virginia regiments resumed the advance under the shelter of the lower hill and sent crashing volleys of Minnie balls into the right flank of the 137th New York. "We though it was our men and holerd at them and told them not to fire," but it became clear these were Rebels said one soldier caught by surprise.[81] The 137th New York had returned fire but didn't know if they could stop the assault.

Seeing this situation, Colonel Ireland reported "At this time I ordered Company A, the right flank company, to form at right angles with the breastworks, and check the advance of the enemy, and they did for some time, but, being sorely pressed, they fell back a short distance to a better position."[82]

Charles Engle saw a wounded corporal and attempted to help him. "The bullets came thick and clost but I got his knapsack off and got him up. I couldent carry him and my gun. I got him to lean on me and got him out the worst fireing," leaving the man on the side of the rock.[83] At least this soldier was safe from the Rebels for the moment. A stone wall was on the 137th New York's flank on the right along the entrenchments and to the rear. The 10th Virginia forced Colonel Ireland to slowly drift back as their fire peppered the ranks of his men.[84] Now the men of Greene's brigade received reinforcements, but not yet from the 6th Wisconsin, 14th Brooklyn and 147th New York that General Greene was personally trying to move towards the 137th New York.

The 71st Pennsylvania had been sent with the 106th Pennsylvania to help General Howard at Cemetery Hill, but the 71st Pennsylvania became lost in the dark and tried to follow the sounds of battle on their right and the light of the moon. Colonel Richard P. Smith had written after the battle, "I could find no general to report to who had command of any portion of the troops." After being met by Captain Craig Wadsworth, a staff officer of the

First Corps, they met Captain Charles P. Horton, Greene's assistant adjutant general who took responsibility and guided the 71st Pennsylvania towards the Union right line.[85]

Horton complained that Smith's men were slow and had to ride back and encourage them to move quickly. With their arrival at the trenches where the 137th New York was currently located, Horton said they gave "three loud cheers" and were fired on by the front and the right "by a few scattering shots." Colonel Smith was concerned about his men and said Greene's staff officer had told him "that all was safe on either flank."[86] This had been true when Horton came across the 71st Pennsylvania, but Colonel Ireland just pulled back his regiment and he stated the 71st Pennsylvania was brought to him by Lt. J.J. Cantine of Greene's staff and Ireland was the one who placed the regiment to keep the Rebels from completely turning the Union right flank.[87]

Yet Colonel Smith made no reference to Ireland (the one officer who was the most knowledgeable one in the group of the current situation) when he tried to justify what happened next. Upon firing a few shots, Captain Horton saw the 71st Pennsylvania get up "and retreated in line, apparently without panic or disorder." They "became engaged with the enemy on the front" wrote Colonel Smith, but he told Horton after fired upon from the right and rear "that he will not have his men murdered," and gave the order to retreat.[88]

The historian of the Philadelphia Brigade tried to give Smith's actions vindication that his position was due to a misunderstanding and not familiar with the ground. There were a few casualties and a number of prisoners from skirmishers. Sergeant Burns may not have agreed with Smith's retreating without orders, but wrote their brief time there "was the heaviest and wickedest musketry fire for about half an hour that I laid under."[89]

Horton urged Smith to go forward, but Smith said "he had received orders to return to his corps," and marched away from the enemy. Officers in the 2nd Corps (Hancock, Webb) said Smith never received orders to return to them and Smith, believed that he may be disciplined for his action, said after the battle "D__n them they had me flanked, it was not my fault." Years later, Greene said it was "desertion" and the Union right flank "had been left in the air."[90]

In truth, the conduct of the 71st Pennsylvania at Culp's Hill jeopardized the collapse of General Greene's line. It was "a blunder on the part of our officers [that] came near costing us dear," which Sergeant Burns frankly admitted.[91] This withdraw forced Ireland to fall back into the traverse that Greene had built on his right as the 19th Virginia had made progress along the stone wall and the 23rd Virginia fired into their right flank from the south. With heavy pressure from the rest of Steuart's Brigade, including two 137th New Yorkers being captured during the retreat by Private George Pile, 37th Virginia took hold of them by their knapsack and sword belt, something needed to be done by Colonel Ireland.[92]

The two companies on the right had been the first to fall back as witnessed by Captain Horton as they "met the flank attack with such a steady fire that the rebels again fell back," but it was only temporary.[93]

Both sides were so close that one 137th New Yorker told his sister that "one of our boys who had fired away all of his ammunition, saw some men and supposed they were our men, and asked for some, but saw they were Rebs, and turned and ran, they pouring a volley after him, but not touching him."[94]

Smoke obscured the men's vision in the moonlight which made it more difficult to see. Because of the poor visibility and concern they may fire on their own men, the Confederates halted their fire now and again.[95]

They were "cautiously feeling for our position and our right," recalled Owen J. Sweet, 1st Lieutenant of Company B. To stabilize their new line and give General Greene the time for the reinforcements coming from Wadsworth's division (First Corps), Colonel Ireland reported on the heroics of Captain Joseph H. Gregg of Company I: "Captain Gregg, in command of a small squad of men, charged with the bayonet the enemy that were harassing us most, and fell, mortally wounded, leading and cheering on his men."

These troops were from the 10th Virginia.[96]

Sergeant Henry Rudy of Company I had survived this sortie against the Rebels and turned his attention to this officer, "our Captain [was] severely wounded in the side and left arm. I helped to carry him off with terrible groans."[97] The surgeon who may have known Gregg when brought to the hospital couldn't operate (also citing illness) and selected another surgeon to "amputate his left arm at the shoulder joint for comminuted fracture of the bone from a bullet." He had succumbed from his wounds and died before the evening of July 3rd.[98]

New documents have surfaced to suggest that while Captain Gregg took part in this sortie, he was not in command, but 1st Lieutenant Owen J. Sweet of Company B. Sworn testimonies given by four Company A & B soldiers, Sweet had asked for volunteers (acquired nearly 100 men) and had gained authorization from the 137th Colonel to make the charge. He made the charge "with uplifted and whirling sword in one hand and hat in the other," driving the Rebels out of the works on his front with fixed bayonets and directed and encouraged them in the most severe part of the fight.[99] They believed he had kept the Rebels in check at this critical juncture when he was slightly wounded by a bullet that grazed his forehead.[100]

Was it possible that Sweet had organized the charge, turned it over to Gregg, and resumed command with his severe wounds? Another possibility is that Sweet and Gregg may have agreed to split command of these volunteers so if one group was captured or communication became difficult during the night fighting, the rest of the men could be pulled back without taking more casualties than necessary. In Owen J. Sweet's statement he said Captain Gregg "volunteered with a number of men to go with me," and since Gregg died of his wounds, we may never find out for certain who was in command.[101]

General George Sears Greene had acquired the time needed, as he heard the fighting on the right and said, "I brought up the reserve." Of the three 1st Corps regiments sent by General Wadsworth, the 147th New York was posted to the left of the

149th New York, to keep the Confederates where they were for the rest of the battle that night.102

A staff officer had directed Lt. Colonel Rufus R. Dawes of the 6th Wisconsin to report to General Greene, who was the first mounted officer he met in the direction of the growing musketry fire. He wrote his name and command on a card taken from his pocket, gave this to Dawes, and ordered the officer to take possession of the empty breastworks on the 137th New York's right flank.103

Since neither man knew that these works were occupied by Steuart's Virginians, Dawes had the men "run with all their might" to avoid the enemy's volley going over the hill. They ran into the 10th Virginia who were as surprised as the 6th Wisconsin, fired blindly, and retreated down the hill. The only casualties were two killed and two wounded.104

The 12th Corps Brigade commander himself was hit from this fire. Dawes had said the works were a few rods down the slope from where he met Greene. It was reported years later that Greene had received a severe contusion from a spent ball that night on Culp's Hill.105 Because of that distance (2 to 3 rods would equal 11 to 17 yards) it is very plausible that the Virginians fire from the lower slope reached Greene since he had bought up the reserve (none of the other Union regiments sent as reinforcements refer to Greene).

Although Dawes hadn't spoke of his men straggling behind as they moved quickly to the right, Greene may have gathered a small number together that became lost in the dark and directed them towards the rest of the 6th Wisconsin.106 I believe that during the three hours of fighting on Culp's Hill on July 2nd, it was here during this most dangerous part of the fighting, that General Greene was near the range of Confederate fire.

While the 6th Wisconsin approached the breastworks, to their right was the other Wadsworth regiment, the 14th Brooklyn, which had been unaware they were nearby during their march to Greene's right flank. Lt. John J. Cantine (who had helped Col. Ireland put the 71st PA in position earlier that evening) came across Colonel

Edward B. Fowler's troops and guided the regiment to the area on Greene's right flank.

Both men were almost captured when a soldier had in their front stepped out from the trees and demanded Cantine's surrender. When he dismounted, Fowler immediately took out his pistol, and shots rang out in the woods enabling the men to escape. Fowler had his regiment face in the direction of the fire and sent two men out (volunteers) to check if those troops were Federals or Confederates. The 14th Brooklyn waited for a period of time, when one of the volunteers, musician John Cox came back in with the information that the other man, Sergeant James McQuire of Company I had been wounded and there were Rebels in their front. This was the 10th Virginia and Fowler gave the order to fire and the 14th Brooklyn rushed forward, which drove the Virginians back in disorder.[107]

Both of these regiments had contributed with the 137th New York to stabilize Greene's right flank and prevented the Rebels from reaching the Baltimore Pike, where they could have taken Meade's artillery reserve and supply wagons and forced the army to pull back. As this action was being decided on Greene's right, the Maryland and North Carolina troops had gained some ground when the 149th had regrouped when they thought the Rebels had gained the rear of their line.

The firing from the 149th New York and 137th New York continued as they had withdrawn to the traverse when they conformed with the rest of the 137th New York, due to the change of front from the right flank. Two North Carolina officers recalled they were "driven from the portion from which we received the oblique fire, and then the fire form the front seemed even more terrific."[108]

Another problem that both sides faced was the lack of ammunition because of the steady fire. It was said the 3rd North Carolina replenished their cartridge-boxes by ammunition from the dead and wounded. Some of their men had only two rounds at one point.[109] One of those wounded was Charles F. Futch, who died a few hours later from being shot in the head while lying down and loading. His brother had stayed with him after he removed him from the firing line.[110]

General Steuart's aide, Lieutenant Randolph McKim had been given orders to bring up the 1st North Carolina Regiment (held as a reserve) to assist the 3rd North Carolina and 1st Maryland Battalion. McKim wrote he was "guided only by the flashes of the muskets," as he heard the bullets fly over the heads from the right. Seeing the fire also in his front, he yelled out "Fire on them, boys; fire on them!" This fire on the right wasn't against Greene's men, but the 3rd North Carolina and the 1st Maryland Battalion as Major William M. Parsley of the 3rd North Carolina ran towards them and shouted, "They are our own men."[111]

Mistaken identity on the battlefield took place and Culp's Hill was no different as soldiers were fired upon or drifted in to the enemies they were fighting by mistake. This happened to a staff officer from the 1st Corps who had asked a Confederate major in the dark the whereabouts of the 12th Corps. He was taken prisoner, surrendered his pistol and sword after the pistol was pointed at him and told of his new status.[112]

Greene's men had held off General Johnson's division and provided assistance from those 1st and 11th Corps regiments as the attacks had lasted until 10pm. Although the rebels under General Steaurt did hold the section of earthworks on the right, they were content to regroup and resupply their brigade and fight only in defense for the rest of the night.

Knowing that his brigade and engineering skills had accomplished more than Meade could have expected, Greene was informed of General Kane's Brigade from Geary's division returning to their old position. He had a staff officer go out and placed them on Greene's right.[113] After they were fired on as they approached their works, one of the volunteers, G.W. Swineford of the 111th Pennsylvania confirmed that it was not Greene's men, but the Rebels. They stayed near the Confederate line and could hear them talk for the rest of the night and into the morning.[114]

Greene was able to get some of his regiments off the frontline so the rest of Geary's division and the earlier reinforcements could take their place. Some of the men rested and replenished their ammunition, while others cleaned their guns.[115]

Around midnight, General Greene was able to rest and then awakened by a soldier who stumbled on him in the dark. After he was told to go to his regiment and to stop moving in the rear, the Commissary Sergeant Edwin R. Follett of the 60th New York, explained he was looking for his regiment to give out rations. Greene pointed out his boys who were asleep on their muskets and stated for their achievement this day, "there they are, give them the best you have, every man deserves a warm biscuit and a plate of ice-cream."[116] His brigade had done well, but he knew the Confederates were going to try again for tomorrow was another day.

SYLVANUS THAYER BY ROBERT W. WEIR, OIL ON CANVAS. THE
SUPERINTENDENT OF WEST POINT WAS A MAJOR INFLUENCE
IN GREENE'S LIFE AND AMERICA'S EXPANSION IN THE 19TH
CENTURY CREDIT: WEST POINT MUSEUM ART COLLECTION,
UNITED STATES MILITARY ACADEMY

THE DAYS FOR CADETS WERE NOT CONFINED TO THE
CLASSROOM, AS GREENE WROTE ABOUT HIS TIME ON THE
PARADE GROUND, SHOWN HERE IN GEORGE CATLIN'S 1828 VIEW
OF WEST POINT, OIL ON CANVAS. CREDIT: WEST POINT MUSEUM
ART COLLECTION, UNITED STATES MILITARY ACADEMY.

PARADE GROUND AT WEST POINT, WITH CADET'S BARRACKS
AND CHAPEL IN BACKGROUND. CREDIT: AUTHOR'S
COLLECTION.

COLONEL WILLIAM B. GOODRICH, 60TH N.Y.S.V. REGT. TOOK COMMAND OF REGIMENT IN MAY 1862 AND KILLED AT ANTIETAM ON SEPTEMBER 17, 1862. CREDIT: FROM THE COLLECTIONS OF THE ST. LAWRENCE COUNTY HISTORICAL ASSOCIATION.

MARTHA AND GEORGE GREENE AT THE TIME OF THEIR
WEDDING IN 1836; THIS WAS HIS SECOND MARRIAGE. CREDIT:
FROM THE BOOK, "THE GREENE'S OF RHODE ISLAND,"
PUBLISHED IN 1903.

1862 SILVER WEDDING ANNIVERSARY HELD IN NEW YORK CITY. GEORGE AND MARTHA GREENE ARE SEATED IN FRONT, WITH DAUGHTER ANNA STANDING (HAND ON FATHER'S SHOULDER) BEHIND HER FATHER AND FRANCIS VINTON STANDING TO THE RIGHT OF HIS MOTHER. SAMUEL DANA, CHARLES T. AND GEORGE SEARS JR., ARE IN THE BACK ROW, WITH THEIR COUSIN, ALBERT R. GREENE TO THEIR LEFT. CREDIT: JOAN PIERPONT OF SOUTHBURY, CT.

SAMUEL DANA GREENE, NAVAL OFFICER OF USS MONITOR
DURING THE CIVIL WAR. CREDIT: JOAN PIERPONT OF
SOUTHBURY, CT.

NEW YORK SENATOR PRESTON KING. HE DENOUNCED
SECESSION BY THE SOUTH AND WAS A FRIEND TO GREENE AND
THE NEW YORK SOLDIERS DURING THE CIVIL WAR. CREDIT:
AUTHOR'S COLLECTION

SGT. JACOB GEORGE ORTH, CO.D., 28TH REGT., PA. VOL. INF. THIS PHILADELPHIA NATIVE CAPTURED A SOUTH CAROLINA REGIMENT. FLAG AFTER BEING WOUNDED IN THE SHOULDER AT ANTIETAM. HE WOULD BE AWARDED THE CONGRESSIONAL MEDAL OF HONOR FOR THIS ACTION. CREDIT: RON BEIFUSS COLLECTION AT U.S. ARMY MILITARY HISTORY INSTITUTE.

SURGEON H. ERNEST GOODMAN, 28TH REGT., PA. VOL. INF.
FIRST SERVED UNDER GREENE'S DIVISION AT ANTIETAM AND
WAS HIS PHYSICIAN (1863-79) THAT HELP SECURE A PENSION IN
1879 FOR GREENE. CREDIT: U.S. ARMY MILITARY HISTORY
INSTITUTE AND CIVIL WAR LIBRARY & MUSEUM MOLLUS,
PHILADELPHIA, PA.

MAJOR JAMES C. LANE, 102ND REGT., N.Y.S. VOL. INF. SERVED
WITH GREENE AT ANTIETAM, CHANCELLORSVILLE, AND
GETTYSBURG. WOUNDED AT CULP'S HILL ON THE NIGHT OF
JULY 2, 1863. CREDIT: ROGER HUNT COLLECTION AT U.S. ARMY
MILITARY HISTORY INSTITUTE.

COURTEOUSY OF PATRICIA STEPANEK / ILLUSTRATION FROM THE BOOK "FLAGS OF THE ARMY OF THE UNITED STATES CARRIED DURING THE WAR OF THE REBELLION, 1861-1865; to designate the headquarters of the different armies, army corps, divisions and brigades." By SAMUEL BECKLEY HOLABIRD PUBLISHED BY PHILADELPHIA, BURK + McFETRIDGE, LITHO. 1888

GREENE'S HEADQUARTERS 3RD BRIGADE FLAG, 2ND DIVISION, 12TH CORPS, ARMY OF THE POTOMAC. CREDIT: ILLUSTRATION PROVIDED BY PATRICIA STEPANEK, PICTURE TAKEN BY AUTHOR.

MAJOR GENERAL HENRY W. SLOCUM, 12TH CORPS
COMMANDER AT CHANCELLORSVILLE AND GETTYSBURG. HE
PRAISED GREENE'S DEFENSE AT GETTYSBURG (CULP'S HILL)
AND FOUGHT FOR HIS RECOGNITION IN THE OFFICIAL
REPORTS, PROMOTION TO MAJOR GENERAL AND GREENE'S
RELIEF BILL IN THE EARLY 1890'S. CREDIT: MASSACHUSETTS
COMMANDERY MILITARY ORDER OF THE LOYAL LEGION AND
THE US ARMY MILITARY HISTORY INSTITUTE.

1ST LT. HENRY RUDY, JR., CO.I, 137TH REGT., N.Y.S. VOL. INF.
TALKED ABOUT MARCH TO GETTYSBURG AND WAUHATCHIE,
WHERE HE WAS WOUNDED AS A SGT. IN HIS DIARY. CREDIT:
SCOTT HILTS COLLECTION AT U.S. ARMY HISTORY INSTITUTE.

CAPTAIN JOSEPH H. GREGG, CO.I, 137TH REGT., N.Y.S. VOL. INF.
MORTALLY WOUNDED ON JULY 2, 1863 IN SORTIE AGAINST THE
CONFEDERATES AT CULP'S HILL. CREDIT: U.S. ARMY MILITARY
HISTORY INSTITUTE AND DIV. OF MILITARY & NAVAL AFFAIRS
NYS ADJT. GEN OFFICE, ALBANY, NY.

MAJOR CHARLES T. GREENE (RIGHT) POSED FOR THE CAMERA WITH LIEUTENANT COLONEL AVERY (LEFT) AND SERGEANT GOODMAN (CENTER). CHARLES LOST HIS RIGHT LEG AT THE BATTLE OF RINGGOLD, GA. IN NOVEMBER 1863. CREDIT: JOAN PIERPONT OF SOUTHBURY, CT.

GEORGE SEARS GREENE BY GEORGE B. BUTLER, OIL ON CANVAS.
CREDIT: WEST POINT MUSEUM ART COLLECTION, UNITED
STATES MILITARY ACADEMY.

FRANCIS VINTON GREENE. HE CHOSE THE MILITARY FOR A
CAREER. LEFT: TO "ANNA M. GREENE FROM F.V. GREENE TAKEN
NOVEMBER 1869," WHEN HE WAS A WEST POINT CADET. RIGHT:
A MEMBER OF THE U.S. MILITARY LEGATION, THE PICTURE IS
DATED, "OCT. 1, 1878 ST. PETERSBURG" RUSSIA. CREDIT: JOAN
PIERPONT OF SOUTHBURY, CT.

MARTH BARRETT (DANA) GREENE IN THE LATE 1870's. CREDIT:
BARBARA AND EDWARD HASSE OF HARRINGTON PARK, NJ.

261 MANHATTAN AVENUE,
BROOKLYN, E.D.

CHARLES THRUSTON GREENE, THE GENERAL'S SON AND
AIDE-DE-CAMP ON HIS STAFF FROM CEDAR MOUNTAIN TO
WAUHATCHIE. TO THE RIGHT IS ADDIE MAUD SUPPLE
GREENE, HIS BELOVED WIFE. CREDIT: JOAN PIERPONT OF
SOUTHBURY, CT.

1876 PORTRAIT OF GEORGE SEARS GREENE. DISTINGUISHED LOOKING AND VERY ACTIVE WITH CIVIL ENGINEERING PROJECTS, THIS 75 YEAR OLD STILL HAD TO BARE THE BURDEN OF PAIN FROM HIS CIVIL WAR WOUND. CREDIT: MASSACHUSETTS COMMANDERY MILITARY ORDER OF THE LOYAL LEGION AND THE US ARMY MILITARY HISTORY INSTITUTE.

GEORGE AND MARTHA GREENE MOVE FROM NEW YORK CITY
TO LIVE WITH THEIR DAUGHTER, ANNA M. (GREENE) DAY AT
MORRISTOWN, NEW JERSEY IN 1883. CREDIT: THE JOINT FREE
PUBLIC LIBRARY OF MORRISTOWN & MORRIS TOWNSHIP

1883 FAMILY GATHERING AT MORRISTOWN, NEW JERSEY HOME. SOME OF THE PERSONS IDENTIFIED ARE: LEFT TO RIGHT, SECOND ROW (SEATED) MARTHA B. D. GREENE, GEORGE SEARS GREENE, EVA WEBSTER RUSSELL, AND HANNIBAL DAY SEATED NEXT TO HIS WIFE AT FAR RIGHT. THIRD ROW, FAR LEFT, ANNA M. (GREENE) DAY AND BACK ROW, CHARLES T. GREENE, ADDIE M.S. GREENE (CHARLES'S WIFE), PORTRAIT OF CALEB GREENE (G.S.G.'S FATHER) AND GEORGE SEARS GREENE, JR. CREDIT: JOAN PIERPONT OF SOUTHBURY, CT.

THE UNIFORM STILL FITS AT THIRTY YEAR REUNION IN
GETTYSBURG. THE PHOTOGRAPH IS SIGNED IN GREENE'S
HANDWRITING, "GETTYSBURG 2 JULY 1893 GEO S GREENE
MAJOR GENERAL BY BREVET." CREDIT: JOAN PIERPONT OF
SOUTHBURY, CT.

CHARLES THRUSTON GREENE. ON REVERSE OF PHOTO: "GETTYSBURG DEDICATION OF N.Y. MONUMENT JULY 1, 2, & 3, 1893. CHARLES THRUSTON GREENE AIDE-DE-CAMP TO BREVET MAJ. GENL. GEO. S. GREENE, HONORARY MARSHALL, BATTLE OF GETTYSBURG JULY 1, 2 & 3, 1863." CREDIT: JOAN PIERPONT OF SOUTHBURY, CT.

FOUR GENERATIONS OF GREENE (1895). LEFT TO RIGHT—ANNA
GREENE BOUGHTON, HER DAUGHTER MARGARET, CHARLES
THRUSTON GREENE (MARGARET'S GRANDFATHER) AND
GEORGE SEARS GREENE (MARGARET'S GREAT GRANDFATHER).
CREDIT: JOAN PIERPONT OF SOUTHBURY, CT.

LAST KNOWN PHOTOGRAPH OF GEORGE SEARS GREENE AT
HOME IN 1897 BEFORE ILLNESS. CREDIT: BARBARA AND EDWARD
HASSE OF HARINGTON PARK, NJ.

VIEW OF GEORGE SEARS GREENE GRAVESITE, WITH CULP'S
HILL. BOULDER IN BACKGROUND, TAKEN IN FEBRUARY 2002.
CREDIT: PAUL HEMPHILL OF NORFOLK, MA.

ANOTHER VIEW OF CEMETERY, SHOWING GEORGE AND
MARTHA GREENE (UPPER RIGHT) WITH OTHER FAMILY
MEMBERS IN WARWICK, RI. CREDIT: PAUL HEMPHILL OF
NORFOLK, MA.

JOHN G. GREENE LT. COLONEL, AUS (RET.) AT US CEMETERY IN
BELGIUM DURING D-DAY OBSERVANCE (JUNE 6, 1998). LIVING
IN WATERLOO, BELGIUM JOHN IS A MILITARY HISTORIAN AND
CONTINUES THE FAMILY TRADITION OF MILITARY SERVICE IN
OUR ARMED FORCES. A PROUD RELATIVE WHO REMEMBERS
THE FORGOTTEN HERO. CREDIT: AUTHOR'S COLLECTION
(SENT TO ME BY JOHN G. GREENE)

ALTHOUGH GREENE COMMANDED NEW YORK TROOPS AT
GETTYSBURG, THE RHODE ISLAND NATIVE IS REMEMBERED
BY WARWICK ART TEACHER JERRY SHIPPEE, HIS STEP-
DAUGHTER SUSAN, AND FELLOW CLASSMATES IN THE MURAL,
"RHODE ISLAND AT GETTYSBURG," COMPLETED IN MAY 2001.
CREDIT: JERRY SHIPPEE OF W. WARWICK, RI.

Chapter Sixteen

Culp's Hill: July 3rd

The return of Geary's Second Division and William's First Division to the right of the Union line meant the danger has passed on the Union left that General Meade had worried about from earlier that day. Greene's men tried to rest and felt good about how they conducted themselves against superior Confederate forces. It was believed that 80 rounds of ammunition were used by the men of Greene's brigade.[1]

While some enjoyed a meal or slept, one 60th New Yorker had claimed a trophy from the Rebels. During the July 2nd fighting, a rebel officer had fallen with sword in hand as he urged his men to scale the breastworks. Leaving the breastworks as the fighting ceased that night, Sergeant Peter Hayne of Company C had retrieved this sword and came across five rebels hiding behind a rock. They followed the Sergeant, who was not carrying his musket due to his scavenger hunt, back to the Union line as prisoners.[2]

Some Rebels lost their way in the dark and became Greene's prisoners as they searched for water to fill their canteens. One of his men even took "a big burly rebel" stealing from the dead and turned him over to his captain.[3] There was some firing on the line in the early morning before light, which caused nervous tension among some in the ranks, but it tapered off and the front remained quiet.[4]

General Robert E. Lee wanted a coordinated attack by his Confederate Army on Meade's flanks to exploit the gains made against the 12th Corps breastworks and with the reinforcements of Pickett's three brigades to General Longstreet, the battle could be won. But the plan fell apart with Longstreet delayed and despite General Ewell reinforcing Johnson's Division with three brigades, he fought alone as Generals Slocum and Williams began the fight at 4:30 am to retake the breastworks on the right.[5]

General Greene didn't have to worry about that part of the line, but he expressed concern for the 66th Ohio Volunteer Infantry that had been under his command at Antietam. They were ordered from Colonel Candy's brigade (placed behind Greene's brigade on their arrival) to go beyond Greene's left and face perpendicular to his line.[6] If the Confederates renewed their attack and followed a straight advance up the slope of Culp's Hill, then their fire from the woods could hit them on their right flank. Virtually isolated and not protected on their flanks if the Confederates turned on them, Greene expressed this to Lt. Col. Eugene Powell, "My God! If you go out there the enemy will simply swallow you!"[7]

In the short time they had gone out beyond Greene's entrenchments, the firing began. General Greene saw the Rebels attack his front and the right of the 12th Corps was "conducted with the utmost vigor."[8]

The Stonewall Brigade under General James A. Walker (left on the Confederate flank on July 2nd) was the first brigade that Johnson had sent in piecemeal fashion to help his beleaguered troops that morning. He followed at 8 am by sending in Edward O'Neal's Alabama Brigade and commit Walker's troops again, by moving them to the right at 9 am. An hour later, General Julius Daniel's Brigade of North Carolinians was ordered to help Steuarts' Brigade against the formidable earthworks on the left of their line.[9]

"The hill in front of this position was, in my opinion, so strong that it could not have been carried by any force," General Daniel wrote in his report.[10] Lt. Col. Randall of the 149th New York may have agreed, but felt concerned about how many lives his regiment had to lose for Daniel's opinion to come true. He offered his officers a drink of whiskey, telling them that this could be the last time they could be together.[11]

The bottle was emptied when the Confederates fired on the right of the Union line.

When the sun came up, darkness no longer concealed the Rebels. Fire was directed towards Greene's men from the trees, in the tree tops and even from behind the dead bodies from yesterday's fight.

"We opened on them at daylight with terrible effect," wrote Henry Rudy of the 137th New York and casualties began to climb among the yells and cries of the wounded. Rudy was lucky because all around him men fell, such as J. Casad who was shot in the head and killed, and Captain Oscar C Williams (the Adjutant) was wounded. "Some places in the trenches," another 137th New York soldier remembered, "the ground was saturated with Human blood" and beyond the breastworks, "the hillside was slippery from human blood."[12]

A 137th New Yorker saw about 50 Rebels come out with a white flag from behind a rock. They stopped firing to allow them into their lines and wrote home to his sister that a rebel said "Napolean with a Million men could not have taken our works or drove us from them."[13] The tenacity of the charging Rebels was remembered by the 149th New York Colonel Henry Barnum; "Twice was our flag shot down, and a rebel first sergeant, in a brave attempt to capture it, fell within two feet of the prostrate banner, pierced with five balls." The flag had received 81 balls through it and 7 in the staff. Barnum spoke of the color-sergeant, William C. Lilly, who spliced the staff and kept it on the works despite his slight wound.[14]

Since Confederate artillery was rendered ineffective to support their advance, they suffered from both Union artillery and infantry along the line. A 53rd North Carolina soldier never forgot how the men fell like leaves from the tree as cannon and musket balls hit their ranks from Greene's entrenchments. "You could see one with his head shot off, others cut in two, then one with his brain oozing out, one with his leg off, others shot through the heart."[15]

General Johnson believed pressure could be relieved from his front by Longstreet's attack on the left flank of the Union line. Instead of changing his tactics against General Greene and the rest of the 12th Corps, he continued the frontal assaults, leaving many killed and wounded on the hill. Some were trapped hiding behind the boulders since the heavy fire from the entrenchments meant no advance or retreat.[16]

Officers from Stonewall's Brigade and Daniel's Brigade reported after the battle of the destructive fire caused by the artillery and infantry and in some cases not able to return the fire.[17]

One Confederate soldier had his ramrod stuck in his gun from the hot barrel due to the rapid fire. Unable to remove it, he shot it at the Yankees and found another gun to use that day.[18] As the sun tried to make its way through the woods and drifting smoke on Culp's Hill that morning, Captain Collins of the 149th New York stated how the men looked with "clothes ragged and dirty, their faces black from smoke, sweat and burnt powder, their lips cracked and bleeding form salt-petre in the cartridges bitten by them."[19]

Except for the 60th New York, the other regiments in Greene's Brigade were relieved at different times and went back over the ridge to eat, make coffee, cleaned their rifles and refilled their cartridge boxes.[20]

General Meade still believed Culp's Hill was not a major concern despite his near fatal order of July 2nd removing the 12th Corps to protect his left. Because the noise level of the battlefield reached his headquarters, Meade jumped to the conclusion that General Geary's division was wasting ammunition. His opinion changed when told of the true nature of the fighting.[21] The failure of General Meade at Culp's Hill on July 2nd and July 3rd had compromised the rest of the line and had created a shadow over their contributions to Union success, which reduced their role in the eyes of history.

General Greene only thought of holding the line and history could judge later what his brigade did for the fighting on Culp's Hill. Casualties increased in the ranks especially the officers of Greene's regiments.

Colonel Randall of the 149th New York was struck in the shoulder by a minie ball as he bent over the wounded Captain Doran, who earlier had been cheering the 122nd New York's arrival to their line with a cap in his uplifted arm.[22] Along their front the dead were left where they fell and the heat made the stench nearly unbearable as the bodies began to putrefy.[23]

As the fighting continued to break down the infrastructure of the attacking Confederates, a Louisiana officer from Williams' Brigade wrote years later, "the roar of musketry was so intense that it was useless to attempt to give commands unless shouted into the men's ears."[24] They gained some relief from Greene's troops as they fired over Williams' Brigade into O'Neal's Brigade of Alabamians and became clear targets as they advanced towards the entrenchments. But they paid a terrible price in helping the Louisianans, many of their men shot down were killed or wounded. It had served no purpose except to increase the fire and casualties.[25]

Still, Greene's men were hit by the Rebels as they moved from the entrenchments to the hollow (at the ridge) and back. Some of the logs caused the bullets to glance if they were round and green, which brought a wound or death in the upper or lower part of the body. However, it was generally the head and upper parts that were injured during the fighting.[26]

One of those regiments that gave General Greene's men a chance to get more ammunition and perhaps a meal (behind the hollow) was the 150th New York Infantry. Writing home to his father, a soldier told him, "this success [Culp's Hill] may be owing to the first entry of the 150th into active service." We can't relate if Greene agreed with this statement, but he agreed with this young man when he asked the "Lord preserve me from such a sight again."[27] Greene felt proud of their discipline just as he was with his own brigade and the other regiments in Geary's division that gave them relief on the line at different times of the fighting.

Many soldiers on both sides were killed without firing a shot or helping others in the ranks. John Hite of the 33rd Virginia didn't get the chance. He told his lieutenant that he felt like there was a dozen balls in his body. John's brother Issac explained to the homefolk about the "ball entering his right side just below his arm, and passing through but very near as the skin turned black."

Knowing his wound was mortal, he "wished to die that he might be relieved of his suffering."[28]

A 25th Virginia soldier risked his life to bring his brother, wounded in the arm, off the rocks along the 60th New York line of fire. Amid the storm of musketry and crashing of shells, he strongly believed "it is due to the hand of a divine providence that we were not both killed."[29]

The severe fighting on the 60th New York's front prevented their withdraw until the fighting ceased at 10:00 am and were aided by the flank fire directed into the Rebels by the 66th Ohio. Donald Brown of the 60th New York felt like he was trapped in the breastworks:

"[Lieutenant] Stanley, who was almost behind me, was in the act of handing me a cartridge, when a bullet, grazing my face, cut his throat. He did not bleed externally but when I looked at him, I knew from his eyes that he would die. He tried to rise, only to topple over, dead. Slap! went a bullet through the body of Sergeant Clark on my left and slap! went another through the hand of Comrade Bullock, beside me."[30]

Fatigue caused some casualties in the 60th as one soldier lost the tops of two fingers after the ball passed through his wrist, the length of his hand when leaning his chin on it, while resting against the breast-works.[31] Like the Rebels, Greene's men could not bring in the wounded because it was almost certain death. Colonel Goddard of the 60th had sent two men to help a severely wounded officer, but they were killed and remained where they fell for the duration of the battle.[32]

Greene's prediction of his old command, the 66th Ohio, being swallowed up by the Confederates proved to be false. Eugene Powell stated "the enemy did not come up on our rear, although shot, shell, and bullets were flying in every direction" as they used the rocks, trees and a fence for protection.[33]

Some of the Ohioans were shot as the Virginians from Jones' Brigade had seen some movement to their right. Two officers, Lieutenants John F. Morgan and Charles E. Butts received multiple wounds.[34]

Although their fire was returned, one officer was mortally wounded and may have alerted inadvertently their presence to their concealment in the woods.

Major J. G. Palmer stood on an outcropping as he reviewed the surrounding left, rear, and front areas with his field glasses to see if the Rebels were trying to get around the regiment. It is a strong possibility that the glare of the sun caught the Major when he moved the field glasses, alerting the Virginians to their presence. He was shot thru the lung and carried back to the main line. Palmer gave encouragement to those near him "Stay with them boys! I will soon be back with you."[35] But he died of his wound one week later and the men believed they had gotten revenge for the Major by killing the sharpshooter that day.[36]

"We directed what fire we could across Greene's front at the enemy in our former entrenchments." as Powell related to Greene's defense of his section of the line.[37]

One young soldier from Company F could not be kept out of the fight as the sounds of gunfire carried past the Baltimore Pike. Stephen Kenneth Gray was just two months shy of being 18 and he was left with the ambulance wagons as the men knew of the danger that they were in outside of Greene's entrenchments.

Stephen left the wagons to share in the danger of his comrades and loaded and fired on the Rebels. General Greene was the one to send in the casualty sheet listing Stephen Kenneth Gray as mortally wounded. Like Major Palmer, he received a gun shot wound to the lung and lingered before death freed his soul back in his home state, Ohio, on November 21, 1863.[38]

They were very effective as the 66th Ohio "held their ground until recalled about 11 a.m., causing considerable execution among the enemy."[39] They moved into Greene's line and allowed one of the New York regiments to rest and refill their cartridge boxes behind the hollow.[40] Greene's men held their fire upon seeing the actions of Captain Edward D. Camden from the 25th Virginia regiment. Moving forward with the picket line, he stopped from the impact of being struck in the face from a minie ball, knocking out some of his upper teeth, the piece of corn bread he had just put in his mouth, and a part of his jawbone.

They saw him from their entrenchments running around in a erratic fashion (feeling the pain & in shock), but he was calmed down by his fellow soldiers, and fired upon when the Captain turned and moved down the hill.[41]

Except for some firing by sharpshooters, Johnson's piecemeal attacks going straight towards the breastworks ended the fighting by 10 am. Many of Greene's men and others in Geary's division witnessed the tragic climax to continue the fight. There were pockets of Rebel soldiers that had stayed behind the boulders and white rags or hankerchiefs were seen waving in the air. From where Greene stood "about fifty of the men got too near to our lines to retreat, and threw down their arms, ran up close to our works, and were allowed to come unarmed into our lines."[42]

One group of 78 Confederates, some of them wounded were invited into the works after showing a white cloth, but as they approached the Union line, an officer appeared. Major Benjamin Watkins Leigh (Chief of Staff to General Edward Johnson) had spurred his splendid mount through the woods and in disregard to his own safety, tried to prevent the surrender of these Stonewall Brigade troops. The Union soldiers fired on man and horse, killing both with numerous balls that struck them at close range. Greene ordered a "soldier's burial" for this brave Confederate officer.[43]

The 12th Corps (along with Longstreet's delay on the left) had disrupted General Robert E. Lee's plan to break the Union line. It was literally a hailstorm of lead that reached even to those non-combatants and animals caught in the mayhem. The regimental band of the 137th New York had three of their drummer boys wounded, along with two captured in trying to bring in their wounded.[44] During the fighting at Culp's Hill, chief musician O. Bingham was nearly killed as he "had his cap shot off his head as he was carrying a wounded sergeant from the line."[45]

One of Greene's men remembered hundreds of birds during the fight come out from the trees and land near the breastworks or on some unsuspecting soldier for their own protection.[46] Calming his mother's fears about him, the 60th New York's Colonel Abel Goddard was more concerned about his horse. "You have learned that my horse was shot at Gettysburg," he told her with detail, "the ball went in about 1/2 an inch below the wind pipe and I came near losing my hors but she has fully recovered. I was standing by her side when she was shot and I had become so attached to her (she stood fire admirably) that I felt badly injured when she was wounded."[47]

Henry Rudy of the 137th New York recorded that morning, the final enemy advance was halted and as they fell back, we "admitted great cheers." Despite the picket firing, "we gave attention to our dead and wounded lying where fallen. The dead Rebels [stay] on the works."[48] A 3rd Wisconsin soldier from General Ruger's Brigade took leave from his regiment on the extreme right of the 12th Corps front to see the area where Greene's brigade had fought. With the dead and wounded everywhere he looked, Van R. Willard saw that some died "as if without a struggle," while there were those "tearing the earth with their hands, dying at last with expressions of the most horrible agony lingering on their distorted features."[49]

Culp's Hill was not be attacked again because the Rebels withdrew behind Rock Creek, but the men faced a new threat from the rear in the afternoon. General Lee had his artillery concentrate their fire on Cemetery Ridge along the center of the Union line to enable Longstreet's attack to split General Meade's army. This became known as Pickett's Charge. Many of those shells had been fired at a higher elevation and went over Cemetery Ridge and landed in the rear of Culp's Hill.[50]

Many of the 149th New Yorkers saw an officer lying behind a tree move abruptly after an unexploded shell had landed at his feet from striking three trees. They laughed as he looked out from behind a tree. "Shells and Solid shot sink among us in all directions," stated Henry Rudy, but casualties were light as "the Corps held its position."[51] With Pickett's Charge turned back late that afternoon, Greene's men dealt with the Rebel pickets for the remainder of the day.

Robert Nelson of the 60th New York had brought into their line a Louisiana officer that he had shot in the hand. Proud of his capture, Nelson came across General Greene and brought his prisoner to him before going to the rear. Before Nelson could get this prisoner to the hospital, Greene told him to "have it cut off."[52] We don't know the reaction of the Louisiana officer to Greene's opinion.

Near midnight on July 3rd, the sleep of Greene's men was disturbed by the moans of the wounded, but firing broke out after a shot had broke the silence in front of the 7th Ohio's breastworks. It was not a renewal of fighting, but the actions of a Confederate sergeant who had tried to take the flag of the 7th Ohio. Being near their works, the sergeant attempted to lift the staff "through the fire space" and have it fall over the head log, but awoke the color sergeant who saw the movement and shot and killed the brave Confederate.[53] Unknown to all, the fighting at Gettysburg was over and by July 5th, General Robert E. Lee began his retreat from Meade to get back to Virginia.

These two days were used to help the wounded and bury the dead. Many soldiers didn't like to be at the hospitals which were usually in large tents or buildings in towns and the fields of local farmers. One of Greene's soldiers saw at a farmhouse a row of dead soldiers laid out side by side who did not survive the saw of the surgeon. Next to them were two mounds of amputated limbs.[54] Some local citizens tried to help the wounded as related by one 60th New Yorker, "one kind lady begged me to let her put a clean bandage on my hand and wrist but as soon as the condition of was exposed to view, she fainted."[55]

A wounded Rebel brought to the 12th Corps hospital believed General Lee could have established his headquarters on the Baltimore Pike with the severe battle taking place on July 3rd (he was brought into the lines on July 2nd), but agreed with his Union counterpart on the work of the surgeons.[56] "The surgeons, with sleeves rolled up and bloody to the elbows, were continually employed in amputating limbs. The red human blood ran in streams from under the operation tables, and huge piles of arms and legs, withered and horrible to behold, were mute evidences of the fierceness of the strife."[57]

There are numerous accounts by the soldiers and citizens of the destruction of the trees and the number of dead they saw for the next two days. "All the trees on the northeast side of the hill were full of bullets way up to their tops, big branches actually cut off by them," Colonel Charles Wainwright had wrote down in his diary. As he continued his walk, the First Corps officer "passed several hundred of the rebel dead lying around among the rocks and boulders."[58] A 66th Ohio soldier described to his father that "the Rebs lay thicker than I ever saw them before," and another in the regiment had sent a letter back home from the pocket of a dead rebel and intended to send it to the writer in the future.[59]

One 78th New Yorker told his brother, "the dead began to smell pretty bad so that we could not hardly stand it to bury them." "The reble [sic] dead lay thick in fromt of our trenches," recorded Henry Rudy and "our troops [will] rifle the pockets and knapsacks of the dead rebles[sic]."

This 137th New Yorker spoke of their dead put "in shallow graves and a head board with name & date at their heads."[60]

They were the fortunate ones for families who came later to bring their loved ones home. Captain Collins had blamed the Rebels for going thru the pockets and knapsacks of their own men, but expressed his amazement of the appearance of the battlefield. Many of the trees were stripped of their leaves and bark with lead mark all over the rocks and flattened bullets covered the ground.[61]

Many of those trees on Culp's Hill died later from lead poisoning due to vast amount of ammunition expended in the two days of fighting. In his report General Geary claimed his division alone on July 3rd fired 277,000 rounds at the Rebels.[62] Before Greene's men left that July 5th afternoon, one of the local farm boys saw the Rebel dead laid out in long narrow trenches, with one on top of the next man, about two feet deep, and covered them just enough to prevent the spread of disease.[63]

General George Sears Greene had achieved more than anyone in the Union high command could have expected. His engineering skills and open mind to the changing tactics of the war justified the respect the men gave him for preventing unnecessary casualties. Breastworks were to be a common feature for the duration of the war in the Eastern and Western theaters. His brigade's casualties were low due to the entrenchments, with 303 men killed, wounded, captured and missing. This was 21% of his strength.[64] In contrast, General Edward Johnson had suffered a 30% rate of casualties, with 373 killed, 1,150 wounded, and 413 missing or captured (totaling 1,936 men).[65]

Johnson didn't change tactics during the struggle and was criticized by a soldier in the Stonewall Brigade; "the whole division suffered through the folly of our hard fighting Johnson. He has none of the qualities of a General, but expects to do everything by fighting."[66] A soldier in the 12th Alabama of O'Neal's brigade didn't criticize Johnson, but could speak for all Southern soldiers at the end of July 3rd, "I thought I had been in hot places before-I though I had heard Minnie balls; but that day capped the climax."[67]

Greene felt that the credit for their victory belonged to General Henry W. Slocum. He stated that Slocum "saw the danger to which the army would be exposed by the movement ordered, and who took the responsibility of modifying the orders which he had received, is due the honor of having saved the army from a great and perhaps fatal disaster."[68]

Greene wrote years later concerning his brigade's action on July 2, 1863 that "had Lee succeeded in penetrating our lines and placing himself square across the Baltimore pike in rear of the center and right wing of the entire army," Meade could have been forced to pull out of Gettysburg and give the Confederates a victory on Northern soil.[69] The hard fought victory on the Union left at Little Round Top would have been nullified that day and the ill-fated Pickett's Charge the next day at Cemetery Ridge would never take place.

History has been unkind in overshadowing Greene's contributions that decided the Battle of Gettysburg [see Chapter One] for the Union. Those officers who are well known for their defense at Little Round Top (Chamberlain) and Cemetery Ridge

(Webb) were awarded the Medal of Honor and are remembered through the great amount of literature written over the years. Greene's Assistant Adjutant-General, Charles P. Horton knew better than anyone what recognition he deserved for July 2, 1863. He hoped that "due credit may be given to the man to whom more than to any other was due the successful events of the fight on the right, and who has never received the honor to which he was entitled."[70]

Chapter Seventeen

Get that gun out of the water

The defeats at Gettysburg in the east and Vicksburg in the west had seriously compromised the Confederacy's chances of obtaining foreign recognition. General Robert E. Lee had made preparations to pull back his army from the battle lines around Gettysburg, leaving behind only those too critical to move. His main concern was getting the Army of Northern Virginia, with its wagon trains of supplies and wounded, across the Potomac River and back into Virginia.

Like his counterpart, General Meade's Army of the Potomac had suffered many casualties and he left the wounded behind, as some surgeons and civilians confronted the aftermath of the battle. With the Confederates having their men on the march, the question was: could Meade prevent Lee's Army from crossing the Potomac River?

For General Greene and his brigade, their pursuit began on their departure on July 5th from Gettysburg at two in the afternoon and marched back to Littlestown, where they were before the battle. No one was on the streets and the rain made the tired troops cold and wet since their woolen blankets had been discarded at Gettysburg.[1] But this was tolerable compared to the suffering and destruction they just left behind. The stench of the battle followed the 12th Corps, however, as Greene's divisional commander, General John W. Geary, summed it up for all of them, "my very clothes smell of death."[2]

Despite their appearance this didn't stop Greene's men from looking for food. Such items as a loaf of bread, biscuits, milk, and cherry pies were offered by some of the local villagers, but at high prices, it caused one officer to call them a "damned Dutch thieves."[3] Sounds of cannon in the distance could be heard and the next day, July 7th, Greene's brigade left camp at 5 a.m. and marched back into Maryland. They covered 28 to 30 miles by keeping off the roads for their use by the artillery and wagon trains and moved through the fields. It was relief to the tired men when they camped at Woodsburough, outside of Fredrick, after trudging through the heavy rain and deep mud, and the delay of knocking down fences in the fields.[4]

Their return to Frederick was not the same festive mood it was in late June 1863 with flags waving and cheering the troops in their march towards Pennsylvania. The rains continued the next day until noon and a 137th New Yorker remembered their appearance as "looking pretty rough, ragged and dirty." They looked to get new clothes in a day or two, a disgruntled soldier in Greene's brigade told his wife "we are getting verry dirty and lousey."[5]

While the men were camped outside of town and dried out their clothes and shoes in the afternoon sun, others hunted through their clothes to rid themselves of this vermin or graybacks that had made a home. Until they could get new clothing and clean their bodies, these little invaders caused discomfort among everyone in the ranks.[6]

The march was resumed that day and camp set up at Jefferson for the night. One sight that greeted Greene's brigade in that short march was a man hanging from a small tree. This man was said to be a Confederate spy hung three days ago by Union cavalry for papers on him on Union forts and movements of the army. Charles Engle of the 137th New York remembered that he bought an item from this man last fall. The body had been stripped by the soldiers for souvenirs, his knees drawn up and badly swollen. No soldier felt sorry for this casualty of war.[7]

By July 9-10th, the distance was narrowed in their approach to the Confederates as they passed through Crampton's Gap and reached the upper end of Pleasant Valley. Greene's troops came near Sharpsburg, the site of the Antietam battlefield and musketry fire and intermittent artillery was heard. General Greene knew if there was to be a fight, his knowledge of the topography from September 1862 could be most valuable to Generals Geary and Slocum, who had missed the Antietam battle. Skirmishers were pushed out front, and passed the graves and scarred trees, but they couldn't see Lee's men and commenced to build breastworks and settled in for the night.[8]

The battle didn't come about as July 11, 1863 saw Greene's men march towards Fairplay and the brigade had sent out skirmishers towards Williamsport. It was here that part of General Robert E. Lee's Army attempted to cross the Potomac River. With the enemy behind breastworks on the top of the hill (and skirmishers out front), they deemed it suicidal to attack and waited for the rest of the 12th Corps to arrive.[9]

On July 12th, the musketry fire grew with additional skirmishers sent into the line, but an they were not ordered to advance because of the formidable earthworks. They were also fatigued and reluctant to attack in heavy rains and thunder and lightning.[10] Another reason was the rising level of the Potomac River, which the Army of the Potomac figured Lee's men could not lay down a pontoon bridge until the water level receded. This allowed Meade's troops to rest for a day and bring more men to the crossing area. The slow movement of the wagon trains (it was believed) would be Lee's Achilles heel and then the earthworks could be overwhelmed and this part of Lee's Army destroyed.

With more artillery brought up and trees felled for breastworks on July 13th, the skirmishers were brought in and the attack was to be made the next day. The rain had stopped on July 14th and when the attack didn't come about that morning, the troops were puzzled over the delay. About noon, one of Greene's men remembered the scene "Generals Geary and Green[e] come riding along from the front with the statement that the rebs had all skedaddled during the night and were safely over the river."[11]

It was a bitter disappointment and surprise that Lee had crossed the river. The men in Greene's brigade varied in reactions. "The boys are out of patience" cried one New York soldier, perhaps to voice his opinion of the Union high command's performance of the last few days. Another had wanted to destroy Lee's Army and others looked forward to end the war right here and return to their families.[12]

The morning of July 15th had Greene's brigade return to Sharpsburg and complete their 14 mile march near Harper's Ferry and camped at Sandy Hook. They were consoled that day with news of the surrender of Port Hudson and the defeat of Johnston by Sherman in Mississippi.[13] Many of the men were happy the next day from their 5 mile march to Pleasant Valley because they had the opportunity to wash their bodies and clothes in the Potomac. General Greene probably didn't get the chance because many of the officers took care of muster and pay rolls, and sent their reports to the War Department.[14]

Edwin P. Farling, a Hospital Steward of the 149th New York, told his friend that "my easy chair is Mother earth," but they had plenty to eat. He felt a special honor to have ate among the doctors and chaplain for they enjoyed such items as chickens, potatoes, onions, and fresh pork. Unlike the hardtack that was a steady diet for men, Farling called their attendants "our foraging brigade for they supply us with the best the land affords."[15]

While they enjoyed their day of rest on July 17th after their long march in chasing after Lee's Confederates, they were reminded of the near capture a few days back. A 12th Corp officer described the scene, "the rocks of the Potomac river are full of the 'debris' of the broken rebel bridges at Williamsport interspersed here and the[re] with a wagon, a dead horse, or a dead man."[16]

It could have been difficult for General Greene to keep his men from bothering civilians or causing destruction of property. Greene's former commander at Antietam, General Alpheus S. Williams described the destruction of Pleasant Valley, "wheat, corn, and potatoes were all standing and as far as the eyes could reach were being desolated by horses, herds of cattle, tramping men, and crushing wagon wheels." [17] Greene and Williams felt the same that discipline needed to be maintained and to respect private property.

There are many stories during the Civil War of Union and Confederate soldiers who served faithfully and worried more about their loved ones. General Greene could not protect them from events at home, but approved help for his men, especially those with families. One of those men was Washington W. Postley of the 78th New York. The 1st Lieutenant & Adjutant had persevered through all the battles with General Greene, but wrote out his resignation due to the following reasons. "My affairs at home are in such a state as to require my presence for the benefit of my motherless children," wrote Postley. Worried about "my eldest boy being dangerously ill," Greene understood Postley's "state of mind" and didn't interfere with losing a valuable officer.[18]

For the past ten days General George Sears Greene enjoyed his reunion with his own son, Francis Vinton, who he had left in Frederick before they had left for Pennsylvania. Seeing his father and brother Charles was a joyful reunion. He resumed the diary entries he kept as father and son rode together on July 19th, "crossed on a pontoon into Harpers [Ferry] & on a suppension bridge over the Shenandoah. Marched up Loudoun Valley 13 miles to within a mile of Hillsboro where we bivouacked for the night after a hot dusty choking march behind the inevitable Second Corps."[19]

During a rest period while the 2nd Corps wagon train had moved ahead on the road, a rebel guerrilla was discovered at a nearby house, identified by his former prisoner. The evidence was found in the rebel's barn with a saddle and saber located under the hay. He was arrested and the barn was burned, the house spared only due to the guards placed there.[20]

Greene's men knew they were in danger if they left ranks due to guerrilla activities. Citizens who were kind to the soldiers may pass on their movements to guerillas upon their departure. This type of warfare was resented by Greene's men and a New York soldier commented, "the troops can hardly be restrained from burning and destroying everything before them."[21]

As Greene's brigade had marched 10 miles on July 20th from the pike which led from Leesburg to Snickersville, foragers were sent out and gathered supplies. Although they were instructed to issue receipts for property taken, Henry Rudy of the 137th New York looked at it as "having revenge on the Rebs." He witnessed one party that returned 20 horses that night. Other items taken included chickens, hogs, sheep, milk, and butter.[22]

General Greene was furious to learn from two ladies that visited him (it was said by the regimental historian of the 149th to be General Geary, but he personally did not see him) that their house was robbed of dresses and other clothing by soldiers in his brigade. The articles were found in the 149th New York's belongings. Calling General Greene a "school teacher," the Surgeon of the 137th New York and Colonel David Ireland heard Greene expressed his chagrin that they could be punished until the guilty party was found.[23]

The thieves gave up after they stood under arms as some privileges were taken away and they marched around the camp with guards by their side and the rogue's march played by the drums and fife.

Greene's victory in restoring discipline wasn't completed as the New York surgeon related what happened "I was standing by our colonel when all at once I saw he was very much disturbed. He called my attention to two of our boys coming into camp with half of a dressed hog upon their shoulders. The colonel made some terrible expression about the _____ fools and someway got the fellows out of sight before the general discovered them."[24]

From every regiment in Greene's brigade, a detail of officers and men were put together at Snickersville to go home and bring the conscripts (from the draft) back to Virginia. Some of the soldiers hated those back home who resisted the draft, but Charles Engle voiced his concerns about the replacements since "we will have to march slow for they can't stand it to march verry hard."[25] If they had to fight a battle, Charles Engle didn't want to be handicapped by these new recruits!

At 8 a.m. on the morning of July 22nd, a party of officers rode up the peak of one of the Blue Ridge Mountains and took in the view of the Shenandoah Valley. General Greene had his son Francis Vinton with him as they joined Generals Geary and Slocum to search for movements of the enemy. They were most fortunate that rebel artillery was not nearby since they made an inviting target with the morning sun behind them.

The party saw rebels in the Millwood—Winchester area, but the opinions varied from "a small cavalry camp" to "a Division of the rebel troops."[26] Regardless, the intelligence gathered put Greene's brigade on the move to prevent their departure and bring them to battle.

They moved through Upperville and passed near Ashby's Gap on July 23rd, a distance of 15 miles that morning. Resuming their march later in the day, they made another 10 miles under a warm sun to Markham station near Manassas Gap. The men rested that evening while laying on their arms.[27] Greene had his troops pass through the gap the next day only to receive orders to countermand their march and return to Markham station. They were to have supported the 2nd, 3rd, and 5th Corps ahead of them and heard firing on the rebels that morning.

Their camp was set up at Piedmont after a march of 22 miles.[28]

Since General Greene's brigade hadn't participated in the skirmish with the Confederates, the march was resumed to White Plains and a thunder shower that evening of July 25th cooled them down in camp.[29]

Apparently one problem the men had in the Shenandoah Valley was good drinking water. It was scarce, one of Greene's men said "we have to drink water that the horses and cattle at the north wouldent touch."[30]

The brigade was more inclined to drink it than ford through it that evening to be on the other side of the stream where the camp was sited by the troops ahead of them. The men were observed as they crossed the log to avoid wet shoes and socks. General Greene felt their attitude was timid and gave orders to move through the stream to avoid delay.

This was ignored by some and General Greene brought his horse next to them to steer them into the water. Using the stones in the stream and his gun, a soldier had leaped-frog over, thus bypassing Greene's discipline method. The men cheered and laughed when Greene shouted "Get that gun out of the water! Get that gun out of the water!"[31] Although no disciplinary action was taken, Greene admired a person who could find a quick solution to an immediate situation.

On their march from Throughfare Gap to Haymarket on July 26th, the men are greeted with houses that had been burned down at the latter place by those in the 11th Corps. Greene's young son, Francis wasn't given concerned about this destruction as he wrote in his diary, "lost Pistol & belt but one of the 5th Ohio brought it to me." He thought about what his father would say if he knew about it.[32]

Because both armies were recovering from their fight at Gettysburg, it appeared that the Generals Meade and Lee were content to maneuver their forces and wait for an opportunity to strike. Greene's brigade started to march south to Cattlet's Station on the Orange and Alexandria Railroad that day, passed through Greenwich and stopped at Warrenton Junction.[33] For the next few days, the men enjoyed their stay in camp and relaxed from the long marches.

General Greene enjoyed a good laugh when a staff member told him at headquarters about an incident in crossing a stream that day. The staff member had taken over for General Greene, who went ahead and kept his troops in contact with the other 12th Corps men. He brought the soldiers over a log and saw a soldier fall. Holding on the log with hands and feet underneath, the soldier dropped his gun in the water as he attempted to get back on the log. One man yelled out "Get that gun out of the water!" He was helped up by his comrades, but not before everyone laughed and remembered General Greene's predicament.[34]

The area of Warrenton Junction was not picturesque, with burned houses (only chimneys remained) and a few small earthworks along the railroad, but was important for bringing clothes and other supplies to the 12th Corps. There was a risk of guerilla activity in the area since the railroad was an ideal target to capture or destroy supplies. Charles and Francis Vinton Greene had wanted to visit an acquaintance they knew lived in the vicinity while in camp, but their father had not allowed it. The 13 year old thought the "General afraid of guerillas."[35]

It was understandable for Greene to be protective. He was proud of his sons and saw how mature they were for their respective ages. Military life appealed to them (like their father), but Francis was only a boy as his father was reminded by his playing with the drummer boys and learned some lessons during their stay in camp.[36]

Greene's brigade left their camp at 5 a.m. the morning of July 31st parallel to the railroad and turned southeast on a road surrounded by scrub pines and other evergreens towards Kelly's Ford. Upon their arrival at 7 pm, Greene's brigade received a guide and separated from the division ordered to march to Ellis Ford that evening. Located on the Rappahannock River, their destination had brought them 29 miles that day, the men fell asleep on the road at times of rest and the 137th New York at one time took the wrong road before rejoining the brigade.[37]

The warm weather combined with a long march made most of the soldiers sleepy. However, a few of Greene's men were hungry and not satisfied with hardtack as related by a 137th New York soldier "last night we stole a two year old stear and kill it," but complained "I do not get enough of stear to eat."[38]

General Greene's men stayed at Ellis's Ford for a long time since neither army wanted to engage in a battle and made preparations for the next campaign in the weeks ahead. At the approach of the Rappahannock River, the Union pickets were located on the shoreline and inside and around the buildings, shops and grist-mill that stood in the open area where the Confederate pickets could view their enemy.

Captain Collins of the 149th New York stated their camp was "located in a piece of woods about a quarter of a mile back from the Ford, and was concealed from view of the enemy by a slight rise of ground between it and the river."[39]

After digging rifle pits near the ford, the pickets of Greene's brigade got along with their counterparts across the river. Having orders not to fire unless the Confederates opened upon them,

Charles Engle described his experience on picket duty "we could talk with the rebel picets if it wasent for a dam a little way above the ford. The water falls 4 or 5 feet and it roars so we cant hear them nor they us. We sometimes salute each other by swinging our caps."[40]

One of the pleasures that many of the men missed was reading the newspapers. Pickets from both sides of the river sometimes traded papers if not prevented by their officers. One of Greene's officers had read about the reports of the Army of the Potomac not doing anything in Virginia and the growing discontent that North Carolina and Kentucky were having for the Confederacy.[41] They even received foreign newspapers as recalled by the 137th New York surgeon, "the London papers don't know what to think of the repulse of Lee [Gettysburg], the Times with its usual malignity assails our cause, but the London Star gives us a very cheering editorial."[42]

Citizens had approached Geary's division to ask for guards for their homes to keep out foragers. One of those homes had made an impression on young Francis Vinton Greene, "visited with Father & Charles an F.F.V. [First Family of Virginia] with two sons in the rebel Black Horse cavalry & her husband dead. One son at home idiotic. Wanted Father to send *one of his sons* for her daughter about a mile off to escort her through the camps." She had told her guest they "had 400 niggers before the war, had sent them all south" and it "had [been] very good living."[43]

Except for their separation at Frederick, Francis Vinton Greene had enjoyed his great military adventure with his father and brother Charles. It left an indelible mark on him that guided him in his pursuit of a professsional career. His military pass expired on August 18, 1863 General Greene enjoyed their time together and wanted to return Francis to his mother and home. After they said their goodbyes, Francis wrote that he "rode to Corps headquarters with father & C[harles] & to Bealton Station with Maj. Rodgers. Left Father waving his hat & rode on the engine to Warrington Junction." He arrived via Alexandria-Washington-New York City at home by 7 o'clock that evening.[44]

Conscripts came into camp to fill the ranks but one soldier felt they "wont be worth much until next spring and by that time half of them will be dead or discharged."[45] This is exactly what General Greene wanted to prevent (understanding a veteran's procrastination), using discipline and drill to make them soldiers. By August 31, 1863 Greene was pleased to find his brigade, as General Geary accompanied him, pass inspection with their guns and equipment in fine order.[46]

The men were mustered in for their back pay in late August, but one New Yorker looked forward to coming home. "I think this war will close in a short time," wrote Joshua Comfort to his parents "for we have got our flags floating over fort sumter and fort wagner and I think it will soon flote over Charl[es]ton."[47] Although Comfort was wrong about Fort Sumter in South Carolina falling in Union hands, he had good reasons to feel optimistic about the end of the rebellion.

Rebel pickets were surprised on August 23rd to see the 78th New York cross the river on a foraging expedition. As they crossed in boats, the colonel had two bullets pass him on the side of the boat and the pickets were driven back. Greene's men had "captured six tons of hay and 15 head of their beef cattle and a grindstone from an old farmer," wrote a participant after they had returned to camp.[48]

Another pastime that some of the men participated in was to visit the ladies in the surrounding area despite orders to the contrary. Some were arrested on their return of conquest and it could have been agreeable to the women, who a soldier in Greene's brigade said "hate us [in] the worst way."[49] The soldiers of the 149th New York were very much excited one morning to see two ladies coming over the hill in front of their camp. They sat on large bags of grain in a two-wheel cart drawn by four oxen as they went their way towards Ellis's Mill to convert the grain into flour.[50]

One of those who came on the scene from the commotion was Edwin P. Farling, the hospital steward. He recalled, "the girls were laughing & talking & seemed to be having a gay time regardless of the hundred eyes leveled at them." Perhaps to alleviate any concern to his female friend back home, Farling told her they "were shockingly out of taste & failed completely in their endeavors to make a favorable impression." It was the driver that garnished his attention however. "What killed me was the darkey, there he sat astride of one of the oxen, hat tipped one side a la Broadway, dressed only as a colored individual can dress driving his gallant charges with a rope and looking about him as though he thought it rare sport."[51]

As September 1863 began, the rebels had their pickets engage in a fight to allow their cavalry to cross the river. This intelligence gathering foray took place about 4 miles down the river from the 149th New York encampment. They were sent by General Greene to help the small squad of Union cavalry that had been surprised, and recovered the horses captured by the rebels before they recrossed the river.

"Near the picket post," remembered a 149th New Yorker, "we found the body of one of our Cavalry shot through the head and while skirmishing in a line up the river his horse was found covered with blood so it seems he must have rode some distance before he fell. His hands were partially closed as if he had grasped the mane & had rode leaning forward & had fallen off from loss of blood."[52]

The time for rest and refitting came to an end on September 15th for General Greene's brigade as they broke camp at 6 p.m. and moved to Kelley's Ford at the Rappahannock River, arriving at 10 pm after a six mile march. For the next two days, Greene lead his brigade across the river on pontoons, made 13 miles before setting up camp near Raccoon Ford on the Rapidan River.[53]

For the duration of their stay at Raccoon Ford, the weather was cold and fires were not permitted due to a sizable rebel force across the river in the open fields. Greene's divisional commander, General John W. Geary, wrote about the rebels "throwing up fortifications on almost every spot of available ground" and were "determined to dispute the passage of the river." Picket duty here was "the most dangerous," called it "the worst place" in Charles Engle's experience. "The rebels fire at us every chance they have," he said as he witnessed a fellow soldier have his gun shot to pieces.

"They have got a bold front and our pickets line lookes more like a line of battle than it does like a picket line."[54]

General Greene took part in the distasteful duty of two men from his brigade, the 78th New York, shot for desertion. The men, seated on their coffins next to the open graves, were not killed by the first volley and had to be shot again before relieving their misery. The division, in a hollow square of three sides, marched past the dead and they were buried without honors.[55] Discipline had to be maintained and for Greene there was no alternative (barring President Abraham Lincoln's intercession).

The executions of September 18th were overshadowed by their movement near Brandy Station on the 25th. Upon moving out at 7 am from camp and arriving at Bealton Station after ten miles, Greene's men remained here until new orders were received. They were to proceed to the freight cars on the Orange and Alexandria Railroad and be issued rations for eight days. Both the 11th and 12th Corps were put under the command of General Joseph Hooker. Their orders were to be transferred 1,200 miles to the Western theater to help General Rosencrans' Army under siege in Chattanooga, Tennessee from the Confederates under General Braxton Bragg.[56]

This change of operations for Greene looked like a good omen for recognition to get promoted.

General Slocum, who was respected by Greene, gave "testimony to his worth" for his performance at Chancellorsville and Gettysburg and felt he was deserving of a promotion to Major General. He had "the entire confidence of all military men."[57] Despite his Corps commander's recommendation to President Lincoln, Greene knew the wheels of justice turned slow.

Greene's brigade of General Geary's division was the last one to board the train's cars on September 28th in the afternoon, putting in to Alexandria at 6 p.m. and then arrived in Washington at 7 p.m., where they were delayed for a few hours. One veteran described some of the men as drunk due to women at the train who "supplied the men with whiskey which they concealed under their skirts." They stopped overnight at the Relay House (outside of Baltimore) and continued on after 1 pm on September 29th to Harpers Ferry and Martinsburg by 4 pm. After they obtained military supplies, with clothing for the officers and men at Martinsburg, they ended their journey that day in Cumberland at midnight.[58]

The men became anxious as they began their movement October 1st, and passed through the towns of Grafton, Fairmont and crossed the Ohio river into Ohio, stopping at Bellair. It was a relief for one soldier of the 137th New York, who felt ill and complained "we are so crowded in the cars we cant lay down." Spencer Jasen took the opportunity to go siteseeing "I went in the coal mine twelve hundred feet under ground. It was a grand sight."[59]

From October 2nd they rode the rails into Columbus, Ohio to proceed into Indiana at Indianapolis and finally arrived at Jeffersonville on October 4th at the Ohio river, General Greene never forgot those people of the West. "Our transit through Ohio and Indiana was a continued ovation; we could not be made welcome enough, and the people vied with each other in hospitality. Whenever the trains stopped refreshments were furnished, officers and men invited to the houses, and songs sung by the children."[60]

The soldiers enjoyed such items as bread, cheese, apples, whisky, and the company of the ladies on their stops. It was the flags displayed, the effects of many battles when unfurled, that gave the citizens their answer for respecting what they had done for their country.[61]

Their train (after they were carried by ferry boat) left Louisville, Kentucky and brought them into Tennessee at the state capital, Nashville. The city had become a main supply depot for the Army of the Cumberland and many of the public buildings were used as hospitals. It was protected by forts that were linked by extensive earthworks. On a visit to one of the hospitals, one of Greene's men had found out that some of the wounded prisoners were from General Longstreet's Corps that had fought at Chickamauga. Knowing of the 12th Corps by the star emblem, he wrote home "they say they would reather fight eney other corps than the star corps as they call it."[62]

The five days (October 7th-12th) that Greene's men were in Nashville gave the Western men a look at their Eastern counterparts. Seeing their neat appearance with paper collars and shoes blacked, the Western men gave them the nickname "paper-collar soldiers." The Army of the Potomac Corps soldiers had to prove themselves in battle to gain their respect.[63]

It rained with "terrible marching in the mud," as Henry Rudy remembered, as they guarded the 11th Corps train (wagons) and stragglers came in to Murfreesboro on October 13th. Like Nashville, the town had forts but his didn't stop guerilla activities as the rebels burned a bridge only a few days ago. Leaving on October 14th, Greene's men marched 25 miles to Shelbyville and left the town on October 16th for Tullahoma over bad roads in a rocky and hilly section. The men tore down a home for firewood to keep warm that cold evening.[64]

This section of Tennessee was known for its guerilla activity. One officer described the contrast from being in the East, "like Virginia, it is entirely denuded of rails, but unlike her barren fields, the country is covered with a most luxurious growth of weeds from 7 to 10 feet in hight, and so dense that a bird could not pass through them." This was good cover for ambushes. General Greene recalled "the river was infested by sharpshooters to such an extent that the roads near it could not be followed," and the mountain passes were natural barriers for defense.[65]

Repairs were made to the tracks that caused a train with supplies to be wrecked near Tullahoma and they proceed to Deckert Station. Greene's brigade was sent in different directions. The 78th New York guarded the bridge over Stone's River, the 137th New York in Wartrace, and the other three regiments ordered to move towards Bridgeport, Alabama by October 22-23rd 1863. By October 25th, the 102nd New York was sent to Nashville to provide protection for the 2nd Division train with the rest of the brigade who stayed in the area due to a torpedo (bomb) that blew up a car on the track.[66]

Greene's brigade (except the 102nd New York) marched 7 miles to Shellmound over the poor roads with rocks and mud from the recent rains. It made for a slow march and the troops used ropes to help pull out a battery that was stuck from time to time. While the men were tired from the difficult march, there was a few at the end of October 27th who ventured over to the Nickajack Cave and saw the place where the manufacture of saltpeter (gunpowder) had been a source for the Confederacy.[67]

With a restful night for Greene's men, they moved out early on October 28th from Shellmound and by noon reached Whiteside (sometimes called Gap or Station). Getting closer to enemy country, skirmishers were sent out in companies a half mile to find out about the enemy and check with General O.O. Howard's 11th Corps that had gone ahead of them on the road. There were no rebels, but no contact with Howard's troops, left an opportunity for the rebels to flank them if they continued their march with no one to guard their rear. To prevent this, General Greene had his old regiment, the 60th New York, detached and left behind.[68]

General George Sears Greene had his men encamped within 6 miles of Chattanooga, near the town of Wauhatchie. With the 60th New York at Whiteside, he was left an under strength brigade and with General Howard's Corps further ahead, basically isolated Geary's division. The General was concerned because a rebel signal officer had been spotted earlier in the afternoon, alerting them to the division's movement. Firing was heard by a rebel battery near the point of Lookout Mountain on General Howard's troops.

With the sun going down in the West and evening draws near, Greene wondered about the close proximity of the rebels. Would they attack them at Wauhatchie or could they help Howard's Corps the next day? He found out the intentions of the Confederates soon enough.[69]

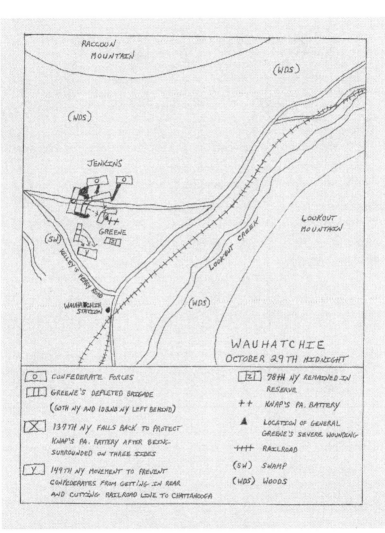

RACCOON
MOUNTAIN

(WDS)

(WDS)

JENKINS

LOOKOUT
MOUNTAIN

GREENE

(SW)

KELLEY'S FERRY ROAD

LOOKOUT CREEK

WAUHATCHIE
STATION

(WDS)

WAUHATCHIE
OCTOBER 29TH MIDNIGHT

☐ CONFEDERATE FORCES

▥ GREENE'S DEPLETED BRIGADE
(60TH NY AND 102ND NY LEFT BEHIND)

☒ 137TH NY FALLS BACK TO PROTECT
KNAP'S PA. BATTERY AFTER BEING
SURROUNDED ON THREE SIDES

☐ 149TH NY MOVEMENT TO PREVENT
CONFEDERATES FROM GETTING IN REAR
AND CUTTING RAILROAD LINE TO CHATTANOOGA

☒ 78TH NY REMAINED IN
RESERVE

+ + KNAP'S PA. BATTERY

▲ LOCATION OF GENERAL
GREENE'S SEVERE WOUNDING

++++ RAILROAD

(SW) SWAMP

(WDS) WOODS

Chapter Eighteen

Your Obedient Servant

"We have no news from the reconnaissance as yet, but as there has been no cannonading to speak of, we assume that our boys have met no considerable fore of the enemy," wrote a newspaper correspondent on October 28, 1863 to the editor of the St. Lawrence Republican.[1] General Greene didn't know what considerable force the enemy had, but wanted to be prepared for any contingency.

The Rebels looked to take advantage of Geary's Division being isolated and planned to make a night attack. Under the command of General Longstreet, the brigades of Micah Jenkins's South Carolinians and Henry L. Benning's Georgians attacked those troops with the other two brigades under Generals Law and Robertson blocked the road that Howard's Corps or other Union troops used to come from Brown's Ferry to help Geary.[2]

On the road they had marched, Greene's men from the 78th New York, put in reserve, faced the rear with the 149th New York on the left flank and the 137th New York in the center of the camp. They gave support to Knap's Independent Battery, which was located on a knoll, its slight elevation had an impact on the gunners that night in the open field. Geary's wagons were parked in the southwest corner, west of the railroad.[3]

Geary had his forces in a horseshoe shaped defense as he first reported hearing picket firing at 10:15 pm, west of the railroad and north of his position. There was a discrepancy in his statement that "the entire command was put under arms at once" and repeated that order when the firing resumed.[4] General Greene had been worried and told his staff to keep their horses saddled and bridled. He had sent an aide, Lt. Albert R. Greene, to ask Geary if the men could sleep on their arms and keep their shoes on. Although Greene was told that Geary thought it wasn't necessary, the General issued the order despite Geary's misgivings.[5]

The 137th New York's Colonel David Ireland didn't comply with Greene's order, feeling they could receive adequate warning from their pickets if the rebels decided to attack them. General Jenkins had kept his soldiers quiet as possible in their march of two to three miles and were in the woods that surrounded the camp. While some of Greene's men turned in to sleep, picket firing was heard with the moonlight overhead as the woods hid those unknown number of rebels in the dark.[6]

It was after midnight when the pickets came in and warned the camp that a rebel column approached. Greene's men began to deploy, but they were taken by surprise by General Longstreet's troops. "It was so dark that they could not be seen," remembered a 12th Corps officer, "but they [the enemy] seemed to know our position perfectly. We distinctly heard the command to those men 'By the left flank . . . . '" The crash of volleys and the sound of the rebel yell carried in the night breeze as Greene's men had returned fire.[7]

Jenkins's South Carolinians were advanced and pushed the disorganized line of Greene's back, but as the rebels stopped to reload, the darkness that aided their advance now began to hinder them. Colonel Asbury Coward of the 5th South Carolina saw the flashes from the muskets on the line ahead of him. Seeing the danger of receiving friendly fire, "I dared not go farther for my men would be in the crossing of our fire from right to left rear." Taking cover on the ground, Coward saw one of his color guard had been hit in the neck who had been next to him. The dying soldier asked the Colonel to "tell my old mammy I died doing my duty for South Carolina."[8]

General Greene saw the muzzle flashes from the rebel line and "had been twice along the line sending in a few stragglers in the rear."[9] The General came alongside Knap's Battery on the knoll, which was out in the open from the woods and became a target from the moonlight showing the battery and soldiers in the dark. A veteran remembered "the flash of the four guns lighted up our whole front, showing for an instant the line coming towards us." It was difficult to know if both Federal and Confederate men were mixed together for the gunners, but "then in the darkness the Flash of rebel muskets marked their line, and the bullets began to come." One of Knap's gunners saw them "advancing in strong force" and wrote in his diary that the rebels "poured a heavy volley into us."[10]

What happened to General Greene at Knap's Battery is related by his son, Francis Vinton:

"Just as it [the gun] was discharged, his horse reared and plunged, and in so doing broke the girth of his saddle. He was alone at the moment, his aides and orderlies having all been sent off with orders.

He dismounted and attempted to repair the broken girth, alternately facing the saddle and turning his face to the left to watch the enemy's movements as disclosed by their fire."[11]

In a flash from the dark a bullet had gone through his upper lip, under the left corner nostril of his nose, passed through his mouth and carried away most of his upper jaw and part of his cheek bone as it exited on the right side. The shock of the impact had knocked him to the ground, but he arose to his feet, and "from loss of blood and of voice," Greene had Colonel Ireland take over command as he left for to the hospital in the rear.[12]

The nature of General Greene's wound was clear, but how it occurred is in dispute. I believe his son's account is the true source, despite the story told four years after the General's death. In a recent study by historian Peter Cozzens on the Chattanooga Campaign, he described the moment of General Greene's wounding had been knocked off his horse.[13]

The two sources he listed didn't stand up to Francis Vinton Greene's account. The first is the Official Records. Greene's report of November 1, 1863 said he was shot (understandable since he was under the doctor's care), but he made no reference on his horse or helped by any staff members to the hospital.[14]

The second source was Albert R. Greene's account, given as a speech and printed in 1890 among fellow veterans of the MOLLUS organization. Although he was an aide to the General, Albert wasn't his son as Cozzens wrote, but his nephew. He could not have witnessed the General's wounding since he had been sent off with orders as the others. Greene does not say he had any of his staff with him when he was wounded. It is speculation at best that Greene's servant helped him to the hospital.[15]

Since there is no testimony from General Greene about receiving help in his records with the National Archives or no eyewitness accounts left by the members of Knap's Battery who could verify what happened, it is plausible that Francis Vinton's story of his father is straightforward. Why had Albert R. Greene change or adlib some of the story of Greene's wounding? The reason may have been a hidden agenda to help his relative, who in 1890, was trying to gather support from Union veterans to have a relief bill presented to Congress to help the aging General. A dramatic pose on a horse, telling his men to stand firm at the very front of battle was told for a political purpose, not for historical accuracy.[16] We don't know if General Greene read this paper, but he couldn't have approved of distorting the facts. Respect and historical facts were too important to the General.

The battle grew in fury as Greene could hear the cannon fire and muskets discharged their bullets into the enemy back at the hospital. The 137th New York was surprised like the others, but they caught the brunt of the attack, along with Knap's Battery. Upon taking some casualties from the rebel fire, they returned their fire and looked for the flashes in the dark from the enemy's line. Sergeant Henry Rudy recalled their "line on our left broke and left many [Rebels] in our left flank."[17]

"The rebs had a least six men to our one," wrote another 137th New York soldier, and compared the rebel style of fighting to "regular Indians." He also spoke of the left, blaming the 149th New York, which "broke and run when the first volley was fired" putting them in a precarious situation.[18] This was not true. In order to prevent the Confederates from moving around his left flank and capturing the railroad (the main objective to prevent supplies from reaching Rosecrans's Army in Chattanooga), Colonel Randall had formed the regiment and marched towards the railroad embankment and fences to use for cover to return fire.[19]

Since this left a gap in the line that the 137th New York could not make the proper realignment while fighting in the dark to cover it, the men of General Jenkins by sheer luck were able to move through and concentrate their musket fire on this regiment and the battery. The situation was critical as they took fire from three sides.[20]

The moonlight and flashes from musket fire contributed to mounting casualties on both sides. Good fortune was Henry Rudy's for a ball passed through his clothes and grazed his neck, but not for James Batcher, as he lied down and was killed when a ball struck him above the left ear in his head.[21] It didn't look better for Knap's Battery. As they used up their shells, the gunners switched to canister to inflict more casualties of the rebels. "We could hear the devils shout, 'Shoot the gunners!' Shoot the gunners!'" reported one observer as they directed their fire from Greene's infantry onto them.[22]

Calling it "one of the heaviest firing I ever saw," Private Mixson of the 1st South Carolina saw his colonel shot while on his knees making observations on the Union line. He died as the minnie ball passed through his heart.[23] The rebel sharpshooters were deadly effective as the gunners "could not find protection any place." The "men & horses wer falling all around" wrote one gunner. The sixty rounds in their cartridge boxes were gone and men were forced to take from the dead and wounded to be resupplied. Bayonets were prepared if it became necessary for a charge to prevent the battery's capture.[24]

The three hour fighting was ended by the withdraw of the Confederates when General Jenkins was informed of Union troops being maneuvered around Benning's Brigade on the right and began attacking his rear. They were aided by the darkness and moved their forces to the Union left behind the swamp where the 149th New York had been initially when the fight broke out. Some of the wagons and supplies captured were set afire by Jenkins's men.

Since Hooker's relief force had broken through General Law's attempted roadblock, their numbers could have cut him off from his escape route.[25]

Greene's men and the rest of Geary's division had given a good account of themselves in this rare night fight of the Civil War. The Confederates looked at the darkness (which had provided them the element of surprise) as hindering coordinating attacks, but it was implied that Law's failure to stop Hooker's relief force prevented Jenkins from delivering the final assault. Perhaps feeling that General Micah Jenkins was not qualified to handle the responsibilities of his new command, General Law was quoted to have said he "could not be expected to furnish silver spurs for Jenkins' new uniform as Major General."[26]

As the 78th New York (which received few casualties, held in reserve) began to build entrenchments with the pioneer corps and searched the dead and wounded for ammunition. General O.O. Howard approached with an escort of cavalry into their camp. He was part of Hooker's relief force and greeted by an officer, "General Greene met me, his head seemingly bound with a napkin, and extended his hand. A bullet had passed through his face carrying away some of his teeth, so that he was unable to speak to me, but he showed me the way to Geary who was beside his slain son [killed while sighting his gun in Knap's Battery].[27]

The battery had suffered many casualties among the officers and enlisted men. The rebels had also shot down the horses, some of them with their harness still on, to prevent the guns removal from the knoll.

Casualties for Greene's brigade were 104, including 90 for the 137th New York that had been nearly surrounded and the Confederates had suffered at least 150 dead that were found by burial details (358 were reported out of 1,800 in the fight as killed, wounded or missing).[28]

"We fold him in his blanket and lower his rude coffin in that hallowed place, a patriot soldier's grave," were the eloquent words that Colonel Barnum used for those at home about the death of Sergeant William C. Lilly, the color-bearer of Gettysburg fame, of the 149th New York.[29] As he lay dying from loss of blood and in pain on an ambulance, in a humane gesture he offered his blanket to a half-naked rebel soldier who was wounded & cold from the rain.[30] With the character of men like Lilly, Greene had every reason to be proud of his brigade.

One of the South Carolinians had waved a flag of truce as he emerged from the woods without his gun towards the camp. Edwin P. Farling and Commissary Sergeant Patterson had spotted him and told him to retrieve his gun he left behind. The rebel left and came back with the gun and was put on guard. Earlier, the hospital steward (Farling) had been approached by a rebel near the hospital to give himself up. The skirmisher was covered in the face with black powder and enjoyed his captor's coffee and hard bread.

Farling told his friend back home "so you see I mixed up a little in the fun—I had worked all night & felt just like taking at least a score of Butternuts."[31]

General George Sears Greene never returned to his brigade again. His wound required a long convalescence and it was unknown how a 62 year old, in good health could respond to treatment. After being treated at field hospital, Greene was sent in an ambulance to Nashville on November 1, 1863.[32] Unless he was awake for the surgery, the doctors used morphine or opium to numb the pain and sleep. Sometimes ether was used, but improbable to use for Greene could have choked due to his wound or suffered respiratory failure.

The news of Greene's wounding had reached his family in New York City during the first week of November and his oldest son, George S. Greene Jr. took passage on the railroads to join his father at the hospital in Nashville. During his son's journey on the rails, Greene was examined and declared unfit for duty by R.D. Lynde, the attending Surgeon on November 4th for a period of 20 days.[33]

Until Greene could be fitted with an upper plate to be able to eat solid foods and allow his wound to heal properly, he was likely to lose weight due to lack of nutrition. His diet consisted of soft foods and liquids of the day such as milk, coffee, brandy, boiled eggs, soup and sweet potatoes. He had to live with the pain for the remainder of his life, but another problem had surfaced that was not repaired. The cheek had been stitched, but the minie ball had caused a salivary fistula, cutting the salivary duct and carrying the ends outward with saliva discharged outside the cheek.[34]

The surgeons did not try to fix it since he remained in a weaken condition and also it was an unusual problem not seen by them in treating various wounds at the hospitals. The General was accompanied by George Jr. on the train, over a 7 day period, stopping by the towns where he had been when the 12th Corps had traveled West to save Rosencrans's Army. Upon their arrival in Washington D.C., they were greeted at the train station by Martha, who had received word from her son to come down from New York.[35]

It was a terrible strain on Martha's nerves that month to see her husband once again. The outpouring of love and tenderness, along with good news to pass on to her family and friends, lifted their spirits. Still, it had been a shock to see him this way since their visit in camp back in June 1863. With the General's medical leave expiring, he was reexamined by the Surgeon W.R. DeWitt, Jr. and continued to suffer from his wounds. Greene had his leave extended another 20 days before he could resume his duties.[36]

Only a week had gone by when George and Martha received word of their son, Charles, being wounded at Ringgold. With the retreat of the Confederate Army at Chattanooga in late November 1863, the pursuit by Union forces was held up by a defensive stand at Ringgold. It was a rebel shell that tore off Charles T. Greene's leg as the brigade crossed the field. Giving comfort to each other and putting their faith in God, the General's resolve was strengthened by his son's outlook of his wounding.[37]

A soldier who commanded the detail that brought Charles to the hospital admired his character. "It was a long trip for him and he suffered much, though the men were exceedingly careful" and through it all Charles did not complain. "What greater glory," wrote Charles to his wife, "or honor can a soldier have than to have a leg taken off by a cannon ball in the glorious cause we fight for."[38]

By December 15, 1863 Greene had recovered enough for light duty as a member of a court-martial.

This obedient servant gave no hint of resigning his commission to recover at home, but it was too early to resume a field command. He reported to the Adjutant General's office in Washington as he was appointed on General Court Martial duty on January 16, 1864, with Major General R. J. Oglesby as President.[39]

It was a different experience for this man who had proven himself in the field. He didn't have any of his staff officers to provide assistance in his new duties while in Washington.[40] As General Greene struggled with his salivary duct problem to regain his strength, there were politicians from New York and Rhode Island who hadn't forgotten Greene and tried to gain his promotion to Major General. In March 1864, with Washington fixated on the Joint Committee on the Conduct of the War hearings of General Meade's conduct of the Gettysburg Campaign, the Secretary of War, Edwin Stanton received two letters supporting Greene's promotion.

Senator Ira Harris of New York stated it was "the unanimous verdict of all" that served with him and that "his services entitled him to expect this promotion." Senator H. B. Anthony was less demanding in his tone to Stanton, but described Greene's service as "distinguished" and "gallant" and agreed with his colleague in support of his promotion to Major General.[41] The timing of those letters, with the hearings in Washington about Gettysburg and Meade's conciliatory letter to Greene over his incorrect reports of the fight at Culp's Hill [see Chapter One] may have given him those two stars that were long overdue.

Greene chose not to play the political game in Washington, compromising his good character, and contributed to ruining a fellow army officer's career for the sake of being promoted to Major General.

Despite this renewed support, nothing came from Harris and Anthony's letters. In May 1864, General Greene's physical problem continued and after talking with family members, decided to request a transfer to the New York City area to get help. The

Secretary of War ordered him to the Eastern Department, under the command of Major General John A. Dix, on May 11, 1864 and was confined to his quarters after a surgical operation.[42]

Looking for permanent relief, the Greene family had decided to consult Dr. William Home Van Buren, a prominent surgeon in New York. Known for his translation of the French literature "Operative Surgery" by Bernard and Huette, this work during the Civil War was distributed to army surgeons by the United States Government. Van Buren had been offered the office of surgeon general by President Lincoln in 1861, but turned him down and gave advice to Lincoln about who to appoint to the office when he was consulted.[43]

Greene had his cheek cut open and have the ends of the salivary duct turned inward. Bandages were applied around the jaw, after his cheek was sewed up, to prevent any movement for three days so the incision could heal. In order to prevent weight loss or further lack of nutrients, liquid food was administered through a glass tube.[44] The wound was slow to heal, but this new or novel approach by Dr. Van Buren had partially corrected the problem. Although the salivary duct was still open from being cut by the bullet, Greene no longer had saliva discharge outside of his cheek.

Regretfully, the pain stayed with him and although the wound finally healed it had left him unable to gain his strength for many months.

Greene's youngest son, Francis, was able to see his father at home and witness his recovery. He noticed after the wound healed "it never gave any serious trouble except at long intervals, when small pieces of lead which had been left in the cheek forced their way out, causing suppuration."[45] Greene attempted to put his affairs in order and informed the Adjutant-General's office of his operation. He forwarded a receipt for reimbursement of lodging and fuel before moving back to his home, greeted by family, friends, and well-wishers.[46]

During those months of recovery in the spring and summer of 1864, General Grant had come East to battle Lee's army toward his march to Richmond and General Sherman had command in the West and marched toward Atlanta against General Johnston's army. Greene read in the newspapers of the terrible casualties and the Union armies being stalemated around Petersburg in Virginia and Atlanta in Georgia. With the fall of Atlanta in September, President Abraham Lincoln was reelected in the November election and Lee's Army remained in a siege at Petersburg. Greene resumed his duties as a member of boards and commissions (court-martial) until late January 1865.[47]

It appeared to everyone that the end of the Confederacy was near, except for those few diehards, and could be decided in the spring campaign. Greene felt he was capable to return to active duty in the field and made inquiries to that effect. On January 21, 1865 General George Sears Greene made preparations for travel by railroad and said goodbye to his loved ones as he was ordered to Nashville, Tennessee and reported to Major General Thomas.[48] The trip took four days and his stay lasted only fifteen days due to new orders. We cannot know what General Thomas had in mind for Greene since neither man left documentation of their time together, but Greene had never given any cause for his superiors to question his capabilities.

His orders for February 11, 1865 were to report to Major General Henry W. Slocum for his new assignment. Slocum was part of General Sherman's army that had left Georgia and moved into the Carolinas. Greene obtained transport to Newbern, North Carolina and became part of General Schofield's expedition that was organized to move west and join with Sherman's army at Goldsborough.[49]

The General "acted as volunteer aide" and "has been with me since we reached Gum Swamp," wrote General Jacob D. Cox who spoke fondly of this aging warrior. There had been no serious opposition to Schofield's movements until rebels at Kingston on March 10, 1865 tried to prevent them from joining with Sherman. Led by General Braxton Bragg, this small force could only hope to delay this Union force for a few days.[50]

Being placed between the Lower Trent road and the railroad, a lieutenant from the 3rd North Carolina artillery found himself "under an incessant fire of artillery and rifles without being able to fire a shot in return." Some of the rebel fire came into General Cox's division. From their horses, Generals Cox and Greene viewed the enemy's fire when Greene had his horse shot under him, and got on another horse as if nothing happened. With the approaching darkness, the rebels broke off contact and moved towards their camp near Kingston.[51]

Greene had temporary command of a division made up of convalescents and recruits under General Cox from March 11th until it was dissolved after Schofield's column met Sherman's army at Goldsborough.

He was given command of the Third Brigade, Third Division of the 14th Army Corps under Brigadier General Jefferson C. Davis. This new command on March 24, 1865 consisted of the 74th Indiana, 18th Kentucky, 14th Ohio, and 38th Ohio.[52]

There would be nothing to stop Sherman's marching columns from moving through North Carolina and joining with Grant in Virginia. On April 12, 1865 Greene's brigade had marched 12 miles and began to settle down in camp at Calton [RR] Station when good news arrived from the railroad. "I was just ready to set down with my plate on the ground to eat supper," wrote Jacob Pontius of Company G, 74th Indiana when "the Whistle of an Engine was heard," delivering the news of the fall of Richmond and the surrender of General Lee's army. Shouts and cheers echoed throughout the area.[53]

Their time together was spent helping to capture the town of Raleigh and participated in the surrender of General Johnston's Army. There were no battles because General Lee's surrender at Appomattox on April 9, 1865 had signaled the end of the Civil War.

For General George Sears Greene, the sacrifice made during the war to preserve the Union was not in vain. The government of the United States had its armies put down the rebellion. Peace was welcomed by both North and South, but it shall be a long healing process for the nation to maintain law and order as the American people cast its eyes to the future.

What thoughts could have gone through Greene's mind as he passed through the battlefields of Virginia? He had to deal with an outbreak of hostilities as related by William Harrison Bowlby of the 74th Indiana from his own soldiers: "He wanted to make us, before we reached Alexandria, Virginia, to march in 4's across a little stream that was swollen by the recent rains. We wouldn't do it. That night, he wouldn't let us have any rations, and was going to make us go without supper. I was standing outside of my tent, and I heard a sort of yell, as I though[t] a charge was going to be. I saw the boys going for General Green's headquarters and the Old Man getting for the brush. So one shot hit him in the thigh, and that was the last of General Green."[54]

While there is no documentation that indicated Greene was wounded in the thigh, his strict discipline (and a newcomer from the east) did not sit well with these tough Westerners, especially with the fighting now at an end. What punishment was received by those who participated in this affair is unknown. With Sherman's Army ordered to the nation's capital in May 1865, the soldiers saw devastation everywhere on their march. They participated in the Grand Review on May 25, 1865 among the dignitaries and citizens to celebrate their victory.[55]

As they left their camp at 7am, Sherman's Army took part in the Grand Review in the Capitol. The warm day had dust filling the air as the soldiers marched down Pennsylvania Avenue to the cheers of the citizens of Washington. One soldier in Greene's brigade said it was "hard work for us to march the distance of six miles & carry our guns in one Position all the time," but had enjoyed himself and "never yet witnessed such crowds of People before." Of all the scaffolds along the parade route, one slogan on white canvas spoke volumes for all, "Welcome Home Brave Boys." By the time they reached their camp at 6pm, Greene's men had marched 20 miles and never forgot this day's celebration.[56]

Before Greene finished his army service upon being mustered out on April 30, 1866 he joined the garrison of defenses of Washington until June 23, 1865 and then served again on Court-martial duty for those remaining days of service.[57] On his arrival in

Washington, the Secretary of War, Edwin D. Stanton had a letter waiting for Greene. He was given the rank of Major General by brevet (an honorary title) to date from March 13, 1865. Sending in his acceptance the next day to the Adjutant-General's office, it could have been a terrible disappointment since others had bypassed him with less seniority or experience in the field.[58]

Although Greene was 64 years of age by war's end, he was the oldest field commander in a young man's war. He had been successful in commanding a regiment, brigade, and a division in battle and his drilling and discipline made them better soldiers on the march and in a fight than other regiments. Overall, casualties were low (except for disease) due to his use of maximum firepower against the Confederates either by offensive (Antietam) or defensive (Gettysburg) measures.

Greene's use of breastworks at Chancellorsville and Gettysburg had shown that advances in weaponry could be negated by saving lives this way. It became a common occurrence in 1864 for both armies in the East and West to dig breastworks, which caused more casualties to the attackers. This obedient servant had done more for the Union than could possibly been imagined, but now it was time for George Sears Greene to be the obedient servant to his family once again.

Chapter Nineteen

No Profession was more Honorable

With the end of the Civil War and his days as a soldier, for the second time in his life, about to end in April 1866, George Sears Greene returned to civilian life with a new job awaiting him. Charles Thurston (who worked at the Treasury Department during their time in Washington D.C.) had wrote to his father of being "delighted with your description of our new home in Croton Valley and the reservoir."[1]

The day after his mustering out of the Army, Greene was put in charge of extension of the Croton Water Works, with the first additional storage reservoir at Boyd's Corners, located in the upper reaches of the watershed in Putnam County. Since the Central Park reservoir had been completed in August 1862, New York City's population continued to grow and made it necessary within a short time to obtain a larger water supply.[2]

The chief engineer, Alfred W. Craven, had the surveys completed and knew his friend and engineering colleague was the best choice for the job. Both families stayed close during the war and Greene may have asked Craven to let him know of any engineering projects while he was on court-martial duty. Charles Thurston had suggested to his father of changing the place from Boyd's Corner to Cravengreene, a sign of their engineering profession and friendship.[3]

Greene's residence was for the next few years in New York and the construction site. He developed new friendships with those experienced and upcoming professionals. This group was with the American Society of Civil Engineers (which Greene helped organize in 1852) and Greene became a member of the Board of Directors in 1867 with its reorganization. He served five terms, became President of the Society 1875-1877 and was elected in 1888 to an honorary membership.[4]

Those personal achievements in later years could not match the enthusiasm he felt when he left Washington D.C. for Putnam County, New York. Greene was so involved with the work at Boyd's Corners in the beginning that he left some personal matters go unattended. Charles Thurston bought a fly cover for his father's grey horse and moved it with his own horses because "they did not take half care" of them at the stable where the General had left it.[5]

"I cannot understand your sending to me for collars," a perplexed Charles wrote, "when they are $1 more here [Washington D.C.] than in New York." His oldest son, George Jr., told his father "you must make your income return on Friday next agenda." Only ten days left, Greene received the papers from his son (after having found missing documents) and directed them to the Accessor office in the Post office at the Morrisania Station.[6] It was a great relief to the General not to be penalized for being late on his income return after saving the Federal Government!

George and Martha were concerned about their grandson Dana and visited him when they came on the train to Morrisania Station. Born on June 27, 1863 (when the General was in Frederick, Maryland with his youngest son, Francis Vinton on the march to Gettysburg) Dana was ill for a time, but George wrote his father that he "has been improving still & is looking very well." But as the summer season began Dana could not have regained his health for his illness resulted in his death on July 17, 1866.[7]

As his oldest son, George Jr., dealt with the grief of losing Dana, the General knew his own grief needed an outlet. He believed that sharing your feelings with family and faith in God were important, but the best immediate remedy was work. It is ironic that work was to begin on the Boyd's Corners Reservoir in July 1866. The farming valley, which received its name from Ebenezer Boyd, a Revolutionary War veteran and tavern keeper, became a 300 acre lake dam. Eleven families were to be relocated along with a church, school, and cemetery.[8]

Considered to be "larger than any built in America up to that time," the dam measured 78 feet in height and 670 feet long at the top. The foundation was made of bedrock and used other materials available "with the least expenditure of time and money," Greene had produced "the most effective results."[9] He became Chief Engineer and Commissioner of the Croton Aqueduct Department on May 11, 1868 with the resignation of Alfred W. Craven. Greene followed through with the project until his removal on April 30, 1870 not because of his work, but due to politics of the Tammany or Tweed Ring organization in Albany.[10]

The Tweed Charter of 1870 had transferred the project to the Department of Public Works. With "Boss" Tweed appointing himself as the Commissioner of Public Works and the intended use of the office gave favors from politicians and kickbacks from contractors, the organization didn't want George Sears Greene interfering with them.[11]

Merit was more important than politics for Greene and was likely relieved (although disappointed not to finish the job) to not have his name tarnished with political corruption. Besides the graft, the reservoir incurred delays because the officials used "heavy earth fill on the upstream face" of the masonry since they were unsure of its stability. Because they didn't make it watertight, it was argued that the pressure against the wall could "weaken the dam rather than strengthen it." Greene's original design proved to be the better model and by April 1873 the reservoir held four billion gallons of water on its completion.[12]

Work was plentiful for Greene in the 1870's as he was involved with the following engineering projects: Central Underground Railroad in New York City, Sewerage System of Washington D.C., Department of Public Parks and construction of Elevated Railway and water meters in New York City, and was a consultant and examined projects in water works for Yonkers, Troy, Detroit (Michigan) and the Sewerage System in Providence, Rhode Island and the Ship Canal from Lake Champlain to the St. Lawrence River.[13]

These community projects showed the growth of those population centers and while some were implemented for immediate effect, others were blueprints for future engineers. Two examples are the Central Underground Railroad and Sewerage System in Providence, Rhode Island. The company for the railroad in 1869 wanted to have a line that ran from City Hall Park to the Harlem River for New York City. The subway was intended to replace the stage routes and horse-car lines that currently existed (including the heavy traffic on Broadway). Greene and the other engineers felt it was economically feasible, the total listed at $17.6 million dollars.[14]

Their report to the company advised using "hot water engines" for better results than the ordinary steam locomotives. They could be used, but the ordinary steam engine had been tried in London and the smoke and dirt caused its rejection. For the hot water engines, "the locomotive would be charged at each end of the line with sufficient water at 470 F to generate steam for the entire trip," thereby no coal could be burned in the subway and improved ventilation. Greene had a sample piece of the line built for a demonstration, but some investors were skeptical and the capital could not be raised. It was going to be constructed in the future, but Greene had laid its foundation.[15]

For the City of Providence, Rhode Island the storms of August 1875 had aggravated the Sewerage System that had been a problem. The discharge of sewage upon the flats and low grounds and the current use of the old dry walled stone square culverts were considered by the city council to be a "danger to the public health." The American Society of Civil Engineers was contacted by the mayor of Providence to provide assistance to their chief engineer two months later and George Sears Greene was part of the three members sent to help them in October 1875.[16]

It could have been most rewarding to Greene to provide help to his native home state and well acquainted with the weather conditions of the Atlantic coastline. Many of the improvements that Providence's engineer, J. Herbert Shedd, began were looked at by Greene and his companions. They agreed with the connecting of sewers by out-falls with the rivers and cove to prevent a build-up of water from a heavy storm, the use of brick and cement in proper proportions, and having the deep water current carry away the sewage at Field's Point.[17]

However, their report to the City Council made a number of commendations. The sanitary condition may improve by removing the drains (which was temporarily collecting sewage from the new sewers) which could have its soil contaminated and replaced with fresh dirt. The flats at low tide should not be a place to discharge sewage but in deep water at the ends of piers or wharves. With the discharge at Field's Point in deep water, this could be done at low tide to preserve the Providence and Seekonk rivers and build a reservoir near the outlet.[18]

Despite the workload that kept him busy into the early 1880's, Greene enjoyed the time spent with Martha and his grandchildren. He took pride in his children's efforts of respected members of society.

George Jr. had become an engineer and for 22 years (appointed in 1875) was in charge of the Department of Docks in New York City. Samuel Dana continued his service in the U.S. Navy and Charles Thurston had gone back into the Army after he left the Treasury Department.[19]

Their youngest children, Anna and Francis Vinton, pursued their goals in life. Anna became a loving young woman and married Murray Sampson Day, a lieutenant in the navy. He was the son of General Hannibal Day, who had been a friend and classmate of George Sears Greene (USMA 1823) at West Point.

After the lieutenant's death on December 27, 1878 aboard the U.S.S. Vandalia, Anna devoted herself to care for her parents and in-laws.

Francis Vinton had decided to follow his father's example (after his boyish adventure of playing soldier with Greene's brigade in 1863), and entered the United States Military Academy. Graduated first in his class (USMA 1870), Francis Vinton went on to have a promising career as a soldier, historian, and civil engineer, which included his attachment with the Military Attaché Legation of the U.S. at St. Petersburg, Russia.[20]

The discipline and work ethic that George Sears Greene had used to overcome the loss of his wife and children from his first marriage, and helped to make soldiers out of farm boys and city dwellers in the Civil War, could not relieve the pain in his jaw. Unlike the pinup sleeve or leg of the Civil War veteran, which many considered a badge of honor, Greene's beard covered his scars, but difficulties always stayed with him.

Such examples as loss of sleep or not being able to eat properly were constant reminders of this malady.

Although there was no indication that Greene missed any time at work, it prevented him from attending social functions. "I should have been very glad to have meet some our old Penn Regts," he wrote to Col. John P. Nicholson (formally of the 28th Pennsylvania), "but last week I was very ill with an abcess on my face & quite unable to go on any duty."[21]

By January 1879, Greene began to slow down with their finances now affected due to his jaw wound and little work. Aware of their parents dilemma, Anna and George Jr. brought their father before a judge of the Superior Court in New York City, on the last day of January, to apply for a pension. This gray-haired, brown eye man of 77 years of age (listed now at 5'8 1/2 feet in height) claimed to be partially disabled from his facial wound at Wauhatchie, Tennessee on October 29, 1863. Copies that pertained to his wound were provided from the 1863 medical leaves told by the two physicians.[22]

To strengthen his case, testimony was given by H. Earnest Goodman, Greene's doctor and former surgeon of the 28th Pennsylvania Volunteers. After he described the wound & the operation of 1864, Goodman stated "the General continues to suffer [the] inability to masticate food, causing impaired nutrition and from time to time an inflammation of the Antrium (known as Neuralgia) which causes a discharge and annoyance from pain." In the 16 years that Goodman prescribed treatment for Greene, he said, "I know of no one who has more patiently borne his disability and more thoroughly deserves a pension."[23]

Greene's claim was reviewed and sent to Washington D.C. for final approval. After months of no decision, Greene had been informed through the mail of the pension being approved on July 28, 1879.

Besides this notification during the first week of August of the awarded $15.00 a month, he also received $2,385.00 to be retroactive to May 1, 1866.[24] This money was welcomed to help supplement their declining income and pay any debts that existed. Even with his partial disability, Greene remained very active.

Some of the organizations he joined and remained a part of included the New York Genealogical and Biographical Society (served as President from 1877 to 1880), the New York Historical Society, the Century Club (since 1868) and the MOLLUS or Loyal Legion (former Union officers dedicated to preserving the memories of the Civil War).[25] He enjoyed the dinners and friendships made over the years. People had sent Greene letters asking help for their family genealogy and it gave him much pleasure to pass on any information. He attempted to gather his own family records in hopes a book could be published in the future (Greene had edited a Revolutionary soldier's letters for publication in 1875).

In May 1881, General Oliver Otis Howard was the superintendent of West Point and pleasantly surprised to read this letter from his old friend at Culp's Hill. "I am appointed a member of the Board of Visitors for the term examination of the present year." This came from the Secretary of War (Robert Todd Lincoln), an honor to the 80 year old, who arrived on May 25, 1881 to perform his duty.[26]

Elected President of the Board, General Greene and the other members gave recommendations to Howard and Lincoln for improvements, if necessary, to the Military Academy. The memories of his cadet days or his son, Francis Vinton, who graduated in 1870 followed him as he looked upon the beautiful scenery of the mountains and Hudson River. The commencement of the graduating class of 1881 began on June 10th with a heavy rain storm that morning, which led the General of the Army to abandon the final parade and review.

The cadets were to have their day in the chapel and took their place in the center pews by 11 am, along with visitors and dignitaries crowded inside the building.[27]

Standing behind the podium and as he studied the attentive crowd, Greene "told them no profession was more honorable, and none required more singleness of purpose than the profession of the Army. It had ceased to be a profession of display and brute force, and required talent and science." Other speeches to follow came from Generals C.C. Augur, William Tecumseh Sherman, and Secretary of War Robert Todd Lincoln. The gloomy weather did not dampen their spirits as they cheered and applauded the wise council taught to them to be a part of their lives.[28]

General Greene enjoyed his time with the cadets and shared reminiscences with other Alumni at the dinner, which included, O.O. Howard, his 1823 classmates Alfred Mordecai and Hannibal Day, and Henry W. Slocum, former 12th Corps commander at Chancellorsville and Gettysburg. While Greene saw the advancements in the Army and in the Nation that took place, he had given some thought to the Secretary's speech to the cadets that day. "You are leaving behind you your most pleasant days. Your dearest recollections will be among them."[29] At this time in his life, General Greene didn't know of what the future could hold for him.

In 1883, George and Martha Greene had left their home of New York City (since 1856) to move in with their daughter Anna in Morristown, New Jersey. After her husband's death in 1878, Anna had built an addition on to the house to care for her in-laws, Mr. & Mrs. Hannibal Day. Two years after Mrs. Day had died, Anna may have discussed the subject with her brothers to have their parents come in with her for financial and health reasons. Greene could have been approached about this subject before and rejected it, determined to maintain their independence, but agreed to it probably for Martha and his children's peace of mind.[30]

If the General had been to Morristown to visit his daughter before the move, he may have learned why the town was growing and popular with outsiders. A New York newspaper described to its readers the conditions of Morristown, "The atmosphere is cool and dry, grateful to weak lungs and pulmonary affections, and a destroyer of chills and fever and the like. The best of water, and plenty of it, gushing from the sides of the Mountains to the West of the town, follows the ducts through every street."[31]

Many New Yorkers had created a building boom in Morristown in the 1880's & 90's. Looking to have a summer residence (and keep cool from the dreaded heat in the city), these Gilded Age millionaires of banking, insurance, and other companies had stately mansions built and increased the services that a city provided for the people. "There is now building everywhere," The Jerseyman proclaimed in 1887 and so it seemed. During the 1880's, for example, over 400 new homes were built alone.[32] Greene could go to New York from Morristown by train (daily if he wished) to see friends, do business, and still feel like he could be near his sons, Francis Vinton and George Jr., who lived in the city.

On a visit to Boston in early December 1883, Greene took time from his schedule to speak with his grandson, Carleton, who was doing well at school, but saw the luxuries of the Gilded Age all around him.

The General tried to give council to the 15 year old about life. He told Carleton that the prizes he wished to have like his Dad, Uncles and Grandfather came "by severe application and hard, through work of preparation." He continued, "the greater the talent bestowed by our maker the greater the obligation to improve that talent to the utmost of our power."[33]

Although Greene was pleased with some changes in his old age, it disturbed him about the lifestyle that money could influence on the younger generation. "It is not pleasant to see so many young men," he wrote Carleton, "acting as if they thought fine clothing, parties, houses, yachts, theaters, &c. were the 'summers bonuses' and chief objects of ambition." That type of life was without purpose or meaning to Greene and his children and Carleton understood this by their example. He told Carleton, "such lives are hardly worth living."[34]

The return to Morristown found George Sears Greene worried over Martha's brief illness. She had been "untiring" and unselfish" in her devotion to George and raised their children and grandchildren, but Martha wasn't able to recover her health and died on December 15, 1883 at the age of 74. "She was much beloved by all who knew her," recalled Francis Vinton almost 20 years later when he spoke of his mother.[35]

Their 46 years of marriage, despite their times of forced separation (ex. Civil War), consisted of love and understanding. The days ahead for George, without Martha as she was laid to rest at Apponaug, Warwick, Rhode Island (Greene's birthplace), were difficult. This time, however, he had the support of family and friends, unlike those bleak days of 1832-33.

It turned out that Greene's son, Samuel Dana, needed more support than himself. By April 25, 1884 Dana was ordered to the Portsmouth Naval Yard (in New Hampshire) as equipment officer. He had been "suffering from mental troubles" in the fall of 1884 it was said due to the recent publications of the naval battle between the Monitor and the CSS Virginia. The old demons resurfaced about letting the Virginia slip away after he defended the ships in Hampton Roads. The General had tried to protect his son in March 1862 from the unwarranted criticism. Dana was attempted to rebuke this alleged black mark against him and wrote a article for publication.[36]

A search was conducted at the naval yard after his absence was reported by Dana's wife to the commandant. On December 16th, the writer reports how they found Samuel Dana to the Army and Navy Register. Finding him dead, near the entrance to the yard in the old Franklin shiphouse, he was "lying on a pile of tree nails, his right hand tightly clasping a Colt's navy revolver." The ball had gone through his head from the right side and exiting over the left ear. The cap was burned from the discharge and was found still on his head.[37]

The loss of Martha and Dana over a year's time was a heavy burden for the old warrior. He never blamed the Navy for creating his son's depression and suicide. In fact, neither Greene Sr. or other members of the family discussed the subject of his death left in any documents. The General and family members were joined by the USS New Hampshire band, a company of marines, and nearly thirty apprentices for Dana's funeral in Bristol, Rhode Island. Firing a volley over his grave, the Navy honored the officer in death for his service that some questioned in life for his conduct in fighting the CSS Virginia.[38] Over 22 years later, the Civil War had claimed another casualty.

Greene tried to keep his mind focused on the activities he enjoyed (ex. read his books, visited the Century Club) and the support of his family. Before Dana's death, Greene was asked by the commissioners of public works to be an advisor for the plans of the New Croton Aqueduct. In 1885-86, Greene was appointed chairman of a Board of Engineers, it consisted of former Generals John Newton, Quincy A. Gilmore, and Greene to investigate charges about the condition of the work in progress.[39]

There were difficulties in building the tunnel, which was located 300 feet below the Harlem River through solid limestone. An earlier attempt had been made to locate the tunnel at 150 feet, but water had come into the tunnel from a pocket of sand that the laborers had breached. The engineers were caught by surprise because of their findings (from test holes) that indicated a 30 foot roof of solid rock. With the new tunnel being constructed, an accident in Shaft Zero (the Croton Dam) had claimed the life of Robert E. Morris, who had just been married and was an assistant engineer.[40]

There were questions raised of the validity of the project. Did the engineers make poor surveys before construction began? Was it economically feasible to continue? Would there be litigation brought against the company and the state if more lives were lost? At 85 years of age, Greene demonstrated his physical vigor (despite his partial disability) "by walking through several of the tunnels between the shafts while his colleagues many years [25] his juniors went to the bottom of the shafts only & there back to the surface."[41].

He was satisfied the project could continue and made his arguments with the lawyers before the board. His determination and vast experience in engineering won over any remaining opposition and the New Croton Aqueduct resumed being built and finished after Greene's participation had come to an end.

This was to be his last engineering service. In a letter to O. O. Howard, George Jr. had remarked that the caretakers of the new reservoir and the gatehouses were amazed by his father's work. Being so well built, they commented "that repairs would not [be] necessary for years and years."[42]

Near the end of the 1880's, George Sears Greene, now 87 years old, returned to his Alma Mater for the last time. He was the presiding officer at the annual meeting of the Association of Graduates in June 1888.

Taking over for his friend and classmate Alfred Mordecai, who died in 1887, Greene recalled the "fixed principles of training and discipline" and the "bond of fellowship" that West Point gave them and continues with today's cadets.[43]

He told his fellow graduates that "duty and loyalty" remained as the fundamental principles of the Academy but improvements were made over the years. Some of those improvements included the change of tactics in Infantry drill, the sciences such as Chemistry and Mineralogy, Cavalry instruction, horses for the Artillery, and practical instruction in Engineering and Ordinance. To this effect, West Point grew from those days in 1823 when Greene had graduated from the Academy.[44]

Greene saw the plain almost doubled in size for drill and the old Mess Hall, the old North and South Barracks and Chapel used for other functions as new structures took their place. Perhaps the cadets could appreciate in time what the Academy did for them as they were "ready to do their duty when occasion calls."[45]

Greene had appreciated it and came to the aid of the nation during times of war and peace. Now in the twilight of his golden years, it was George Sears Greene, who required the aid of his fellow soldiers and the nation he fought to preserve.

Chapter Twenty

A Priceless Heritage

During the last two decades of the 19th Century, many of the Civil War veterans began to preserve their memories of the Great Rebellion, as the nation looked to forge ahead and put Reconstruction behind. For North and South, it was a time of healing and creating strong bonds of friendship among the ex-soldiers (although there were some who remained bitter or unreconstructed because of their experience as soldiers or civilians).

George Sears Greene didn't publish his memoirs for financial gain or to justify actions taken during the Civil War (and blame others) as some prominent Generals as Ulysses S. Grant, Joseph E. Johnston, William T. Sherman, and John B. Hood. Although Greene furnished Century Magazine with an article on Culp's Hill in the 1880's, his involvement to preserve the history of the battle began earlier while he was in Washington D.C. In March 1866, Greene had encouraged the future historian John B. Bachelder, concerning the battle of Gettysburg, to send him a good topographical survey of Culp's Hill, and to contact the officers of his former brigade for information of the fight.[1]

Later in the 1870's, he reviewed three maps sent to him by Bachelder on Gettysburg and felt they were fair for the topography, but lacked in accuracy. "I supposed that I was on the field," Greene told Bachelder in a light-hearted tone, "but I do not find my name on the 3d days map and so covered with much of that of the 2d day as not to be distinguished. It was a dark night but we could be heard if not seen."[2] Just as he had fought for recognition in 1863-64 for their part in the Gettysburg reports against General Meade, Greene did not want those laurels won on the field misrepresented.

Reunions were a popular venture among the veterans. The General attended his first one back in November 1873 with the 28th Pennsylvania and Knap's Battery.[3] Memories were exchanged of their fight at Antietam and the night attack against Knap's Battery, where Greene was wounded at Wauhatchie. While he saw his former soldiers and renewed friendships gave him fulfillment, the growing recognition of Greene brigade and the man came at a reunion in 1888 at Gettysburg.

It was the first time that Confederate veterans had come to Gettysburg and participated with Union veterans in a ceremony. General James Longstreet, who had sent reinforcements against Greene's left flank at Antietam in the early afternoon of September 17, 1862 told the crowd at the dedication of the monument to Greene's brigade about what they did here. Stating the success of Greene's men had prevented "the Confederates from turning Meade's right flank," Longstreet came to realize as he studied Greene's military record and learned about the character of him that "there was no better officer in either army."[4]

Greene enjoyed retirement with trips to New York, helping interested parties with their genealogical researches, and came back in the summers during the 1890's to Narragansett Bay in Rhode Island to visit friends and relatives. Although he was a transplanted New Yorker living in New Jersey, Greene never forgot the love of his native state. He told his children that Narragansett Bay was "the most beautiful sheet of water in the world, and the climate of its islands and shores the most salubrious."[5]

Despite these activities in Morristown and abroad, he wrote to a friend, "it would be a nice thing for me to be a little more comfortable in the few years which will be given to me."[6] Greene had not spoke about his health, but was referring to his finances. This problem had come to light in 1879 when he applied for a pension and he received a limited income from working. Now Greene no longer was employed and his only income was the pension of $15.00 a month.

Greene left no documents (or family members) of why he suffered for money. Providing for his family (even with the loss of income from civil engineering during the Civil War) had never been a problem. Did their bank fail, with the loss of their savings, during the depression of 1873? Were there bad investments over the years? Perhaps George and Martha gave money to needy loved ones as charity. We may never know why except the reason could be that Greene didn't think he could live long enough to even worry about this problem.

The sharing of expenses in the Morristown home were affected by the death of Greene's friend, General Hannibal Day in 1891. They had enjoyed their days of West Point and conversed on many subjects from their families, literature, the military and events of the day. Religion had been one of those subjects they discussed since Francis Vinton stated Greene's belief "was never shaken" and followed "its precepts in his daily life."[7]

Looking upon the end of life, Hannibal may have told Greene (as he stated in his will) "believing as I do in the immortality of the soul, it is a matter of much indifference to me where my bones are laid after death."

Beside leaving behind fond memories, Hannibal had bequeath to his friend the easy chair in the parlor to enjoy conversations with guests and reading books from the library they had shared over the years.[8]

By the winter of 1892, George Sears Greene had friends who came to his aid and looked to Congress for help. During the 1st session of the 52nd Congress, a Relief bill (H.R. 7487) was introduced by Halbert S. Greenleaf on March 22nd in the House of Representatives "to place George S. Greene on retired list after appointment to captain of engineers." The purpose of this bill was to have the law suspended and have money for relief given to him for service in the army since his resignation in 1836.[9]

By May 5, 1892 Senator J. R. Hawley of New York presented the Relief Bill (S 3075) in the Senate to the Committee of Military Affairs. The bill that was introduced in both houses was created by General Henry W. Slocum, Greene's friend and former 12th Corps commander. At this stage of his life, Greene's reluctance to enter the political realm was cast aside. "I am very much interested in its passage," he told a fellow comrade and inquired "can our friends of the Loyal Legion in Phila. do anything in the way of asking members of Congress to see to its passage."[10]

Greene's life in the military and civil engineering fields were detailed with letters of support by Generals Wagner Swayne, Henry W. Slocum, and Major William F. Smith in the bill. As Greene approach- ed his 91st birthday, Swayne commented on the testimony of Generals Howard and Slocum on Greene's service to the nation. He could only add that Greene "is widely known and much beloved by those of us who have occasion to cherish memories of the war, and our interest in anything that does him honor or occasions him pleasure is strong or abiding."[11]

Slocum had wanted the Congressmen to know that "the total income of Gen. Greene is less than $800 per annum, including his pension." If Greene had not obtained the $15.00 a month pension in 1879, his total income would have been $620 per year. Smith had realized that Greene was very poor and could no longer work due to his age and wrote to support passage of the bill. "I do not think there is a person alive who served in the war who rendered more good service that Gen. Greene, and I trust he will receive some substantial token of the appreciation by Congress of his intelligent, faithful, loyal and continuos services during the war."[12]

Although Greene was honored by the support of his friends and attempts made to have former Union soldiers lobby their Congressmen, he told a friend, "I know it will be up hill work." Greene apprehension about a speedy passage of the relief bill was correct. A week after Senator Hawley introduced the bill in the Senate, J.C. Kelton, President Harrison's Adjutant-general, notified the Secretary of War that Greene held the highest rank of 1st lieutenant (in 1836) in the Army, not Captain of Engineers. He told the secretary, however, the provisions of June 11, 1890 act showed "a precedent was established (Horatio P. Van Cleve, 2nd LT.) of authorizing appointments in such cases to the grade formerly held in the U.S. Army."[13]

What did this mean for Greene? It meant that the law didn't have to be suspended since there was a recent precedent, but the bill had to be rewritten and presented again to both houses for approval to be placed on retired list after appointment to 1st lieutenant of artillery. This was delayed until the next session of the 52nd Congress because of the full docket of bills that awaited approval.

The government decision may have been a surprise, but there had been no opposition by any Congressmen. Greene remained hopeful even as he was confronted with a problem from his old employers in Morristown. For the years since Greene had moved to Morristown, he enjoyed the water that came through the ducts from the Mountains outside of town. As the Morris Aqueduct installed water meters at the residential homes, their inspector reported Greene had "rather objected to having one inserted."[14]

Back in the early 1870's it was Greene who played a part in New York City having water meters and now he found himself protesting this intrusion into his home. H. C. Pitney, the President of the Morris Aqueduct, wrote to the General that he could not make an exception in his case. "I fully appreciate the value of the professional advice you have given us and am willing to pay for it," but the respect that Pitney had for Greene could not outweigh the harm to "knowingly resist." As a favor, Pitney asked him not to harass the plumber![15]

Greene wrote back to Pitney, told him of other homes without water meters and did not ask for compensation for his advice. These issues were addressed by Pitney about "a few homes had been furnished with modern improvements" and they were catching up with the other homes because of the adoption of their present rules. In the meantime Greene was sent receipted water bills before the company could send another man out to the home. The advances in technology had been a part of Greene's work, but this modern improvement was something he could not keep out.[16]

The Relief bill was resubmitted (S3075) with the correction of military grade on February 9th and May 5th of 1893 by the principal sponsors of both houses.[17] Again, the constituents for

Greene were stymied in their efforts due to the great panic of 1893 (inflation of the currency from the Silver Purchase Act and loss of gold reserves to Europe) that became a priority for Congress. Other issues such as tariff revision and failure or instability of the banks and railroads forced the 2nd session of the 52nd Congress to let the Relief bill go without a vote.[18]

Unknown to the American people during the spring and early summer of 1893 was President Grover Cleveland's operation off the coast of New Jersey. The removal of the cancerous tumor (along with the entire upper jaw) had temporarily incapacitated Cleveland and this secret was even kept from Adali Stevenson, his Vice-President.[19] Even if the bill was voted for passage for General Greene, it could not have been reviewed by the President to become law, with or without his signature.

As Greene entered his nineties, his life began to get noticed in the newspapers of the day. Events such as birthday celebrations at the Century Club and the homes of Greene Jr., and Francis Vinton were mentioned.

He enjoyed speaking at the 25th anniversary of the New York Genealogical Society. Yet despite his pain that remained after the 1864 operation, Morristown's The Jerseyman reported, "he walks with a firm, elastic step, retains all his mental powers, and has the appearance of a gentleman of seventy years." Another newspaper referred to the General as "hearty" and "jolly" surrounded by his friends in army and club circles.[20]

Even if the prospects looked bleak for Greene's Relief Bill in Congress, it hadn't dampened his spirits as he went with his son Charles to Gettysburg for the dedication of the New York State Monument in July 1893. Over 10,000 citizens, with 3,500 former Union soldiers were in attendance for the first three days of festivities, as they listened to speeches and sang patriotic songs. The General was made the honorary Grand Marshal of the parade (escorted by 25 soldiers of his brigade) and the oldest living participant (92 years old) from the battle of Gettysburg.[21]

The last day, July 3rd, saw the ex-soldiers of the 12th Corps formed in columns that hot Sunday morning in the center square of Gettysburg. Followed by General Greene, his son Charles Thurston, and General Slocum by carriage, they marched to Culp's Hill with their torn and tattered flags that Greene's brigade had carried through the battles. On the little platform where Greene stood to introductions by Slocum, he was received with prolonged cheers.[22]

Not since that terrible day at Antietam when his soldiers cheered him as he rode down the line could he understand the recognition that the efforts here by his brigade were not forgotten. Greene told the audience of the events of those days at Culp's Hill, praised Generals Slocum and Kane for their roles "in the hour of her [country] greatest need," and "we thank God that so many of [you] are present at this time in health & in vigor & able to rejoice in a happy & united country."[23]

Like Generals Slocum, Sickles (who was in charge of the Board of Commissioners of New York State for Gettysburg Monuments), and the veterans of the Army of the Potomac, he wanted the future generations to remember what they did here. "A priceless heritage" were the words used by Governor Roswell P. Flower to describe their actions and he told the crowd at the end of his speech that Greene "looks as fresh as a summer rose" and hoped "every one of you may live as long as he." General Sickles concurred with the Governor that if only he could be as handsome and as good as General Greene was.[24]

Not only did Greene enjoy seeing many of his soldiers since 1863, but he benefited in meeting a new supporter when he left the reunion. Meeting General Daniel Sickles for the first time, this 74 year old spellbinder had been elected to Congress in 1892 and he had pursued legislation for Gettysburg to be a federally protected park.[25] Greene supported this movement and Sickles had many contacts in the various veteran military organizations and could use his influence with the Congressmen to obtain passage of the relief bill.

For the third time, now with the 53rd Congress in session, Greene's Relief Bill was submitted in the House (H.R. 4416) on December 4, 1893 and in the Senate (S1513) on January 29,

1894. Senator Hawley had been an old supporter, but the sponsor of the bill in the House was a fellow Civil War veteran, General Newton Curtis of New York. In December 1893, the New York Times told its readers about Greene being the oldest surviving West Point graduate, and its support of this "tardy act of justice" for the bill.[26]

By the summer of 1894, Congress had voted in favor of Greene's Relief Bill and it was presented to President Grover Cleveland for his approval. The proviso attached to the bill made Greene forgo his pension and it couldn't bar any claims from his children or other heirs for a pension after his death. This bill, approved in early July, was received on the 20th by the President for his signature.[27]

The last obstacle was perhaps the worst time for Greene for the bill could be vetoed by Cleveland, who had vetoed many pension bills during his first term in the late 1880's. Since he did sign many bills for pensions Cleveland's reputation for eliminating waste expenditures had been used by the Grand Army of the Republic (GAR) in the political climate of the day as being against the veterans. Apparently the President was reluctant to commit himself in the 30 days from the passage of the bill because it became law without his approval.[28]

Cleveland chose not to return the bill to Congress within the time prescribed by the Constitution which allowed it to be a law and avoided any backlash from supporters and opponents when he was seeking support for the administration. Senator Hawley notified the Secretary of War, Daniel S. Lamont on August 6th, so he gave the good news to the General and his son, Francis Vinton, where they had visited East Greenwich, Rhode Island.[29]

It had been a long journey and his friends, such as Henry W. Slocum who didn't live to see his brigade commander obtain relief, had fought the good fight for one so deserving. By Special Orders No. 192 from the Sec. of War and Adjutant-General George D. Ruggles, Greene's commission was dated from August 11, 1894 and it now remained for Greene to contact Ruggles.[30]

Francis Vinton had traveled with his father through the New England states and told of the government's decision to loved ones on winning the 2 1/2 year battle when they arrived in Pomfret, Connecticut and replied to Ruggles. The General had sent a telegram through Western Union on August 17th to accept his appointment as 1st Lieutenant of Artillery and placement on retirement list and took the oath of office the next day.[31] As Francis and other eyewitnesses surrounded Greene, the Notary Public had sworn in the oldest active duty soldier (93 years) in United States History.

It was ironic that Pomfret held this special event. It could have crossed his mind upon raising his right hand when he became a lieutenant again. Those days that he courted his first wife, Elizabeth Vinton and took their vows here as a young man while a 2nd lieutenant just finished teaching at the Academy. Over 65 years later, Greene ended his army career, respected and praised for his accomplishments, and thankful for God's mercy that saw him through the many trials of life.

After he verified with the paymaster dates from his visit to Bar Harbor, Maine with the Adjutant- General's office, Greene no longer worried about his finances anymore.[32] Greene maintained an active life despite his age by long walks and travel when the opportunity presented itself. He often jumped on and off street cars while in motion, which caused distress to his children and they made Greene pledge not to do that anymore.[33]

Beginning in 1897, George Sears Greene had asked the Adjutant-General's office for a copy of the new law about brevets and if it affected him.[34] Brevets had been introduced as an honorary award to be used during social functions and for service during the Civil War. It was used as compensation for lack of promotions, but grew to be a problem due to issues of pay, seniority and other military functions. This process was left over and stayed with the Regular Army.

The brevets were phased out over a period of time, but those that existed (such as Greene's brevet of Major General) remained. The Assistant Adjutant-General told Greene that the revised statues concerning brevets provided that "no officer shall be addressed in orders or official communications by any title other than that of his *actual rank*."[35]

Being relieved, as he read this communication that he retained his honorary rank, Greene could laugh at the letter he received 5 days later in his mail. In his haste to reply to the General, the AAG had inadvertently sent all his records from the file on Greene along with the letter. Because he had no proof of his existence, the young man asked for their return.[36] Now they both had good reasons to be relieved!

Even now when many of those he loved and respected had departed this life, there were many young people who sought him out. From 1894, Greene had been the oldest surviving graduate of West Point and relished the conversations with young men "about their plans, their projects, and their prospects" along with being "a most helpful counselor."[37]

At the time he received the information about the brevets, the General had been confined to his home in Morristown due to illness. Francis Vinton blamed it on his visits in New England to family and friends, which fatigued that boundless energy he had always retained. Upon his return home, he had been walking down one of New York City's streets when he sank to the ground, possibly from a heart attack. Given only a few days to live by his physicians, Greene rallied, but never could leave his home again.[38]

The mind was sharp, but his body was slowly failing him as he was restricted later to one floor and then to his room. When America declared war against Spain in 1898, Greene followed the events in Cuba and the Philippines where his son, Francis Vinton lead troops as a General. On his return home, Francis Vinton had shared with his father that January 1899 what had transpired overseas during the war.[39]

"Sitting up in his room" remembered Francis Vinton was the disciplinarian who took pleasure in seeing him, but now his mind started to betray him. "When I saw him ten days later, he was insisting on writing a somewhat incoherent letter to a friend who had been dead for twenty years." Greene's children saw their father confined to his bed a week later and the effects of old age had released his soul from this earth on January 28, 1899 at 1 o'clock in the morning. His death was reported immediately to the wire service and people awoke to read about this distinguished American in cities such as Boston, Chicago, San Francisco, and Washington D.C.[40]

George Sears Greene's life was told by the newspapers in New York, Rhode Island, and his hometown where he lived for the last 16 years, emphasis made of his Civil War record. One editor told his readers that Greene "leaves to his countrymen the precious legacy of his example, and to those whose privilege it was to know him the memory of a sound and manly and gentle character." Friends and relatives gathered, including a delegation from the Loyal Legion, and said goodbye to their fellow Christian on January 31st at St. Peter's Episcopal Church in Morristown, New Jersey.[41]

They celebrated Greene's life as the Rev. Dr. Hibbard and Rev. William P. Taylor gave the sermon and joined uplifted voices from the heart as they sang with the choir in his memory. The next day Greene was put aboard a special train, accompanied by his sons, Francis Vinton, George Jr., and Charles Thurston, and relatives where they arrived at 9:30 that morning at the East Greenwich depot.[42]

The weather was bitter cold that day as the funeral procession made its way through the town and as they left Main Street came to Apponaug, where George was interred next to his beloved Martha in the family burial plot. Located on a knoll about a quarter of a mile north of the town, it was here that he grew up and enjoyed the scenery that was his boyhood. The pallbears, included associates from the Civil War such as General O.O. Howard (left with one arm) and Captain L. L. Buck (soldier in the 60th New York & engineer), carried his casket to his grave. After a brief service by Rev. F.B. Whitecomb and Rev. Daniel Goodwin, Greene was laid to rest and the procession departed.[43]

The General had thought about a Will during these years when his health was good and the Relief bill had stalled in Congress in the early 1890's. The arrangements had been witnessed and made legal in February 1894 and now Greene's wishes were made known to his relatives. Although he wanted any debts paid immediately, Greene wanted his books distributed among his relatives and asked them to complete his "Greene Genealogy" which he had commenced since the end of the Civil War.[44]

George Sears Greene had his request honored by his children, by employing Mrs. Louise Brownell Clarke who edited the papers and had the collection published in 1903 in book form. He requested his manuscripts and genealogical books donated to the Rhode Island Historical Society and for his sons and daughter to share his estate equally. Greene had further stated that Anna, who had cared for her parents, be provided by a Trust, with this income managed by her brothers.[45]

A few days after Greene's will was probated, Francis Vinton and George Jr., had two appraisers take inventory of their father's estate. The items ranged in value from 50cents for a small table to $8,750.00 dollars for 70 shares of capital stock of the Barber Asphalt Paving Co. The total value of his estate was $12,789.19.[46] Since we are aware of his poor financial state during the early 1890's, it is reasonable to think he tried to invest his income from the Relief bill so he and Anna could live off the dividends.

As a final memorial to their father, Francis Vinton had contacted General Daniel Sickles for permission to remove a boulder from Culp's Hill that Sickles, along with General Butterfield and Major Zabriske had viewed. It was explained to these members of the New York Battlefield Commission that he wished to place it on his father's grave and offered to pay for all expenses. The request being approved, Sickles wrote that "George Sears Greene deserve[s] every possible recognition." With the boulder's removal by the stone cutter, C. W. Ziegler, it was loaded on to the freight car in the summer of 1899 and the train carried it straight through from Gettysburg to Apponaug, Rhode Island. The General would have approved of this distinguished honor.[47]

The state of New York and Rhode Island thought Greene should not be forgotten as living memories of him faded into history. In mid-May 1903, New York's Governor Odell had signed a special appropriation act for a bronze statue of the General at an estimated cost of $8,000 dollars.[48]

The dedication took place in Gettysburg on the Culp's Hill battlefield in September 1907. One of the speakers was General Alexander S. Webb, who received the Medal of Honor for his actions on July 3, 1863 in repulsing Pickett's Charge. "The desperate nature of your struggle with superior forces," Webb told the onlookers, made his men "understand the importance of your holding this position" that evening of July 2nd. He believed Greene and his brigade deserved more consideration in the annuals of history.[49]

A Rhode Island newspaper called George Sears Greene "the best unknown of the leading native sons of the State." During the 1912 session of the General Assembly in the State House, a tablet in Greene's memory had received funding, but there had been little fanfare. No ceremony. No official announcement. People took little notice of it located in the Corridor of the State House when it was unveiled in May 1913.[50]

Even as late as 1998, when it was reported of Greene's bronze sword replica and plaque being recovered from vandals who removed it from his grave, some facts of his life were misrepresented in the newspaper.[51] His life deserves more attention as a role model for future generations than a mere footnote in history. The principal theme of his life was discipline. From being educated, raising a family, his days in the Army, Civil Engineering, and how he coped over the loss of loved ones, it shaped his character.

In 1903, New York State Historian Hugh Hastings spoke of General Greene as being a forgotten hero of Gettysburg as "it is possibly the only battle of the war where the issue of the battle and the fate of the Union Army dependent on the good judgment exercised by a single general officer."[52] In war and in peace, George Sears Greene gave the people and the nation, the best of his talents, for a better tomorrow. "What do not our people owe to him?," wrote his friend O. O. Howard.[53] What indeed.

Appendix A

Civil War Medical Treatment of Jaw Fractures

Unlike the age factor and the complications afterward in dealing with General George Sears Greene's wound of the jaw, there was the added factor of infection from germs from the minie ball or carrying a piece of foreign material into the body.

As the war dragged on into years, a pattern had developed on both sides as explained by Mr. Terry Reimer, Research Coordinator at the National Museum of Civil War Medicine, in treating jaw fractures:

"On the Union side, most jaw fractures were treated by cleaning out the wound, setting the fragments in place, applying adhesive plasters or bandages, and securing it all with straps. Different interdental 'splints' were used to hold the jaw in place and keep the teeth in alignment.

Stitches were manly used to stop bleeding vessels, not the way we use them today. Wiring was tried but rarely used."

"The Confederates had a more uniform apparatus which was designed by James Baxter Bean. He developed a gutter percha (rubber) splint which was formed to fit the teeth perfectly. It was then inserted and held firmly in place by a metal and wood compress and occipito-frontal bandages.

The compress and bandages were like a retainer, holding the jaw and teeth in place during healing. Patients could take liquid food with the apparatus in place.[1]

Notes: Appendix A

1   Mr. Terry Reimer to Author August 9, 2001.

Appendix B

The Death of Preston King

Too often in history when a war is ended and peace is restored, people are weary and look to put the recent conflict behind them. Yet there are casualties that occur months afterward that tend to be forgotten.

This is the case of former Senator Preston King of New York. A friend of the Union soldier and supporter of George Sears Greene, King had been deeply disturbed by the high casualties and doubtful about staying in politics.

Having suffered a mental breakdown earlier in his life during the late 1830's, King had recovered, but now by 1864-65, after serving as a delegate in the 1864 Republican Convention and appointed collector of the port of New York in the summer of 1865, things had changed. The Ogdensburg Daily Journal reported "Mr. King was unable to stand the pressure of his official position. Every allegation of misconduct in subordinates disturbed him. The officers and soldiers asking for situations, excited his sympathies."[1]

Preston King had told friends of his intentions to resign and broke down mentally. He sought medical treatment for his affliction. But on the morning of November 12, 1865 Preston King had left the Astor Hotel and obtained passage on the Hoboken ferry boat. A little girl and boy witnessed him jump overboard and drowned, leaving behind his hat on the deck. Described as a "honest, earnest man," King's death was confirmed by Thurlow Weed, when he was shown his hat by the children. It was only yesterday that

Weed and two colleagues had been with King when he told them "death, if it could be reached without crime, would be a relief."[2]

Notes: Appendix B

1.   _____, History of St. Lawrence Co., New York p.190; Ogdensburg Daily Journal November 16 & 17, 1865.
2.   Ogdensburg Daily Journal November 15, 16, & 17. 1865.

List of Abbreviations

ADCH: Attack and Defense of Culp's Hill
B&L: Battles and Leaders of the Civil War
BEHS: Buffalo and Erie County Historical Society
BUL: Brown University Library
CHS: Colorado Historical Society
DAB: Dictionary of American Biography
DHS: DeWitt Historical Society of Tompkins County
DU: Duke University
FSNMP: Fredericksburg and Spotsylvania National Military Park
         GC Gettysburg College
GNMP: Gettysburg National Military Park
HHL: Henry E. Huntington Library
KHS: Kennebec Historical Society
LC: Library of Congress
MHS: Massachusetts Historical Society
NARA: National Archives and Records Administration
NYGB: New York Genealogical and Biographical Record
NYGM: New York Gettysburg Monuments
NYPL: New York Public Library
NYSA: New York State Archives
OR: Official Records of the Union and Confederate Armies
         in the War of the Rebellion
RIHS: Rhode Island Historical Society
SLCHA: St. Lawrence County Historical Association
TCHS: Tioga County Historical Society
USAMHI: United States Army Military History Institute
USMA: United States Military Academy
UVL: University of Virginia Library

Endnotes

Notes: Chapter One

1. Balch, William M. "Did General S. Greene win Civil War at Battle of Gettysburg?" National Tribune, August 20, 1931.

2. United States War Department The War of the Rebellion: A Compilation of the Union and Confederate Armies. Government Printing Office; 1880-1901, Vol.27, pt.1, pp.114-119. (Hereafter cited as O.R.); Fennell, The Attack and Defense of Culp's Hill, p.7 (Hereafter cited as ADCH).

3. Quaife, Milo M. (ed) From the Cannon's Mouth: The Civil War Letters of General Alpheus S. Williams Wayne State University Press 1959, p. 271; Pfanz, Gettysburg-Culp's Hill & Cemetery Hill p.381

4. Henry W. Slocum to George S. Greene, December 30, 1863. The New York Historical Society. Slocum had thought about asking for a court of inquiry. See letter to his friend, Col. Joseph Howland located at the New York Historical Society Manuscript Department.

5. Henry W. Slocum to George G. Meade, December 30, 1863 (copy) Ni849, Henry E. Huntington Library.

6. O.R., Vol.27, pt.1, pp. 763-765; Fennell, ADCH, p.8

7. Ibid, p. 769-770; Ibid, p. 9-10

8. Ibid

9. George G. Meade to George S. Greene, March 10, 1864 Ni849, HHL

10. U.S. Congress, Joint Committee on the Conduct of the War. Reports—Testimony of General George G. Meade, March 5, 1864.

11. Meade, George G. Jr. The Life and Letters of George Gordon Meade Charles Scribner's Sons, 1913. Volume 2, p. 179; Cleaves, Freeman Meade of Gettysburg University of Oklahoma Press, 1960, p. 225

Notes: Chapter Two

1. In Memoriam: George Sears Greene, Brevet Major-General, U.S.V. 1801-1899. J.B. Lyon Company, State Printers 1909, p. 62-63; Fennell, ADCH, p. 29; Clarke, Louise Brownell The Greenes of Rhode Island: With Historical Records of English Ancestery, 1534-1902. The Knickerbocker Press 1903, p. X; New York Times January 28, 1899.

2. Ibid; Ibid; Ibid

3. Clarke, The Greenes of Rhode Island, p. X;

4. A Biographical Dictionary of American Civil Engineers, ASCE Historical Publication No.2, 1972, p. 52. A number of Biographical Dictionaries and Encyclopedias give two names for Sarah's maiden name: Weekes and Wickes. I felt the source listed above was the best since Greene helped create the ASCE.

5. Clarke, The Greenes of Rhode Island, p. X-XI; Fennell, ADCH, p.29; Stephen W. Sears to Author August 15, 2000; The Warwick Beacon August 21, 1984.

6. Ibid, p. XI

7. Brodie, Fawn M. Thomas Jefferson: An Intimate History W.W. Norton & Company Inc. 1974, pp. 415-418.

8. Ibid, p. 418; Jones, Maudwyn The Limits of Liberty, American History 1607-1980 Oxford University Press 1983, p. 98-99.

9. Johnson, Allen & Malone, Dumas (ed) Dictionary of American Biography Charles Scribner's Sons, Volume 7 1946, p. 566; Clarke, The Greenes of Rhode Island, p. XI; The Warwick Beacon August 21, 1984; The New York Genealogical and Biographical Record Volume 30, No. 2, 1899 p. 69.

10. Clarke, The Greenes of Rhode Island, p. XI

11. Ibid; In Memoriam, George Sears Greene, p. 62; Warwick Beacon August 21, 1984; Fennell, ADCH, p. 31; Johnson & Dumas, DAB, p. 566; Motts, Wayne E. "To Gain a Second Star: The Forgotten George Sears Greene" Gettysburg Magazine, No. 3 July 1990, p. 65

12. George Sears Greene to John C. Calhoun, April 17, 1819 Cadet application papers (copy), United States Military Academy Library.

13. Clarke, The Greenes of Rhode Island, p. XI; NYGB, p. 69; Fennell, ADCH, p.31.

Notes: Chapter Three

1. "Address by Gen. George S. Greene, at the Annual Meeting of the Association of Graduates, West Point, N.Y., June 11, 1888." p.1-2, Box 2, Folder 14, The William and Marion Sluys Collection of Greene Family Manuscripts, Rhode Island Historical Society.

2. Ambrose, Stephen E. Duty, Honor, Country: A History of West Point The John Hopkins Press 1966, p. 148.

3. Ibid, p.90, 124

4. "Address by Gen. George S. Greene," p.3 Box 2, Folder 14, WMSC, RIHS.

5. Ibid, p. 148.

6. Register of the Officers and the Cadets of the U.S. Military Academy, June 1820-1823 p. 12-14. There are 89 cadets listed in Motts's article, "To Gain a Second Star" Gettysburg Magazine No. 3, July 1990.

7. Ibid, p. 14.

8. Clarke, The Greenes of Rhode Island, p. XI.

9. "Address by Gen. George S. Greene," p.2, Box 2, Folder 14, WMSC, RIHS.

10. Ambrose, Duty, Honor, Country p. 148.

11. Ibid, p. 163-164; Fleming, Thomas West Point: The Men and Times of the United States Academy William Morrow & Company 1969, p.92-93.

12. Register of the Officers and Cadet, p. 9-11.

13. Clarke, The Greenes of Rhode Island, p. XI.

14. Ibid; Register of the Officers and Cadets, p.6-7; NYGBR, p. 69; The Biographical Cyclopedia of Representative Men of Rhode Island National Biographical Publishing Co., 1881, p. 292.

15. Motts, "To Gain a Second Star," p.67.

16. Ibid; Clarke, The Greenes of Rhode Island, p. XI.

17. Cullum, Biographical Register, p. 301; Howard, O.O. Thirtieth Annual Reunion of the Association of the Graduates of the U.S. Military Academy, Seemann & Peters, Printers and Binders 1899, p. 136.

18. Ibid, p. 301-302; Ibid; Pension Records of George Sears Greene, National Archives and Records Administration; NYGBR, p. 69; Fennell, ADCH, p. 31. He split his teaching duties from September 21, 1823 to June 16,

1824 and October 6, 1824 to August 29, 1826 with Mathematics and taught Engineering from August 29, 1826 to April 20, 1827.

19.   Fennell, ADCH, p. 31; Cullum, Biographical Register, p. 301; Pension Records of GSG, NARA.

20.   Clarke, The Greenes of Rhode Island, p. XII; Providence Sunday Journal May 25, 1913.

21.   Grant, John and Lynch, James and Bailey, Ronald West Point The First 200 Years The Globe Pequot Press, 2002, p. 53-54; McCullough, David John Adams Simon & Schuster, 2001 p.635. Adams had treated the cadets to an outdoor dinner and was given a performance afterwards by the West Point band.

22.   Freeman, Douglas Southall (edited by Richard Harwell) Lee: An Abridgment Charles Schribner's Sons, 1961 p. 13, 15-16.

Notes: Chapter Four

1.   Clarke, The Greenes of Rhode Island, p.XII; Cullum, Biographical Register, p. 302; Fennell, ADCH, p. 31; Pension Records of GSG, NARA.

2.   Ibid.

3.   Klunder, William Carl Lewis Cass and the Politics of Moderation The Kent State University Press 1996, p. 64-65.

4.   Ibid; George S. Greene note March 21, 1831 Letter book 1831-1841 Box 1, Folder 9, George Sears Greene Papers, RIHS.

5.   Clarke, The Greenes of Rhode Island, p. XII; Fennell, ADCH, p.31-32

6.   Johnson & Malone, DAB, p. 566.

7.   Web Site: WWW.FamilySearch.org (George Sears Greene); Clarke, The Greenes of Rhode Island, p. 474. Their birth dates are June 3, 1829, December 17, 1830 and August 10, 1832.

8.   Ibid.

9.   Special Orders No. 85, June 20, 1832 Letter book 1831-1841 Box 1, Folder 9 GSG Papers, RIHS.

10.   George S. Greene to R. Jones August 19 and September 6, 1832 Letter book 1831-1841 Box 1, Folder 9 GSG Papers, RIHS.

11.   George S. Greene to Thomas J. Jessup September 30, 1832 Letter book 1831-1841 Box 1, Folder 9 GSG Papers, RIHS.

12. Web Site: WWW.Family Search.org (George Sears Greene); Clarke, The Greenes of Rhode Island, p. 474.

13. Ibid; George S. Greene to Thomas J. Jessup November 1, 1832 Letter book 1831-1841 Box 1, Folder 9 GSG Papers, RIHS.

14. Fennell, ADCH, p. 32.

15. Clarke, The Greenes of Rhode Island, p. XII.

16. Ibid.

17. Cullum, Biographical Register, p. 302.

Notes: Chapter Five

1. Clarke, The Greenes of Rhode Island, p. XII.

2. Ibid.

3. Ibid.

4. Ibid.

5. Swift, Lindsay (ed) The Great Debate Houghton Mifflin Company, 1898, p.22.

6. Clarke, The Greenes of Rhode Island, p. XIII.

7. Ibid.

8. NYGB, p. 72.

9. Ibid.

10. Clarke, The Greenes of Rhode Island, p. XIII; Swift (ed), The Great Debate, p. 22.

11. Ibid, p. 19, 22.

12. Map of Part of the Frostburgh Coal Field Compiled from actual surveys by George Sears Greene 1842, Hagley Museum and Library (Here as known as FCF map).

13. George S. Greene to B. Murray undated, Letter book 1831-1841 Box 1, Folder 9 GSG Papers, RIHS. Unless it required the company to buy the property, the majority of the negotiations were to obtain the mineral rights.

14. Ibid.

15. Bowen, Mary "Mt. Savage History" (speech presented to the Homemakers Club) 1953.

16. Ibid.

17. NYGB, p. 72.

18. Baptismal Certificate, Greene applicant file, U.S. Military Academy
19. NYGB, p. 72.
20. Greene, FCF map.
21. Bowen, "Mt. Savage History"
22. Stakem, Patrick H. "The Mount Savage Iron Works: Western Maryland's Industrial (little) Giant," Western Maryland Chapter, NRHS, Inc.
23. Ibid.
24. Bowen, "Mt. Savage History," 1953.
25. Stakem, "The Mount Savage Iron Works"
26. Ibid.
27. NYGB, p. 72.

Notes: Chapter Six

1. Clarke, The Greenes of Rhode Island, p. XIII.
2. Kennebec Journal June 13, 1845.
3. Ibid, July 4, 1845.
4. Ibid, July 11, 1845.
5. Ibid.
6. Ibid, January 9, 1846.
7. Ibid, October 30, 1846.
8. North, James W. History of Augusta, Clapp & North 1870 p.644.
9. Ibid, p. 645.
10. Clarke, The Greenes of Rhode Island, p. 474
11. North, History of Augusta, p. 645.
12. NYGB, p. 72.
13. John T. Anderson to R. Williams, December 22, 1850 Nash Collection, Kennebec Historical Society.
14. Financial document (Anderson & Clark, Engineers), November 13, 1850 NC, KHS.
15. Tabulation figures (John T. Anderson), NC, KHS.
16. Cullum, Biographical Register p. 303; Shelley Wallace to Author November 14, 2000. The company attempted to get financial help in a appropriation bill in 1859 for $200,000, but Governor Edwin D. Morgan vetoed the measure, citing the granting of loans violated the Constitiution of 1846. Later attempts during the Civil War proved

unsuccessful for the Albany and Susquehanna Railroad. For more information see Rawley, James A. Edwin D. Morgan 1811-1883 Merchant in Politics Columbia University Press 1955, p. 90-91, 173.

17.   Clarke, The Greenes of Rhode Island, p. XIII.

18.   Report of a survey of a Railroad from Bristol and Warren to Providence by George Sears Greene, May 13, 1852 p. 11.

19.   Ibid.

20.   Ibid, p. 13-16.

21.   Clarke, The Greenes of Rhode Island, p. 476.

22.   Ibid.

23.   Wisley, William H. The American Civil Engineers 1852-1974; The History, Traditions, and Development of the American Society of Civil Engineers founded 1852, American Society of Civil Engineers, 1974, p. 13-14.

24.   Ibid.

25.   Clarke, The Greenes of Rhode Island, p. XX.

26.   Foster, G. L. The Past of Ypsilanti: A Discourse delivered on leaving the old Presbyterian Church Edifice, Lord's Day, September 20th, 1857. Fleming & Davis, Book Publishers 1857, p. 31.

Notes: Chapter Seven

1.   Galusha, Diane Liquid Assets: A History of New York City's Water System Purple Mountain Press 1999, p. 35.

2.   Ibid.

3.   _____, A Biographical Dictionary of American Civil Engineers, ASCE 1972 p.52;

_____, "Early Presidents of the Society," Civil Engineering Volume 6, Number 10, October 1936, p.710.

4.   Ibid.

5.   Ibid.

6.   Ibid.

7.   DAB, p. 567.

8.   Clarke, The Greenes of Rhode Island, p. XIV.

9.   Galusha, Liquid Assests, p.35.

10.   Ibid; New York Times June 11, 1861.

11.   _____, History of St. Lawrence Co. New York L.H. Everts & Co. 1878, p. 190.

12.   Preston King to John Bigelow May 10, 1860 Preston King letters, Ogdensburg Public Library.

13.   Ibid, December 25, 1860.

14.   Ibid, January 26, 1861.

15.   Clarke, The Greenes of Rhode Island, p. XIII.

16.   Ibid.

17.   Ibid.

Notes: Chapter Eight

1.   Clarke, The Greenes of Rhode Island p. XIII-XIV.

2.   Fennell, ADCH p. 40.

3.   Reminiscences of a Civil War Veteran by Donald Brown, Colorado Historical Society and From the Collections of the St. Lawrence County Historical Association.

4.   Jordan, William B. (ed) The Civil War Journals of John Mead Gould 1861-1866 Butternut and Blue 1997, p. 7.

5.   Ogdensburg Advance December 13, 1861.

6.   Jordan, Civil War Journals, p. 76.

7.   Ibid, p. 77.

8.   Ogdensburg Advance December 27, 1861.

9.   Ibid, December 13, 1861, December 27, 1861; January 23, 1862; St. Lawrence Republican January 14, 1862.

10.   Ibid.

11.   Ibid.

12.   Ibid.

13.   Toomey, Daniel Carroll The Patapsco Guards, Independent Company of Maryland Volunteer Infantry Toomey Press 1993; William Knight records, National Archives.

14.   "A Hero at Sixty-two" miscellanous article, EG Box 22, HHL.

15.   Bartlett, John Russell Memoirs of Rhode Island Officers who were engaged in the service of their country during the Great Rebellion of the South Sidney S. Rider & Brother, 1867 p. 140.

16.   St. Lawrence Republican February 4, 1862.

17. Rawley, James A. Edwin D. Morgan p. 167-168.

18. Eddy, Richard History of the Sixtieth Regiment, New York State Volunteers from the Commencement of its Organization in July 1861, to its Public Reception at Ogdensburg as a Veteran Command, January 7, 1864 Chrissy & Markley 1864 p. 75.

19. St. Lawrence Republican February 4, 1862.

20. Ibid.

21. Eddy, History of the Sixtieth Regiment, p.76.

22. Livingstone, Charles Brandegee Charlies Civil War: A Private's Trial by fire in the 5th New York Volunteers—Duryee Zouaves and 146th New York Volunteer Infantry Thomas Publications 1997, p. 11.

23. St. Lawrence Republican February 4, 1862.

24. Eddy, History of the Sixtieth Regiment, p. 76.

25. E.L.Crane to Parents & Sister January 31, 1862 Stockholm Historical Society.

26. St. Lawrence Republican February 25, 1862.

27. Clarke, The Greenes of Rhode Island, p. XIV.

28. George Sears Greene to Francis Vinton Greene February 17, 1862 Francis Vinton Greene Papers, Manuscripts and Archives Division, The New York Public Library, Astor, Lenox and Tilden Foundations.

29. Ibid.

30. Ibid.

31. St. Lawrence Republican February 25, 1862.

32. Potsdam Courier and Freeman February 19, 1862.

33. George Sears Greene to Martha Greene February 22, 1862, FVG Papers, NYPL.

34. Ibid.

35. Lester S. Willson to Parents February 19, 1862 Willson Family Papers, Merrill G. Burlingame Special Collections, Montana State University.

36. George E. Elderkin to Stewart Allen March 19, 1862 Allen Civil War Letters Collection, St. Lawrence County Historical Association.

37. Luther L. Gates to Hatty Gates March 8, 1862 Luther L. Gates Letters, The Robert W. Woodruff Library, Emory University.

38. St. Lawrence Republican March 3, 1862.

39. Eddy, History of the Sixtieth Regiment p. 98; J.C.O. Redington to Richard Eddy June 9, 1864 Property of Dennis Buttacavoli.

40.   Ibid; Ibid; J.E. Wilson to Richard Eddy March 22, 1863 Property of Dennis Buttacavoli.

41.   J.E. Wilson to Richard Eddy March 25, 1863 Property of Dennis Buttacavoli.

42.   George Sears Greene to Francis Vinton Greene March 12, 1862 FVG Papers, NYPL.

43.   Ibid.

44.   Johnson & Malone, DAB, p. 570-571.

45.   George Sears Greene to Martha Greene March 22, 1862 FVG Papers, NYPL.

46.   George Sears Greene to Francis Vinton Greene March 12, 1862 FVG Papers, NYPL.

47.   George Sears Greene to Martha Greene March 22, 1862 FVG Papers, NYPL.

48.   Ibid.

49.   St. Lawrence Republican March 18, 1862.

50.   Luther L. Gates to Hatty Gates March 20, 1862 Luther L. Gates Letters.

51.   Ibid, April 25, 1862.

52.   Ibid; Eddy, History of the Sixtieth Regiment p. 95.

53.   Potsdam Courier and Freeman April 23, 1862.

54.   Special Order 101 April 14, 1862 and Special Order 105 April 18, 1862.

55.   Eddy, History of the Sixtieth Regiment p. 98.

56.   Ibid, p. 99.

Notes: Chapter Nine

1.   Record Group 94, Records of the Adjutant General's Office, Letters Received by the Commission Branch, file G-24-CB-1867 (m1064, Roll 335) NARA, Telegram May 23, 1862 to Whalen & King (hereafter referred to as RG 94).

2.   RG 94, War Department to Senator King May 23, 1862.

3.   RG 94, Pay Voucher for May 1862.

4.   O.R., Volume 12, Pt. 1, p.552.

5.   Samuel Dana Greene to Martha May 31, 1862 Civil War Miscellaneous Collection, United States Army Military History Institute.

6. Fox, William In Memoriam: Henry Warner Slocum 1826-1894 J.B. Lyon Company, Printers 1904 p. 127.

7. Clarke, The Greenes of Rhode Island, p. XIV.

8. Quint, Alonzo H. History of the 2nd Massachusetts James P. Walker, 1867 p. 93

9. Richard Cary to Helen June 1, 1862 Massachusetts Historical Society.

10. Ibid, June 13, 1862.

11. Fox, In Memoriam Henry Warner Slocum p. 128.

12. Charels F. Morse to Father June 12, 1862 MHS.

13. Richard Cary to Helen June 13, 1862 MHS.

14. Charles F. Morse to Father June 15, 1862 MHS.

15. Henry Comey to Sister June 17, 1862 American Antiquarian Society.

16. Henry Bruce Scott to Lizzie June 15, 1862 MHS.

17. Richard Cary to Helen June 13, 1862 MHS.

18. Ibid.

19. Ibid, June 19, 1862 MHS.

20. George Sears Greene to E.D. Morgan June 17, 1862 The Western Reserve Historical Society.

21. Ibid.

22. Fox, William In Memoriam: George Sears Greene p.66-67.

23. Richard Cary to Helen June 21, 1862 MHS.

24. Charles F. Morse to Robert June 27, 1862 MHS.

25. Charles P. Horton Pension Records, NARA.

26. Clarke, The Greenes of Rhode Island, p. XIV; Fennell, ADCH p. 37.

27. Luther L. Gates to wife July 25, 1862 Luther L. Gates Letters, RWL, EU.

28. George Sears Greene to Alexander Dallas Bache July 12, 1862 RH1410, HHL.

29. Eddy, History of the Sixtieth Regiment, p. 148-149.

30. O.R., Volume 12, Pt. 2 p. 157; In Memoriam, Greene p. 69.

31. George S. Greene Report August 14, 1862 Nathaniel P. Banks Papers, Library of Congress, Manuscript Division; Krick, Robert K. Stonewall Jackson at Cedar Mountain University of North Carolina Press 1990 p. 127.

32. Editors of Time-Life Books, Voices of the Civil War: Second Manassas 1995, p. 27-28.

33. Edward Wiggin Jr. (Ned) to May September 28, 1862 Property of Dennis Buttacavoli of Hasbrouck Heights, New Jersey.

34.   George S. Greene Report August 14, 1862 LC; Krick, Stonewall Jackson at Cedar Mountain p. 99-100.

35.   Ibid; Foote, Shelby The Civil War: A Narrative Fort Sumter to Perryville Vintage Books, 1986, p. 600-601; Time-Life Books, Second Manassas p. 32

36.   Ibid, p. 28-29; Foote, Fort Sumter to Perryville p. 601-602.

37.   O.R., Volume 12, Pt.2, p. 134, 159.

38.   Charles E. Jayne to Parents August 11, 1862 Charles E. Jayne Papers The Three Village Historical Society.

39.   Edward Wiggin Jr. (Ned) to May September 28, 1862 Property of Dennis Buttacavoli.

40.   O.R., Volume 12, Pt. 2, p. 227, 236; McClendon, William A. Recollections of War Times by an Old Veteran Paragon Press 1909, p. 94-95; Krick, Stonewall Jackson at Cedar Mountain p. 281.

41.   Foote, Fort Sumter to Perryville p. 602; Time-Life Books, Second Manassas p. 28-29.

42.   Ibid.

43.   George S. Greene Report August 14, 1862 LC.

44.   New York Times August 20, 1862.

Notes: Chapter Ten

1.   O.R. Volume 12, Pt.2, p.252-53.

2.   Jordan, Civil War Journals p. 184.

3.   O.R. Volume19, Pt.2, p.279.

4.   O.R. Volume 14, Pt. 1, p. 179-80.

5.   Merwin Eugene Cornell to Brother & Sister September 9, 1862 Merwin Eugene Cornell Papers, Ontario County Historical Society and Museum.

6.   Ibid.

7.   Henry Hayward to Father September 12, 1862 MS-009/9-1.59, Papers of Ambrose Henry Hayward, Musselman Library, Gettysburg College.

8.   Editors of Time-Life Books, Voices of the Civil War: Antietam Time-Life Books, p.11; Thackery, David T. A Light and Uncertain Hold: A History of the Sixty-Sixth Ohio Volunteer Infantry The Kent State University Press 1999, p. 102.

9.   Brown, "Reminiscences" CHS and SLCHA.

10. Ibid; Thackery, A Light and Uncertain Hold p. 102.

11. Wilson, Lawrence Itinerary of the Seventh Ohio Volunteer Infantry, 1861-1864 Neale Publishing Company 1907, p. 204.

12. Brown, "Reminiscences" CHS and SLCHA; Quaife, From the Cannon's Mouth, p.125.

13. Brown, "Reminiscences" CHS and SLCHA.

14. O.R., Volume 19, Pt. 1, p.475.

15. Ibid.

16. Ibid, p. 504.

17. Ibid, p. 504-505.

18. Brown, "Reminiscences" CHS and SLCHA.

19. Poughkeepsie Eagle September 23, 1862 (Courtesy of Joel Craig).

20. O.R., Volume 19, Pt. 1, p. 515-516.

21. Brown, "Reminiscences" CHS and SLCHA.

22. Poughkeepsie Eagle September 23, 1862; Brown, "Reminiscences" CHS and SLCHA.

23. Ibid.

24. Ibid; St. Lawrence Republican October 7, 1862.

25. Quaife, From the Cannon's Mouth p. 128.

26. Ibid.

27. Brown, "Reminiscences" CHS and SLCHA.

28. Poughkeepsie Eagle September 23, 1862.

29. St. Lawrence Republican October 7, 1862.

30. Brown, "Reminiscences" CHS and SLCHA.

31. Editors of Time-Life Books, Antietam p. 60-61.

32. O.R., Volume 19, Pt. 1, p. 505.

33. Ibid, p.511-512; McIntosh, W. H. History of Ontario County, New York Everts, Ensign, and Everts 876, p.243.

34. O.R., Volume 19, Pt. 1, p. 1023; Sears, Stephen W. Landscape Turned Red: The Battle of Antietam Ticknor & Fields, 1983 p. 209-210.

35. Time-Life Books, Antietam p.87.

36. O.R., Volume 19, Pt.1, p. 507, 512.

37. Sears, Landscape Turned Red p. 209-210; J.M. Smither, 5th Texas, Antietam Collection Darthmouth College Library.

38. Mieyal, Timothy J. "A Story of Valor: The 7th Ohio Volunteer Infantry" MA Thesis, Kent State University 1998 p.158.

39.   O.R., Volume 19, Pt.1, p. 507.

40.   Mieyal, "A Story of Valor" p.158.

41.   Thackery, A Light and Uncertain Hold p. 104-105; Sears, Landscape Turned Red p. 210-211; Eugene Powell 66th Ohio Antietam Collection; Mieyal, "A Story of Valor" p.158.

42.   Cornet, Joseph L. "The 28th Pennsylvania at Antietam." Grand Army Scout and Soldiers' Mail September 22, 1883.

43.   Sears, Landscape Turned Red p.213.; Private W.H. Witcher 6th Georgia Antietam Collection.

44.   John P. Murphy Pension records, NARA; Congressional Medal of Honor Society document (postmarked June 14, 2000).

45.   Erie Weekly Gazette October 9, 1862.

46.   Ibid.

47.   Ibid; Time-Life Books Antietam p.87: O.R., Volume 19, Pt. 1, p, 512.

48.   Thackery, A Light and Uncertain Hold p.105; Wood, George L. The Seventh Regiment-A Record James Miller 1865 p. 138; Mieyal, "A Story of Valor" p. 158.

49.   Wilson, Itinerary f the Seventh Ohio p. 208.

50.   Cornet, "The 28th Pennsylvania at Antietam" September 22, 1883.

51.   Thackery, A Light and Uncertain Hold p.105; O.R., Volume 19, Pt. 1, p.507; Mieyal, "A Story of Valor" p. 159; Time-Life Books, Antietam p.78; Sears, Landscape Turned Red p. 213.

52.   Monroe, J. Albert "Battery D, First Rhode Island Light Artillery at the Battle of Antietam, September 17, 1862." Personal Narratives of the Events of the War of the Rebellion, Rhode Island Soldiers and Sailors Historical Society, Third Series, No. 16, Providence 1886 p. 125-27; Sears, Landscape Turned Red p. 219.

53.   O.R., Volume 19, Pt. 1, p. 507; Mieyal, "A Story of Valor" p.159

54.   Cunningham, D. and Miller W.W. Report of the Ohio Antietam Battlefield Commission Springfield Publishing Company, 1904 p. 47-48.

55.   Ibid; Priest, John Michael Antietam: The Soldiers Battle White Mane Publishing Company 1989 p.122; Thackery, A Light and Uncertain Hold p.105; Wiley, Bell Irwin The Life of Billy Yank, The Common Soldier of the Union Louisiana State University Press 1952, p.58

56.   O.R., Volume 19, Pt.1, p. 505,507,513; Eric Weekly Gazette October 9, 1862; Priest, The Soldiers Battle p. 122.

57. Wyckoff, Mac A History of the 2nd South Carolina Infantry: 1861-1865 Sergeant Kirkland's Museum and Historical Society, Inc. 1994 p.47.

58. O.R., Volume 19,Pt.1, p.513.

59. Ibid; Incidents in the life of a Private Soldier in the war waged by the United States against the Confederate States 1861-1865 by Robert Wallace Shad, Company C, 2nd SCV p.90 South Caroliniana Library University of South Carolina.

60. Cunningham and Miller, Antietam Battlefield Commission p. 47-48.

61. Priest, The Soldiers Battle p.122; Huyette, Miles C. The Maryland Campaign and the Battle of Antietam Hammond Press 1915, p.40.

62. Wyckoff, Mac A History of the Third South Carolina Infantry 1861-1865 Sergeant Kirkland's Museum and Historical Society, Inc. 1995 p. 76,78.

63. Congressional Medal of Honor document (postmarked June 14, 200); A. Henry Hayward to Brother September 28, 1862 MS-009/9-1.63 Papers of Ambrose Henry Hayward, ML,GC.

64. O.R., Volume 19, Pt.1, p.506-507; Mieyal, "A Story of Valor" p.160; Sears, Landscape turned Red p.215; Time-Life Books, Antietam p. 78-79.

65. Stinson, Jr. Dwight E. "Analytical Study of Action of Greene's Division" Antietam National Battlefield Site February 2, 1961 p.9-10.

66. Ibid.

67. O.R., Volume 19, Pt1, p.509; Hattaway, Herman General Stephen D. Lee University Press of Mississippi 1976 p. 56-57.

68. Joseph A. Moore, Moore Family: PA "Save the Flag" Collection United States Army Military History Institute.

69. Thackery, A Light and Uncertain Hold p.106.

70. Cleveland Herald October 10, 1862; Mieyal, "A Story of Valor" p. 161.

71. Ibid, October 3, 1862; Ibid; A. Henry Hayward to Father September 18, 1862 MS-009/9-1.61 Papers of AHH, ML,GC; Wood, The Seventh Regiment p.138-141; Cleveland Leader October 2, 1862.

72. O.R., Volume 19, Pt.1, p.505.

73. Brady, James P. (ed) Hurrah for the Artillery! Knap's Independent Battery "E," Pennsylvania Light Artillery Thomas Publications p. 153, 158-159.

74. Ibid, p.159.

75. Ibid, p.162.

76. Armstrong, Marion V. "Sumner at Antietam" Antietam National Battlefield Park.

77. Greene, G.S. "Battle of Antietam" Box 1, Folder 8 George Sears Greene Papers, RIHS. He stated Williams either advised or ordered him to find Hancock.

78. O.R., Volume 19, Pt.1, p. 506.

79. Time-Life Books, Antietam p. 90.

80. Smith, James O. "My First Campaign and Battles, A Jersey Boy at Antietam—Seventeen Days from Home." Blue and Gray 1 (1893) p.285.

81. Ibid, p. 286; Crowell, Joseph The Young Volunteer G.W. Dillingham Co., Publishers 1906, p.126-127; Swords, Robert S. Historical Sketch of Company "D" Thirteenth Regiment New Jersey Volunteers, Part of the 3d Brigade, 1st Division, 12th Army Corps D. H. Gildersleeve & Company, Publishers 1875 p.17; Toombs, Samuel Reminiscences of the War, Comprising a Detailed Account of the Experiences of the 13th Regiment New Jersey Volunteers, In Camp, the March and in Battle Journal Office 1878, pl 20-21.

82. Poughkeepsie Eagle September 23, 1862.

83. O.R., Volume 19, Pt. 1, p. 915-916.

84. Sears, Landscape Turned Red p. 232.

85. Gettysburg National Military Park Newspaper Clippings, Volume 6 p. 69; Fennell, ADCH p.38: Motts, "To Gain a Second Star" p.67-68.

86. Hector Tyndale Pension Records, NARA.

87. Henry Hayward to Brother September 21, 1862 Papers of AHH, ML, GC.

88. Moore, "Save the Flag" Collection USAMHI.

89. Quaife, From the Cannon's Mouth p.129.

90. Time-Life Books, Antietam p.95.

91. Mieyal, "A Story of Valor" p.164; Cleveland Herald October 3, 1862; O.R., Volume 19, Pt.1, p.505.

92. Ibid, p. 505-506.

93. Charles T. Greene to Susan M. Dana September 19,1862 Civil War Miscellaneous Collection, USAMHI.

94. Ario Pardee, Jr. to Father September 18 and 23 1862 Pardee/Robison Collection, USAMHI; Hayward said they had counted 167 dead South

Carolinians on one part of the field. AHH to Father September 18,1862 MS-009/9-1.61 Papers of AHH, ML, GC.

95. Thackery, A Light and Uncertain Hold p. 108-109; Joseph Diltz to Sidney Milledge October 10, 1862 Duke University.

96. Thackery, A Light and Uncertain Hold p. 109; William Sayre to Ziba Sayre September 25, 1862 Sayre Collection, USAMHI.

97. Brown, "Reminiscences" CHS and SLCHA.

98. Edward Wiggin, Jr. (Ned) to May September 28, 1862 Property of Dennis Buttacavoli.

99. Smith, "My First Campaign and Battles" p.288.

100. O.R., Volume 19, Pt. 1, p.504.

101. Mieyal, "A Story of Valor" p. 165; Greene, "Antietam" Box 1, Folder 8 GSG Papers, RIHS.

Notes: Chapter Eleven

1. Scharf, J. Thomas History of Western Maryland; Being a History of Frederick, Montgomery, Carroll, Washington, Allegany, and Garrett Counties from the Earliest Period to the Present Day; including Biographical Sketches of their Representative men L. H. Everts 1882, p.258.

2. Erie Weekly Gazette October 2, 1862.

3. Bates, Samuel P. History of Pennsylvania Volunteers, 1861-1865; prepared in compliance with acts of legislature B. Singerly, state printer 1869-71 p.1014.

4. Binghamton Daily Republican January 22, 1889.

5. Collins, George K. Memoirs of the One Hundred and Forty-ninth Regiment New York Infantry, 3rd Brig., 2nd Div., 12th and 20th A.C. Published by author 1891 pl 24.

6. Binghamton Daily Republican January 22, 1889; Brown, "Reminiscences" CHS & SLCHA.

7. St. Lawrence Republican October 14, 1862.

8. O.R., Volume 19, Pt.2, p.25-26.

9. Blair, William Allan (ed) A Politician Goes to War: The Civil War Letters of John White Geary The Pennsylvania State University Press 1995, p.67-68.

10.   Ibid, p.60.

11.   William A. Blair to Author, January 1, 2001.

12.   Blair, A Politician Goes to War, p.58-60, 69; When Geary came into the camp of the 28th PA, the boys cheered and made a rush toward him. The soldier said Geary's "arm is yet tied up in a sling." A. Henry Hayward to Brother September 28, 1862 MS-009/9-1.63 Papers of AHH, ML, GC.

13.   George Sears Greene Military Record, NARA.

14.   Howard, Thirtieth Annual Reunion p.138.

15.   George Sears Greene to E.D. Morgan November 2, 1862 The Gilder Lehrman Collection, The Pierpont Morgan Library.

16.   Ibid.

17.   Collins, Memoirs p. 77.

18.   Ibid, p.43; Binghamton Daily Republican January 23, 1889.

19.   Collins, Memoirs p.47-48.

20.   Thackery, A Light and Uncertain Hold p.111; Blair, A Politician Goes to War p.65.

21.   Binghamton Daily Republican January 23, 1889; Collins, Memoirs p.50-51.

22.   Ibid.

23.   Fox, William F. (ed) New York Monuments Commission of the Battlefields of Gettysburg and Chattanooga. Final Report of the Battle field of Gettysburg. Volume 3 1902, p. 938 (Hereafter known as NYG).

24.   Collins, Memoirs, p. 52.

25.   Oliver Ormsby to Parents November 14, 1862 (Permission of Jeff Ollis).

26.   Charles Engle to Charlotte November 23, 1862 (Property of Judy Coy).

27.   Ibid.

28.   Binghamton Daily Republican January 24, 1889.

29.   Ibid; Collins, Memoirs p. 55.

30.   Ibid, p. 56-57.

31.   Ibid, p.57-58; Binghamton Daily Republican January 24,1889.

32.   Charles Engle to Charlotte December 7, 1862.

33.   Binghamton Daily Republican January 24, 1889.

34.   Charles Engle to Charlotte December 7,1862.

35.   Collins, Memoirs p. 61.

36.   Oliver Ormsby diary December 5, 1862.

37. Collins, Memoirs p.61.

38. Ibid, p.63.

39. Ibid, p.64-67; Binghamton Daily Republican January 24,1889; Charles Engle to Charlotte December 13, 1862.

40. Lysander Welman Diaries of the Neville Public Museum of Brown County, December 13,1862.

41. Collins, Memoirs p.69.

42. Binghamton Daily Republican January 25, 1889.

43. Collins, Memoirs p. 71-72.

44. Lysander Welman Diaries December 18, 1862.

45. Thackery, A Light and Uncertain Hold p. 115; Union County Gazette January 1, 1863; Lysander Welman Diaries December 18, 1862.

46. Ibid, p. 116; Ibid; Ibid

47. Richard Eddy to Preston King December 20, 1862 RG94 NARA.

48. A.S. Williams to E. M. Stanton December 20, 1862 RG94 NARA.

49. E.D. Morgan to E.M. Stanton December 25, 1862 RG94 NARA.

50. George S. Greene to Senator Preston King December 24, 1862 (copy) Box1, Folder 1 GSG Papers, RIHS.

51. Preston King to E. M. Stanton January 2, 1863 RG94 NARA.

52. George Sears Greene to Frank January 5, 1863 FVG Papers, NYPL.

53. Ibid.

54. Blair, A Politician Goes to War p.69.

55. St. Lawrence Republican December 9, 1862.

56. Kaplan, Justin (ed) Complete Poetry and Collected Prose by Walt Whitman Library of America 1982, p. 714.

57. Lysander Welman Diaries December 20, 1862.

58. Binghamton Daily Republican January 28, 1889.

59. Ibid.

60. George Sears Greene to Frank January 5, 1863 FVG Papers, NYPL.

61. Ibid.

62. Charles Engle to Charlotte January 12 & 18, 1863; Oliver Ormsby to Parents January 14, 1863; Binghamton Daily Republican February 4, 1889.

63. Ibid; Lysander Welman Diaries January 21, 1863.

64. Collins, Memoirs. p. 86.

65.   Binghamton Daily Republican February 4, 1889; Charles Engle to Charlotte January 26, 1863; Lysander Welman Diaries January 21&22, 1863.

66.   Taylor Elmore diary January 22, 1863 Gettysburg National Military Park Library.

67.   Eddy, History of the Sixtieth Regiment p.207.

68.   Lysander Welman Diaries January 21, 1863.

69.   Binghamton Daily Republican February 5, 1889.

Notes: Chapter Twelve

1.   Blair, A Politician Goes to War p.88

2.   Binghamton Daily Republican February 18, 1889; Joshua Comfort to Father and Mother February 19, 1863 Joshua and Merrit Comfort Papers, Rare Book, Manuscript, & Special Collections Library, Duke University, Durham, North Carolina.

3.   Charles Engle to Charlotte February 22, 1863.

4.   Binghamton Daily Republican February 18, 1889.

5.   Joshua Comfort to Father and Mother March 2,1863 JMC Papers, DU.

6.   Charles Engle to Charlotte February 25,1863.

7.   Fennell, ADCH p.52-53; Motts, "To Gain a Second Star" p.68.

8.   Charles Engle to Charlotte March 8, 1863; Oliver Ormsby to Friend March 5, 1863.

9.   Ibid, March 14, 1863; Charles Engle to Charlotte March 11, 1863.

10.   L. Frick to McArthur March 28, 1863 Sullivan F. McArthur Collection, Buffalo and Erie Historical Society.

11.   Ibid.

12.   St. Lawrence Republican March 18,1863.

13.   Ibid, March 24,1863.

14.   Memoriam, GSG p. 76; Motts, "To Gain a Second Star" p.68.

15.   St. Lawrence Republican March 31,1863.

16.   Ibid, April 7, 1863.

17.   Clarke, The Greenes of Rhode Island p. XVI.

18.   Oliver Ormsby to Parents April 11, 1863.

19.   Charles Engle to Charlotte April 12, 1863.

20.   J. E. Wilson to R. Eddy March 25, 1863 Property of Dennis Buttacavoli.

Notes : Chapter 13

1. Brown, "Reminiscences" CHS & SLCHA.
2. Sears, Stephen W. Chancellorsville Houghton Mifflin Company 1996, p.142; Charles Engle to Charlotte May 8, 1863.
3. Quaife, From the Cannon's Mouth p. 179.
4. Ibid, p. 180.
5. Greene, George "Story of a Brigade" United States Magazine IV October 1865 p.303.
6. Charles Engle to Charlotte May 8, 1863; Quaife, From the Cannon's Mouth p.182-183; Greene, "Story of a Brigade" p.303.
7. O.R., Vol. 25, Pt. 1, p.764; Collins, Memoirs p. 104.
8. Ibid, p.757.
9. Ibid, p.757, p.764; Collins, Memoirs p.104-105; Oliver Ormsby to Parents May 16, 1863.
10. Ibid.
11. Charles Engle to Charlotte May 8, 1863.
12. Collins, Memoirs p.105; Oliver Ormsby to Parents May 16, 1863.
13. Greene, "Story of a Brigade" p.303.
14. Ibid.
15. O.R., Vol. 25, Pt.1, pl.729; Fennell, ADCH p.53.
16. Oliver Ormsby to Parents May 16, 1863.
17. Brown, "Reminiscences" CHS & SLCHA.
18. O.R., Vol.25, Pt. 1, p. 764.
19. In Memoriam, GSG p.78; Motts, "To Gain a Second Star" p.68.
20. O.R., Vol. 25, Pt1, p. 758.
21. Oliver Ormsby to Parents May 5, 1863.
22. Greene, "Story of a Brigade" p.303.
23. Collins, Memoirs p.107.
24. O.R., Vol.25, Pt.1, p. 758.
25. Charles Engle to Charlotte May 8, 1863.
26. O.R., Vol.25, Pt.1, p.758.
27. Brown, "Reminiscences" CHS & SLCHA.
28. Charles Engle to Charlotte May 8, 1863.
29. Oliver Ormsby to Parents May 5, 1863.
30. Caius C. Lord Pension Record, NARA.

31.   O.R., Vol.25, Pt.1, 769.
32.   Brown, "Reminiscences" CHS & SLCHA; Collins, Memoirs p. 108.
33.   O.R., Vol.25, Pt. 1, p.769.
34.   Collins, Memoirs p. 109.
35.   O.R., Vol.25, Pt.1, p.758.
36.   Ibid, p.760.
37.   Sears, Chancellorsville p. 340; Charles Engle to Charlotte May 8, 1863.
38.   Samuel R. Lusk to Parents May 8, 1863 137th N.Y. Letter Volume 117, Fredericksburg and Spotsylvania National Military Park; Furguson, Ernest B. Chancellorsville 1863-The Soul of the Brave Alfred A. Knopf, Inc. 1992, p.246.
39.   St. Lawrence Republican May 26, 1863.
40.   O.R., Vol.25, Pt.1, p.760; Lewis, William C. "Greene's Brigade" The National Tribune November 19, 1908.
41.   Ibid, p. 765.
42.   St. Lawrence Republican May 26, 1863; Brown, "Reminiscences" CHS & SLCHA.
43.   Ibid.
44.   O.R., Vol.25, Pt.1, p.760.
45.   Ibid, p.758.
46.   Samuel R. Lusk to Parents May 8, 1863 FSNMP.
47.   Ibid.
48.   Collins, Memoirs p.110-111; O.R., Vol.25, Pt.1, p.758-759,762,765,767-768.
49,   Quaife, From the Cannon's Mouth p.199.
50.   Collins, Memoirs p. 111-112.
51.   Ibid, p.112-113.
52.   O.R., Vol.25, Pt.1, p.759.
53.   Ibid, p.759, 765.
54.   Collins, Memoirs p.113.
55.   Ibid; O.R., Vol.25, Pt.1, p.759.
56.   Washington A. Roebling to John Bigelow December 9, 1910 Bigelow Papers, Library of Congress; Furguson, Chancellorsville 1863 p. 129-130; Thackery, A Light and Uncertain Hold p.132.
57.   Charles Engle to Charlotte May 12, 1863.
58.   Oliver Ormsby to Parents May 16, 1863.

59. O.R., Vol.25, Pt.1, p.758, 761.

60. Ibid, p.763.

61. Ibid, p. 76.

62. J.C.O. Redington to Richard Eddy June 9, 1864 Property of Dennis Buttacavoli.

63. Statement of Thomas Elliot, Lester S. Willson, Hugh Smith, Michael Law, John Delany, and P.S. Sinclair to Richard Eddy June 29, 1864 Property of Dennis Buttacavoli.

64. Ibid.

65. Joshua Comfort to Father and Mother May 10 & 23, 1863 Joshua and Merrit Comfort Papers Rare Book, Manuscript, & Special Collections Library, Duke University, Durham, North Carolina.

66. In Memoriam, GSG p.79; Motts, "To Gain a Second Star" p.68.

67. O.R., Vol.25, Pt. 1, p.759.

Notes: Chapter Fourteen

1. Couch, Darius N. "The Chancellorsville Campaign" Battles and Leaders of the Civil War, Thomas Yoseloff Volume 3, 1956 p.168.

2. Collins, Memoirs p. 116.

3. Copy of Obituary February 3, 1924 Sullivan F. McArthur Collection, BECHS.

4. Hiram Bloomer to Hopkins May 24,1863 New York State Library.

5. Charles Engle to Charlotte May 22, 1863.

6. Ibid, May 31,1863; Joshua Comfort to Father and Mother June 5, 1863 Joshua and Merrit Comfort Papers, DU.

7. William Gray to Hellen Gray June 3, 1863 GNMP.

8. Charles Engle to Charlotte June 3, 1863.

9. Ibid; Greene, "Story of a Brigade" p.306.

10. Ibid.

11. Schroyer, M.S. "Snyder County Historical Society Bulletins" Volume 2, Number2 1939.

12. Collins, Memoirs p. 116.

13. Joshua Comfort to Father and Mother June 5, 1863 Joshua and Merrit Comfort Papers, DU.

14. Collins, Memoirs p.117.

15. George S. Greene to Horatio Seymour June 11, 1863 Property of Dennis Buttacavoli.

16. H.W. Benham to Horatio Seymour June 10, 1863 Property of Dennis Buttacavoli.

17. O.R., Vol.25, Pt.1, p.761.

18. Sword, Wiley (ed) "Wiley Sword's War Letters Series-Army General George Greene Attempts to Solve The Navy's Problem With Rebel Torpedoes" Blue & Gray Magazine Volume XIX, No.4 p. 22-23.

19. Diary of Francis Vinton Greene June 13,1863 University of Virginia Library.

20. Diary of Spencer H. Jasen, 137th New York Infantry Regiment for the year 1863, June 13,1863 Tioga County Historical Society.

21. Quaife, From the Cannon's Mouth p.212.

22. Diary of Francis Vinton Greene June 14,1863 UVL.

23. Collins, Memoirs p.119.

24. Diary of Francis Vinton Greene June 14, 1863 UVL.

25. Charles Engle to Charlotte June 16, 1863; Collins, Memoirs p. 120; Diary of Francis Vinton Greene June 14, 1863 UVL.

26. Fox, In Memoriam-Slocum p.172.

27. Charles Engle to Charlotte June 16, 1863.

28. Diary of Francis Vinton Greene June 15, 1863 UVL.

29. NYG, Volume 2, p.491.

30. Steuben H. Coon to Father August 14, 1863 Civil War Miscellaneous Collection, USAMHI.

31. Wilson, Itinerary of the Seventh Ohio Volunteer Infantry p. 250.

32. Collins, Memoirs p. 119-120; Charles Engle to Charlotte June 16, 1863.

33. St. Lawrence Republican June 30, 1863.

34. Joshua Comfort to Father and Mother June 21,1863 Joshua and Merrit Comfort Papers, DU.

35. Collins, Memoirs p.121; Charles Engle to Charlotte June 16, 1863.

36. Diary of Francis Vinton Greene June 16, 1863 UVL.

37. Ibid, June 17, 1863; Collins, Memoirs p.121.

38. Quaife, From the Cannon's Mouth p. 214.

39. Collins, Memoirs p. 122.

40. Diary of Francis Vinton Greene June 18, 1863 UVL; Binghamton Leader March 2, 1892; Eddy, History of the Sixtieth Regiment p.253.

41. Collins, Memoirs p.122; Diary of Francis Vinton Greene June 18, 1863 UVL.

42. Ibid, p.123.

43. Diary of Francis Vinton Greene June 19, 1863 UVL.

44. Eddy, History of the Sixtieth Regiment p.263-264; Quaifc, From the Cannon's Mouth p.217; Collins, Memoirs p.123-124; Binghamton Leader March 2, 1892.

45. Fennell, ADCH p.100-101; An example of Deserters who had been pardoned in the 137th New York Regiment before June 19, 1863 is given in the Binghamton Leader March 2, 1892 issue.

46. Collins, Memoirs p. 125-126; Diary of Spencer H. Jasen June 20, 1863 TCHS; Binghamton Leader March 2, 1892; Diary of Francis Vinton Greene June 19, 1863 UVL.

47. O.R., Vol.27, Pt.3, p.223.

48. Collins, Memoirs p.126.

49. Ibid, p.126-127.

50. Binghamton Leader March 2, 1892.

51. Taylor Elmore Diary June 22, 1863 GNMP.

52. Charles Engle to Charlotte June 24, 1863.

53. Ibid.

54. Fennell. ADCH p.82-83.

55. Binghamton Leader March 2, 1892; Collins, Memoirs p. 127.

56. Ibid; Ibid.

57. James S. Hyde Diary June 26, 1863 Norwich Civil War Roundtable Collection, USAMHI.

58. Collins, Memoirs p.128-129; Diary of Francis Vinton Greene June 27, 1863; Binghamton Leader March 3, 1892; Diary of Spencer H. Jasen June 27, 1863 TCHS.

59. Ibid; Ibid; Ibid; James S. Hyde June 27, 1863 USAMHI.

60. Ibid, p. 129; Ibid, June 28,1863; Ibid; Diary of Spencer H. Jasen June 28,1863 TCHS; Fennell, ADCH p. 86.

61. Diary of Francis Vinton Greene June 29, 1863 UVL.

62. Fox, In Memoriam GSG p. 86.

63. Jorgensen, Jay "Holding the Right: The 137th New York Regiment at Gettysburg," Gettysburg Magazine Number 15, July 1996 p.61; James S. Hyde Diary June 29, 1863 USAMHI; Collins, Memoirs p.130-131;

_____, Letters Home: A Collection of Civil War Soldiers Letters Garden Spot Gifts, Inc. 1996 p. 17-18.

64. Diary of Spencer H. Jasen June 29,1863 TCHS.

65. Collins, Memoirs p.131.

66. Jorgensen, "Holding the Right" p.61; James S. Hyde Diary June 30, 1863 USAMHI.

67. Diary of Spencer H. Jasen June 30, 1863 TCHS; O.R., Vol.27, Pt. 1, p. 859.

68. Fennell, ADCH p.89-90; Collins, Memoirs p. 133-134; Jorgensen, "Holding the Right" p.61.

69. Charles P. Horton to John B. Bachelder January 23, 1867 in David L. and Audrey J. Ladd, The Bachelder Papers: Gettysburg in Their Own Words 3 Volumes Morningside Books, 1994-95, 1: p. 290.

70. Collins, Memoirs p.134-135.

71. Jorgensen, "Holding the Right" p. 62.

72. Henry Rudy Diary July 1, 1863 The DeWitt Historical Society of Tompkins County; Schroyer, "Snyder County" Vol. 2, No. 2.

73. James S. Hyde Diary July 1, 1863 USAMHI.

74. Eggleston, George Cary A Rebel's Recollection University of Indiana Press 1959 p. 130; Coddington, Edwin B. The Gettysburg Campaign: A Study in Command Charles Scribner's Sons 1968, p. 196-197.

Notes: Chapter Fifteen

1. Pfanz, Harry W. Gettysburg: Culp's Hill & Cemetery Hill The University of North Carolina Press 1993, p109-110; Collins, Memoirs p. 136-137.

2. Motts, "To Gain a Second Star," p.68; James, Jessie H. "The Breastworks at Culp's Hill" B&L, Vol. 3, p.316.

3. O.R., Vol.27, Pt. 1, p.856.

4. Ibid; Jorgensen, "Holding the Right" p.62; Motts, "To Gain a Second Stat" p. 68-69; O'Brien, Kevin E. "A Perfect Roar of Musketry: Candy's Brigade in the fight for Culp's Hill" Gettysburg Magazine No.9, July1993 p.84.

5. Fox, In Memoriam GSG p. 43.

6. Jones, "Breastworks of Culp's hill" p.316.

7.   Pfanz, Culp's Hill & Cemetery Hill p.316.

8.   Ibid; Collins, Memoirs p.137; Charles P. Horton to John B. Batchelder January 23, 1867 Ladd, The Batchelder Papers 1:293; NYG, 3: 1013.

9.   Lewis, William C. "Greene's Brigade" The National Tribune November 19, 1908.

10.   Pfanz, Culp's Hill & Cemetery Hill p. 118.

11.   Jorgensen, "Holding the Right" p.62; Elmore, Thomas L. "Courage against the Trenches: The Attack and Repulse of Steaurt's Brigade on Culp's Hill Gettysburg Magazine No. 7, July 1992, p.85.

12.   Ibid; Charles P. Horton to John B. Bachelder January 23,1867 Ladd, The Bachelder Papers, 1:293.

13.   Tallman memoirs, USAMHI.

14.   Binghamton Leader March 4, 1892.

15.   O.R., Vol. 27, Pt. 2, p.543.

16.   Ibid, Pt.1, p. 856; Motts, "To Gain a Second Star" p.69; Jorgenson. Jay "Joseph W. Latimer, The 'Boy Major'! At Gettysburg," Gettysburg Magazine No. 10. January 1994 p. 29-34.

17.   O.R., Vol.27, pt.1 p.862;_____Greene's brigade. The thirtieth Anniversary 1863-1864, Souvenir of the Reunion, July, 1-3 1893, of its Greene's Brigade, 3rd Brigade, 2nd Division, 12th Corps, the 60th,78, 102nd, 137th and 149th New York Volunteers, who alone at Culp's hill in the Days' Battle Saved the Right at Gettysburg J.C.O. Redington 1893 p.5 (Hereafter referred to as Greene's Brigade)

18.   O.R., Vol. 27, Pt.1 p. 863.

19.   Greene's Brigade, p, 6; Fennell, ADCH p. 116.

20.   Eddy, History of the Sixteen Eddy, History sixtieth p.260: Collins, Memoirs p,138.

21.   Pfanz, Culp's Hill & Cemetery Hill p.194.

22.   Ibid, p.194-195; Alpheus S. Williams to John B. Bachelder November 10,1865 Ladd, Bachelder Papers, 1:215.

23.   Ethier, Eric "King of the Hill" Civil War Times Illustrated Vol.36, No.6 December 1997, p.66.

24.   Motts, "To Gain a Second Star" p.69; Busey, John and Martin, David Regimental Strengths and Losses at Gettysburg Longstreet house 1986, p.151.

25.   O.R., Vol.27, Pt.2, p. 518; Motts, "To Gain a Second Star" p.69.

26.   Busey and Martin, Regimental Strengths and Losses, p.151.

27.   Henry W. Slocum to Messrs. T.H. Davis & Co., September 8, 1875 Northern Commanders and Staff, Robert L. Blake Collection, USAMHI; O.R., Vol.27, Pt. 1, p.759, 833; Shotwell, Mike and Sword, Wiley "Two New York Swords in the Fight for Culp's Hill: Col. James C. Lane's and Capt. Nicholas Grumbach's" Gettysburg Magazine No. 10, January 1994 p.37.

28.   Olmsted, M. L. "Recitals and Reminiscences" in Fighting Them Over: How the Veterans Remembered Gettysburg in the Pages of the National Tribune, Edited by Richard A. Sauers Butternut and Blue, 1998 p.365.

29.   O.R., Vol.27, Pt.1, p.862; Fennell, ADCH p. 127.

30.   Charles P. Horton to John B. Bachelder January 23, 1867, Ladd, Bachelder Papers 1: 293-294.

31.   Greene, George S. "The Breastworks at Culp's Hill" B&L, Vol.3 p. 317.

32.   Steuben H. Coon to father August 14, 1863 Civil War Miscellaneous Collection USAMHI.

33.   Ibid.

34.   Henry Rudy Diary, DHS; Greene, B&L, p. 317.

35.   Jorgensen, "Holding the Right" p.64; Sauers, Fighting Them Over p. 366; Ethier, "King of the Hill" p.68.

36.   O.R., Vol.27, Pt.1, p.862.

37.   Pfanz, Culp's Hill & Cemetery Hill p.213.

38.   Steuben H. Coon to Father August 14, 1863, USAMHI; Collins, Memoirs p.138; Perry Norton to Father July 9, 1863 Norton Brothers Letters, USAMHI.

39.   O.R., Vol. 27, Pt.1, p. 856, 863.

40.   Ibid, Pt.2, p.532; Pfanz, Culp's Hill & Cemetery Hill p.210; Motts, "To Gain a Second Star" p.69; Fennell, ADCH p.128-129.

41.   Nevins, Allan (ed) A Diary of Battle: The Personal Journals of Colonel Charles S. Wainwright, 1861-1865 Stan Clark Military Books 1992, p.244-245.

42.   O.R., Vol.27, Pt.2, p.504; Lewis, "Greene's Brigade" November 19, 1908; St. Lawrence Republican July 14,1863; Brown, "Reminiscences" CHS & SLCHA.

43.   O.R., Vol.27, Pt.2, p.537.

44.   Jones, Jessie H. "Save the Day," The National Tribune March 7, 1895; Ibid, "A Pair of Breastplates," The National Tribune June 6, 1901.

45. Brown, "Reminiscences" CHS & SLCHA.

46. "Memoirs of Benjamin Anderson Jones, Virginian, Civil War Experiences," Virginia Historical Society; Sharples, Edward "History of Company B, 60th New York," USAMHI.

47. Steuben H. Coon to Father August 14, 1863 USAMHI.

48. O.R., Vol. 27, Pt. 1, p.860.

49. Pfanz, Culp's Hill & Cemetery Hill p. 216; Motts, "To Gain a Second Star" p.71; Fennell, ADCH p.131.

50. O.R., Vol.27, Pt.1, p.533, 537, 539.

51. Ryan, George F. "Greene's Brigade at Culp's Hill," The National Tribune November 29, 1923; Fennell, ADCH p.131-132.

52. Logan Hill to Author June 12, 1999.

53. Steuben H. Coon to Father August 14, 1863 USAMHI.

54. St. Lawrence Republican July 14, 1863.

55. Shotwell & Swords, "Two New York Swords," p.38.

56. Collins, Memoirs p.139.

57. Tom Brooks to Author June 22, 1999; Pfanz, Culp's Hill & Cemetery Hill p.216.

58. O.R., Vol.27, Pt.2, p.513.

59. Collins, Memoirs p.409.

60. Ibid, p.417.

61. Shotwell & Swords, "Two New York Swords," p.38.

62. Ibid, p.39.

63. Fox, In Memoriam GSG p.46.

64. Collins, Memoirs p.139.

65. Ibid; O.R., Vol. 27, Pt.1, p.868; Shotwell & Sword "Two New York Swords," p.38-39.

66. Greene, B&L, p. 317.

67. O.R., Vol.27, Pt.1, p.856; Dawes, Rufus R. Service with the Sixth Wisconsin Volunteers Morningside 1984, p.181-182; NYG, Vol.1, p.381; Vol.3, p.1001-1003.

68. Motts, "To Gain a Second Star" p. 73.

69. Howard, Oliver Otis Autobiography of Oliver Otis Howard, Major General United States Army Baker and Taylor Co., Vol.1, 1907 p. 428.

70. Pfanz, Culp's Hill & Cemetery Hill p.213-214.

71. O.R., Vol.27, Pt. 2, p.504; Ibid, Pt1, p. 856; Clemens, Thomas G. "The

Diary of John H. Stone, First Lieutenant, Company B, 2nd Maryland Infantry, C.S.A.," Maryland Historical Magazine Vol.85, 1990 p.131; Elmore, "Courage against the Trenches," p.83.

72.   Zollinger, William P. Hollyday, Lamar and Howard, D.R. "General George H. Steaurt's Brigade at the Battle of Gettysburg" Southern Historical Society Papers Vol. 2 1876 p.105-107.

73.   O.R., Vol.27, Pt.2, p.510; Elmore, "Courage against the Trenches" p.85-86; Jorgensen, "Holding the Right" p.64-65.

74.   Zollinger, "Steuart's Brigade" SHSP, p. 105-107.

75.   Goldsborough, W.W. The Maryland Line in the Confederate Army 1861-1865 Guggenheim, Weil, and Co. 1900 p.103-104.

76.   Elmore, "Courage against the Trenches" p.86.

77.   _____, Letters Home p.18.

78.   Pfanz, Culp's Hill & Cemetery Hill p.218.

79.   "Charles Anderson Raines Memoirs," 23rd Virginia Regiment FSNMP.

80.   The Windsor Standard June 29, 1894.

81.   Charles Engle to Charlotte July 12, 1863.

82.   O.R., Vol.27, Pt1, p.866.

83.   Charles Engle to Charlotte July 12, 1863.

84.   Motts, "To Gain a Second Star" p.71.

85.   R. Penn Smith to Isaac Wistar July 29, 1863 File 3/3.2.7, Wistar Institute; Charles P. Horton to John B. Bachelder January 23, 1867 Ladd, Bachelder Papers 1: 294-295.

86.   Ibid; Ibid, p.295; O.R., Vol.27, Pt. 1, p.432.

87.   O.R., Vol. 27, Pt. 1, p.856; Motts, "To Gain a Second Star" p.71.

88.   R. Penn Smith to Isaac Wistar July 29, 1863 File 3/3.2.7, WI; Charles P. Horton to John B. Bachelder January 23, 1867 Ladd, Bachelder Papers 1: 295.

89.   Banes, Charles H. History of the Philadelphia Brigade J. B. Lippencott & Co., 1876 p. 186; William J. Burns "Civil War Diary" Robert L. Brake Collection, USAMHI.

90.   Charles P. Horton to John B. Bachelder January 23, 1867 Ladd, Bachelder Papers 1: 295; R. Penn Smith to Isaac Wistar July 29, 1863 File 3/3.2.7, WI; O.R., Vol.27,Pt. 1, p. 427; Greene, B&L p. 317; Jorgensen, "Holding the Right" p.66.

91.   Burns Diary, USAMHI.

92. O.R., Vol.27, Pt.1, p.866; Greene, B&L p.317; Jorgensen, "Holding the Right" p.66; Pfanz, Culp's Hill & Cemetery Hill p.221.

93. Charles P. Horton to John B. Bachelder January 23, 1867 Ladd, Bachelder Papers 1: 295.

94. _____, Letters Home p.18.

95. Fennell, ADCH p.140.

96. "Statement of distinguished service of Owen J. Sweet," 137th New York Regt 1896 Box 29, Folder 4, Regimental History Survey Files, New York State Archives; O.R., Vol.27, Pt. 1, p.866; Motts, "To Gain a Second Star" p.71.

97. Henry Rudy Diary, DHS.

98. Binghamton Leader March 4, 1892.

99. Owen J. Sweet Papers, 137th New York Regt 1896 Box 29, Folder 4, Regimental History Survey Files. The men listed as witnesses are: Company A-Sergeant Alexander Carmen, Company B-Sergeant Eli B. Carter, 1st Lieutenant Hoffman W. Ensign, and Leroy M. Parsons. NYSA.

100. Owen J. Sweet statement, Box 29, Folder 4, RHSF, NYSA.

101. Ibid.

102. Greene, B&L p.317; Pfanz, Culp's Hill & Cemetery Hill p.222; Charles Fennell believed in his study of Culp's Hill that the 147th New York supported the 102nd New York. ADCH, p. 143.

103. O.R., Vol.27, Pt.1, p.827, 856; Dawes, Sixth Wisconsin p.181-182.

104. Ibid, p.182; Rufus R. Dawes to John B. Bachelder March 18, 1868 Ladd, Bachelder Papers 1: 326.

105. Ibid; RG 94, House of Representatives Report 1080 [attached to bill H.R. 7487] 52nd Congress, 1st Session NARA.

106. _____, "A Hero at Sixty-two," George Sears Greene Papers EG Box 22, HHL. This person I believe was a part of the group, but confused about the fighting part of the story since there is no confirmation coming from Union or Confederate sources.

107. O.R., Vol.27, Pt.1, p.287; Tevis, C.V. and Marquis, D.R. The History of the Fighting Fourteenth Brooklyn Eagle Press 1911. p.91; Edward B. Fowler to John B. Bachelder May 8, 1878 and October 2, 1889 Ladd, Bachelder Papers 1: 549; 3: 1637-1638; Pfanz, Culp's Hill & Cemetery Hill p.222

108. Clark, Walter (ed) Histories of the Several Regiments and Battalions from

North Carolina in the Great War, 1861-1865 E. M. Uzzell, Printer and Binder 1901 p.195.

109.   Ibid.

110.   Pfanz, Culp's Hill & Cemetery Hill p.218.

111.   McKim, Randolph H. "Steuart's Brigade at the Battle of Gettysburg" SHSP Vol. 5 1878 p.293; Ibid, A Soldier's Recollections: Leaves from the Diary of a Young Confederate Zenger Publishing Co., Inc. 1983 p.195-196.

112.   Pfanz, Culp's Hill & Cemetery Hill p.220.

113.   O.R., Vol.27, Pt.1, p.857.

114.   Swineford, George W. "On Culp's Hill," The National Tribune August 3, 1916; Boyle, John Richards Soldiers and True: The Story of the 111th Pennsylvania Veteran Volunteer Infantry, 1861-1865 Eaton & Mains 1903, p.125.

115.   O.R., Vol.27, Pt.1, p.863,867; Collins, Memoirs p.139-140.

116.   Curtis, Newton Martin From Bull Run to Chancellorsville G.P. Putnam's Sons 1906 p.188-189.

Notes: Chapter Sixteen

1.   Sauers, Fighting Them Over p. 366; Collins, Memoirs p.139.

2.   Brown, "Reminiscences" CHS & SLCHA; Ryan, "Greene's Brigade"

3.   Ibid; Sauers, Fighting Them Over p.366.

4.   Collins, Memoirs p.140; St. Lawrence Republican July 14,1863.

5.   Fennell, ADCH p.163; Pfanz, Culp's Hill & Cemetery Hill p.287, 291.

6.   Thackery, A Light and Uncertain Hold p. 147.

7.   Ibid; Eugene Powell to John B. Bachelder March 23, 1886 Ladd, Bachelder Papers, 2: 1248.

8.   Greene, B&L, p.317.

9.   O'Brien, "A Perfect Roar of Musketry" p.87-90.

10.   O.R., Vol.27, Pt. 2, p.568.

11.   Collins, Memoirs p.140.

12.   Brown, "Reminiscences" CHS & SLCHA; Steuben H. Coon to Father August 14, 1863 USAMHI; Henry Rudy Diary, DHS; Unidentified 137th NY soldier to Father & Mother July 7, 1863 137th file, GNMP.

13.   _____, Letters Home p.18.

14.   O.R., Vol. 27, Pt.1 p.868.

15.   Leon, L. Diary of a Tar Heel Confederate Soldier Stone Publishing Company 1913, p.36.

16.   O'Brien, "A Perfect Roar of Musketry" p.90.

17.   O.R., Vol.27, Pt. 2, p.572, 573, 574; Caldwell, Willie Walker Stonewall Jim: A Biography of General James A. Walker, C.S.A. Northcross House, Publishers 1990 p.89-90.

18.   Leon, Diary of a Tar Heel p.37.

19.   Collins, Memoirs p.143.

20.   Sauers, Fighting Them Over p.367; Ibid, p.140-141.

21.   O.R., Vol.27, Pt. 1, p.770; Pfanz, Culp's Hill & Cemetery Hill p.297.

22.   Collins, Memoirs p.142.

23.   Ibid, p.143.

24.   Zable, David "Paper Read before the Army of Northern Virginia, Louisiana Division December 12, 1903." GNMP.

25.   Ibid; Pfanz, Culp's Hill & Cemetery Hill p.300.

26.   Collins, Memoirs p. 144.

27.   Kaminsky, Virginia Hudges (ed) A War to Petrify the Heart: The Civil War Letters of a Dutchess County, N.Y. Volunteer Richard T. Van Wyck Black Dome Press 1997, p. 106; Topps, David "The Dutchess County Regiment" Gettysburg Magazine, No. 12, January 1995 p. 50-54.

28.   Jessup, Harlan R. (ed) The Painful News I have to Write: Letters and Diaries of Four Hite Brothers of Page County in the Service of the Confederacy Butternut & Blue 1998, p.148.

29.   King, John R. "My Experience in the Confederate Army and in Northern Prisons" Stonewall Jackson Chapter No. 1333, United Daughters of Confederacy 1917, p. 6-7 (Reprinted by Martha Stump Benson 1994).

30.   Brown, "Reminiscences" CHS & SLCHA.

31.   Ibid.

32.   St. Lawrence Republican July 14, 1863.

33.   Eugene Powell to John B. Bachelder March 23, 1886 Ladd, Bachelder Papers, 2: 1248; O'Brien, "A Perfect Roar of Musketry" p.92.

34.   Pfanz, Culp's Hill & Cemetery Hill p.296.

35.   Thackery, A Light and Uncertain Hold p.149.

36.   Ibid.

37.   Eugene Powell to John B. Bachelder March 23, 1886 Ladd, Bachelder Papers, 2: 1248.

38.   Information compiled on Stephen K. Gray, 66th Ohio, by Rev. John Gray. The federal, state, and medical records he checked on his relative listed SKG being wounded on all three days. We believe the 3rd of July is correct and it is unknown why Greene had personally sign off on SKG casualty sheet since he was not in his brigade. He may have known him back in the Antietam campaign or saw him & heard his story from the chaplain.

39.   O.R., Vol.27, Pt. 1, p.837.

40.   Thackery, A Light and Uncertain hold p.149.

41.   Edward D. Camden Diary, 25th Virginia Infantry FNMP; Pfanz, Culp's Hill & Cemetery Hill p. 297.

42.   Greene, B&L, p.317.

43.   Ibid; Wilson, Lawrence The Washington Post July 9, 1899; Bertholf, G. D. "The Twelfth Corps. The Part they took in the Big Battle of Gettysburg" The National Tribune May 11, 1893; Pfanz, Culp's Hill & Cemetery Hill p. 326.

44.   Jorgensen, "Holding the Right," p.67.

45   _____, History of the DeWitt Guard, Company A, 50th Regiment, National Guard, State of New York Andrus, Mc Chain and Company 1866 p. 75.

46.   Sauers, Fighting Them Over p.367.

47.   Abel Goddard to Mother August 1863 Civil War Miscellaneous Collection USAMHI.

48.   Henry Rudy Diary, DHS.

49.   Raab, Steven S. (ed) With the 3rd Wisconsin Badgers: The Living Experience of the Civil War through the Journals of Van R. Willard Stackpole Books, 1999 p. 199.

50.   Collins, Memoirs p. 146.

51.   Ibid; Henry Rudy Diary, DHS.

52.   Don Nelson (interviewed by Stan Maine) to author May 11, 2001. He thought it was one of the Louisiana Tigers, but this had to be of Williams' Brigade men since the Tigers were located at Cemetery Hill area and town of Gettysburg.

53.   Wilson, Lawrence The Washington Post July 9, 1899.

54. Brown, "Reminiscences" CHS & SLCHA.

55. Ibid.

56. Barziza, Decimus et Ultimus The Adventures of a Prisoner of War The University of Texas Press, 1964 p. 54.

57. Ibid.

58. Nevins, A Diary of Battle p.251. There was 2,000 guns picked up by the 12th Corps from the field, see Ethier's "King of the Hill" p.72.

59. O' Brien, "A Perfect Roar of Musketry" p.95; Thackery, A Light and Uncertain Hold p.153.

60. William Gray to Charles Gray July 17, 1863 (copy) GNMP; Henry Rudy Diary, DHS.

61. Collins, Memoirs p.148-149.

62. O.R., Vol.27, Pt.1, p.833.

63. Martz, Jason A. "It was not a happy time: What the Civilians of Gettysburg saw and heard during the battle" Gettysburg Magazine No.18 January 1998 p.126.

64. Busey and Martin, Regimental Strengths p.257.

65. Ibid, p. 285-286.

66. Bean, W.G. The Liberty Hall Volunteers The University Press of Virginia 1964 p.151.

67. Mobile Evening News July 24, 1863.

68. Greene, B&L, p.317.

69. Ibid.

70. Charles P. Horton to John B. Bachelder January 23, 1867 Ladd, Bachelder Papers, 1: 298.

Notes: Chapter Seventeen

1. Collins, Memoirs p. 151; Henry Rudy Diary, DHS; Spencer H. Jasen Diary, TCHS.

2. Blair, A Politician Goes to War p.100.

3. Collins, Memoirs p. 152.

4. Ibid; Charles Engle to Charlotte July 9, 1863; Spencer H. Jasen Diary, TCHS.

5. Binghamton Leader March 5, 1892; Charles Engle to Charlotte July 9, 1863.

6.   Collins, Memoirs p. 152-153.

7.   Ibid, p. 153-154; Charles Engle to Charlotte July 9, 1863; Spencer H. Jasen Diary, TCHS.

8.   Ibid, p. 155-156; Ibid; Ibid.

9.   Ibid, p. 156.

10. Ibid; Binghamton Leader March 5, 1892.

11. Binghamton Leader March 5, 1892.

12. Spencer H. Jasen Diary, TCHS; Charles Engle to Charlotte July 18, 1863; Collins, Memoirs p. 158.

13. Ibid; Binghamton Leader March 5, 1892.

14. Ibid; Ibid; Collins, Memoirs p.159.

15. Edwin P. Farling to Julia July 16, 1863 Massachusetts Historical Society.

16. Blair, A Politician Goes to War p. 101.

17. Quaife, From the Cannon's Mouth p.236.

18. Washington W. Postley to Adjutant-General July 18, 1863 Military and Pension Records NARA. It is ironic that he was considered AWOL in November 1862 when he was ill in the hospital and the Judge Advocate dismissed those charges on March 28, 1863 due to the record of the trial lost from the wagon overturned and spilled out the contents of the desk during the march to Dunfries, Virginia. At Gettysburg, the Lt. Col. of the 78th New York said Postley "was conspicuous for the coolness and zeal with which he kept the regiment supplied with ammunition under a very hot fire." O.R., Vol. 27, Pt. 1, p. 864.

19. Diary of Francis Vinton Greene July 19, 1863 UVL.

20. Henry Rudy Diary, DHS; Collins, Memoirs p.161; Binghamton Leader March 5,1892.

21. Ibid.

22. Ibid; Diary of Francis Vinton Greene July 20, 1863 UVL; Collins, Memoirs p.162.

23. Binghamton Leader March 5, 1892; Collins, Memoirs p.162-163.

24. Ibid.

25. Binghamton Leader March 5, 1892; Charles Engle to Charlotte July 21,1863.

26. Diary of Francis Vinton Greene July 22, 1863 UVL; Blair, A Politician Goes to War p.102-103.

27. Ibid, July 23, 1863 UVL; Ibid, p.104; Spencer H. Jasen Diary TCHS;

Collins, Memoirs p. 165; Binghamton Leader March 5, 1892.

28. Ibid, July 24, 1863 UVL; Ibid; Ibid; Ibid; Ibid.

29. Ibid; Spencer H. Jasen Diary, TCHS.

30. Charles Engle to Charlotte July 28, 1863.

31 Collins, Memoirs p. 166-167.

32. Quaife, From the Cannon's Mouth p.244; Binghamton Leader March 5, 1892; Diary of Francis Vinton Greene July 26, 1863 UVL.

33. Collins, Memoirs p. 169; Binghamton Leader March 5, 1892; Spencer H. Jasen Diary, TCHS.

34. Ibid.

35. Ibid, p.170; Diary of Francis Vinton Greene July 27 & 28, 1863 UVL.

36. Ibid.

37. Ibid; Collins, Memoirs p.170-171; Spencer H. Jasen Diary, TCHS; Binghamton Leader March 5, 1892.

38. Joshua Comfort to Father and Mother August 1,1863 Joshua and Merrit Comfort Papers, DU.

39. Collins, Memoirs p. 173.

40. Charles Engle to Charlotte August 8, 1863.

41. Binghamton Leader March 5,1892.

42. Ibid.

43. Diary of Francis Vinton Greene August 1, 1863 UVL.

44. Ibid, August 18, 1863 UVL.

45. Charles Engle to Charlotte August 23, 1863.

46. Collins, Memoirs p.176; Spencer H. Jasen Diary, TCHS.

47. Joshua Comfort to Father and Mother August 30, 1863 Joshua and Merrit Comfort Papers, DU.

48. William Gray to Mother August 30, 1863 (copy) GNMP.

49. Collins, Memoirs p.174-175; Charles Engle to Charlotte August 23, 1863.

50. Ibid, p. 177.

51. Edwin P. Farling to Julia September 13, 1863 MHS.

52. Ibid; Collins, Memoirs p. 178.

53. Collins, Memoirs p. 178; Spencer H. Jasen Diary, TCHS.

54. Ibid; Blair, A Politician Goes to War p. 115; Charles Engle to Charlotte September 21, 1863.

55. Ibid; Ibid.

56. Spencer H. Jasen Diary, TCHS; Charles Engle to Charlotte September 27,

1863; Greene, Albert R. "From Bridgeport to Ringgold by way of Lookout Mountain" MOLLUS Rhode Island Chapter 1890. p.272-273.

57.   RG 94, H.W. Slocum to Gen. S. Thomas September 15, 1863 NARA.

58.   Greene, "From Bridgeport to Ringgold" p. 275; Spencer H. Jasen Diary, TCHS; Collins, Memoirs p.180-181.

59.   Charles Engle to Charlotte October 1, 1863; Ibid.

60.   Greene, "Story of a Brigade" p.307.

61.   Collins, Memoirs p. 184-186.

62.   Ibid, p. 187; Charles Engle to Charlotte October 7, 1863.

63.   Ibid, p.188-189.

64.   Henry Rudy Diary, DHS; Charles Engle to Charlotte October 14 & 17, 1863.

65.   Blair, A Politician Goes to War p. 124; Greene, "Story of a Brigade" p. 308.

66.   Collins, Memoirs p.190; O.R., Vol. 31, Pt. 1, p. 129-130; Henry Rudy Diary, DHS; Spencer H. Jasen Diary, TCHS.

67.   Greene, "From Bridgeport to Ringgold' p.281-282; Greene, "Story of a Brigade" p. 308.

68.   Ibid, p.282-283.

69.   O.R., Vol. 31, Pt. 1, p. 130; Greene, "Story of a Brigade" p. 308.

Notes: Chapter Eighteen

1.   St. Lawrence Republican November 10, 1863.

2.   Swisher, James K. Brigadier General Micah Jenkins C.S.A. Prince of Edisto Rockbridge Publishing Company 1996 p.109.

3.   Collins, Memoirs p.197; Greene, "From Bridgeport to Ringgold" p.286-287.

4.   O.R., Vol.31, Pt.1, p.112.

5.   Greene, "From Bridgeport to Ringgold" p.287-288; Jones, Jessie H. "Lookout Mountain: An Account of the Battle by a Fighting Parson," National Tribune October 21, 1889; Cozzens, Peter The Battles for Chattanooga: The Shipwreck of their Hopes University of Illinois Press 1994 p.76.

6.   Ibid, p. 288; Mixson, Frank M. Reminiscences of a Private J.J. Fox, Inc. 1990, p.45.

7. Skinner, George W. Pennsylvania at Chickamauga and Chattanooga: Ceremonies at the Dedication of the Monuments Erected by the Commonwealth of Pennsylvania to Mark the Positions of the Pennsylvania Commands Engaged in the Battles William Stanley Ray, State Printer 1900 p. 379; Cozzens, The Battles for Chattanooga p. 84.

8. Bond, Natalie Jenkins and Coward, Osmun Latrobe (ed) The South Carolinians: Colonel Asbury Coward's Memoirs Vantage Press 1968 p.89

9. O.R., Vol. 31, Pt. 1, p. 127.

10. Greene, "From Bridgeport to Ringgold" p.289; Cozzens, The Battles of Chattanooga p.84; Brady, Hurrah for the Artillery! P. 309.

11. Clarke, The Greenes of Rhode Island p. XVIII-XIX.

12. Ibid, p. XIX; Greene, "From Bridgeport to Ringgold" p. 289-290; O.R., Vol. 31, Pt. 1, p.127.

13. Cozzens, The Battles for Chattanooga p. 84.

14. O.R., Vol. 31, Pt. 1, p. 127.

15. Ibid; Greene, "From Bridgeport to Ringgold" p. 289-290.

16. Ibid, p. 289.

17. Henry Rudy Diary, DHS.

18. Charles Engle to Charlotte November 1 & 4, 1863.

19. Collins, Memoirs p. 198.

20. Swisher, Prince of Edisto p. 110; Henry Rudy Diary, DHS; Blair, A Politician Goes to War p. 131-132; Fullerton, Joseph S. "The Army of the Cumberland at Chattanooga" B&L, Vol. 3 p.720.

21. Henry Rudy Diary, DHS.

22. Greene, "From Bridgeport to Ringgold" p.290.

23. Mixson, Reminiscences of a Private p.46.

24. Brady, Hurrah for the Artillery! p. 309; Greene, "From Bridgeport to Ringgold" p.290-291; Henry Rudy Diary, DHS.

25. Bond & Coward, The South Carolinians p. 90; Swisher, Prince of Edisto p. 111.

26. Ibid, p. 90-91; Ibid, p. 112-114.

27. Greene, "From Bridgeport to Ringgold" p.292; Howard, Thirtieth Annual Reunion p.141.

28. Ibid; Henry Rudy Diary, DHS; O.R., Vol. 31, Pt. 1, p.130; Collins, Memoirs p. 199-200; Swisher, Prince of Edisto p. 111.

29. Syracuse Journal November 11, 1863.

30. Collins, Memoirs p. 376.

31. Edwin P. Farling to Julia November 16, 1863 MHS.

32. Greene Pension Records, NARA.

33. Clarke, The Greenes of Rhode Island p. XIX; RG94, medical certificate NARA; Greene Pension Records, NARA.

34. Ibid; Ibid.

35. Ibid.

36. Greene Pension Records, NARA.

37. Greene "From Bridgeport to Ringgold" p.311.

38. Brookfield Journal May 25, 1961; O.L.F. Browne to George S. Greene (Fragment of letter) in 1890's Box 1, Folder 8, George Sears Greene Papers RIHS.

39. RG94, George S. Greene to General Thomas January 31, 1864; Greene Pension Records, NARA.

40. Ibid, February 29 & March 31, 1864 NARA.

41. Ibid, Ira Harris to Edwin Stanton March 18, 1864 and H.B. Anthony to Edwin Stanton March 21, 1864 NARA.

42. Ibid, George S. Greene to General Thomas May 31, 1864 NARA.

43. Walsh, James J. (ed) The Catholic Encyclopedia Robert Appleton Company Vol. 15, 1912.

44. Clarke, The Greenes of Rhode Island p. XIX.

45. Ibid.

46. RG94, George S. Greene to General Thomas May 31, 1864; Abstract of Commutation of Quarters and Fuel May 31, 1864 EG Box 22, HHL. Greene's list of cost included fuel for a servant. Since he did not have any of his staff, this may be a "contraband" slave that we know had been with him in May 1862.

47. Clarke, The Greenes of Rhode Island p. XIX; Cullum, Biographical Register p. 302.

48. Ibid; O.R., Vol.65, Pt. 2, p.623.

49. Ibid, p. XIX-XX; O.R., Pt.1, p. 694.

50. Ibid; Jacob D. Cox Diaries 1864-65, p. 89 Box 11, Series 4, Jacob Dolson Cox Papers Oberlin College.

51. Ibid; Ibid; Coski, John M. and Coski, Ruth Ann (ed) "Many are delighted" Two Confederate Diaries From the Last Weeks of the War,

North & South Vol. 3, No. 4, p. 62. One source had indicated he was wounded, but this is not supported by any collaborating papers or published works. Biographical Cyclopedia p. 292.

52. Ibid; Ibid, p. 92

53. Pontius, Phillip (ed) "Uncle Jake in the Civil War," Bridgebuilder, The National Pontius Association Magazine February 1968.

54. Nadeau, Mildred (transcribed) Diary of William Harrison Bowlby Property of Florence Kring.

55. Clarke, The Greenes of Rhode Island p. XIX; Cullum, Biographical Register p.302.

56. Pontius, "Uncle Jake" Bridgebuilder.

57. Clarke, The Greenes of Rhode Island p.XIX; Cullum, Biographical Register p. 302.

58. RG94, George S. Greene to General Thomas May 26, 1865 NARA.

Notes: Chapter Nineteen

1. Charles T. Greene to George S. Greene June 7, 1866 George Sears Greene file copy, USMA.

2. Clarke, The Greenes of Rhode Island p. XX; Cullum, Biographical Register p. 302;_____, "Early Presidents of the Society" p.710.

3. Charles T. Greene to George S. Greene June 7, 1866 George Sears Greene file copy, USMA.

4. Clarke, The Greenes of Rhode Island p. XX;_____, "Early Presidents of the Society" p.710-711; NYGB, p. 72.

5. Charles T. Greene to George Sears Greene June 7, 1866 George Sears Greene file copy, USMA.

6. Ibid; George S. Greene Jr. to Father June 3, 1866 Francis Vinton Greene Papers, NYPL.

7. Charles T. Greene to Father July 1866 George Sears Greene file copy, USMA.

8. Galusha, Liquid Assets p. 39.

9. _____, "Early Presidents of the Society" p. 710.

10. Clarke, The Greenes of Rhode Island p. XXI; Cullum, Biographical Register p. 302; NYGB, p.71.

11. Ibid; "In Memoriam, George Sears Greene" MOLLUS Papers, January 31, 1900.

12. _____, "Early Presidents of the Society" p. 711; Galusha, Liquid Assets p.41.

13. Clarke, The Greenes of Rhode Island p. XXI; Cullum, Biographical Register p. 302-303; NYGB p. 71; The Providence Journal May 25, 1913; Johnson & Malone, DAB p. 567; Howard, Thirtieth Annual Reunion p. 141-142.

14. Ibid; _____, "Early Presidents of the Society" p. 711.

15. Ibid; Ibid; The Providence Journal May 25, 1913.

16. Committee of the American Society of Civil Engineers, "Report of the System of Sewerage in the City of Providence—Presented August 7, 1876." p. 3-6 Brown University Library.

17. Ibid, p. 8-9 BUL.

18. Ibid, p. 9-10 BUL.

19. Johnson & Malone, DAB p. 560, 567.

20. Ibid, p. 563; Clarke, The Greenes of Rhode Island p. XXII; NYGB, p. 72.

21. George S. Greene to John P. Nicholson November 27, 1871 John Page Nicholson Papers, RB51097 HHL.

22. Greene Military and Pension Records, NARA.

23. Ibid.

24. Ibid.

25. NYGB, p. 71-72. Joining in April 10, 1869 he was also Vice-President in 1873-76, 1883 and Trustee in 1870, 1874-85. Clarke, The Greenes of Rhode Island p. XX.

26. George S. Greene to Oliver O. Howard May 10, 1881 O.O. Howard Papers, Bowdoin College Library; "In Memoriam." MOLLUS Papers January 31, 1900; Cullum, Biographical Register p.303.

27. Army and Navy Journal June 18, 1881.

28. Ibid; Howard, Thirtieth Annual Reunion p.142.

29. Ibid.

30. Clarke, The Greenes of Rhode Island p. XXII.

31. Cavanaugh, Cam In Lights and Shadows: Morristown in Three Centuries The Joint Free Library of Morristown and Morris Township 1986, p. 116-117.

32. Ibid, p.142.

33. George S. Greene to Carleton Greene December 8, 1883 Box 2, Folder

1, The William and Marion Sluys Collection of Greene Family Manuscripts, RIHS.

34. Ibid. Carleton Greene listened to his grandfather and used his relatives as role models. He became an engineer and was a member of the American Society of Civil Engineers, serving as a Director in 1920-1922._____, "Early Presidents of the Society" p.711.

35. The Jerseyman December 21, 1883; Clarke, The Greenes of Rhode Island p. 473-474.

36. Army and Navy Register December 20, 1884.

37. Ibid.

38. Ibid.

39. _____, "Early Presidents of the Society" p. 711; George S. Greene Jr. to O.O. Howard June 2, 1899 O.O. Howard Papers, Bowdoin College Library; Clarke, The Greenes of Rhode Island p. XXI.

40. Galusha, Liquid Assets p. 66.

41. George S. Greene Jr. to O.O. Howard June 2, 1899 O.O. Howard Papers, Bowdoin College Library; _____, "Early Presidents of the Society" p. 711; "In Memoriam." MOLLUS Papers January 31, 1900.

42. Ibid.

43. Greene, "Address" p. 4-6, Box 2, Folder 14, WMSC, RIHS.

44. Ibid.

45. Ibid.

Notes: Chapter Twenty

1. George S. Greene to John B. Bachelder March 8, 1866 Ladd, the Bachelder Papers, 1: 242.

2. Ibid, May 8, 1878 Ladd, the Bachelder Papers, 1: 542-543

3. George S. Greene to John P. Nicholson August 26, 1873 RB97865, Vol.1, p. 318 HHL.

4. Ethier, "King of the Hill" p.77.

5. Clarke, The Greenes of Rhode Island p. XXII; The Providence Journal May 25, 1913.

6. George S. Greene to John B. Bachelder May 1, 1890 Ladd, the Bachelder Papers, 3: 1721.

7. Clarke, The Greenes of Rhode Island p. XXII.

8.   Will of Hannibal Day, Morris County, New Jersey State Archives. He asked not to be cremated or buried in the Ocean.

9.   RG 94, HR7487 NARA.

10.   Ibid, S3075 NARA; George S. Greene to John B. Bachelder June 20, 1892 Ladd, the Bachelder Papers, 3: 1846-1847; George S. Greene to John P. Nicholson undated, John Page Nicholson Papers Ni127, HHL.

11.   Ibid.

12.   Ibid.

13.   Ibid, J.C. Kelton to Sec. of War May 12, 1892; George S. Greene to John P. Nicholson undated, John Page Nicholson Papers, Ni127 HHL.

14.   H.C. Pitney to George S. Greene April 27, 1892 Box 1, Folder 5 George Sears Greene Papers, RIHS.

15.   Ibid.

16.   Ibid, May 2, 1892 Box 1, Folder 5 George Sears Greene Papers, RIHS.

17.   RG94, S3075 February 9 and May 5, 1893 NARA.

18.   Nevins, Allan Grover Cleveland: A Study in Courage Dodd, Mead and Company 1932, p. 524-525.

19.   Ibid, p. 528-532.

20.   New York Times May 6, 1891, February 28, 1894, May 7, 1895; The Jerseyman May 12, 1893; Newspaper clipping (unknown) May 7 or 14, 1895 EG Box 22, HHL.

21.   Gettysburg Star and Sentinel July 4, 1893; The Providence Journal May 25, 1913.

22.   Ibid.

23.   Greene, George S. "Speech on Gettysburg" Box 1, Folder 6 George Sears Greene Papers, RIHS.

24.   Gettysburg Star and Sentinel July 4, 1893.

25.   Swanberg, W.A. Sickles the Incredible Charles Scribner's Sons 1956, p. 366.

26.   RG94, HR4416 (December 4, 1893) and S 1513 (January 29, 1894); New York Times December 16 and 24, 1893.

27.   George S. Greene Pension Record NARA.

28.   Ibid; Nevins, Grover Cleveland p. 327-329.

29.   RG 94, J.R. Hawley to Sec. of War August 6, 1894 NARA.

30.   Ibid, Special Orders No. 192 August 16, 1894 NARA.

31.   Ibid. George S. Greene to Adjutant-General Ruggles August 17 and 18, 1894 NARA.

32.   Ibid, August 31, 1894 NARA.

33.   New York Times July 3, 1898.

34.   RG94, George S. Greene to Adjutant-General February 23, 1897 NARA.

35.   Ibid, Assistant Adjutant-General to George S. Greene August 28, 1897 NARA.

36.   Ibid, September 2, 1897 NARA.

37.   New York Times July 3, 1898.

38.   Ibid; Clarke, The Greenes of Rhode Island p. XXIII.

39.   Clarke, The Greenes of Rhode Island p. XXIII.

40.   Ibid; Boston Globe January 28, 1899; Chicago Tribune January 28, 1899; San Francisco Chronicle January 28, 1899; The Washington Post January 28, 1899.

41.   New York Times January 28, 1899; Rhode Island Pendulum February 2, 1899; The Jerseymen February 3, 1899.

42.   Rhode Island Pendulum February 2, 1899; The Jerseyman February 3, 1899.

43.   Ibid; Ibid.

44.   Will of George Sears Greene, Morris County, New Jersey State Archives.

45.   Ibid.

46.   Ibid. He also owned stocks and bonds in a second asphalt company and in a Silver mine. It is possible that Greene suffered reverses on Wall Street in the 1880's that led to his financial difficulties.

47.   Francis V. Greene to Daniel E. Sickles May 31, 1899 (including attached note from Sickles June 2, 1899), A. J. Zabriskie to B. H. Griswold July 6, 1899 George S. Greene file, GNMP.

48.   New York Times May 24, 1903.

49.   In Memoriam GSG, p. 52.

50.   The Providence Journal May 25, 1913.

51.   Ibid, February 21, 1998.

52.   New York Times May 24, 1903.

53.   Ibid, February 2, 1899

Bibliography

Manuscript Sources

American Antiquarian Society Worchester, Massachusetts
    Henry Comey Letter
Bowdoin College Library Brunswick, Maine
    O.O. Howard Papers, Special Collections & Archives
Brown University Library Providence, Rhode Island
    Sewerage System Report for Providence
Buffalo and Erie County Historical Society Buffalo, New York
    Sullivan F. McArthur Collection
Colorado Historical Society Denver, Colorado
    Donald Brown Reminiscences (Original)
Dartmouth College Hanover, New Hampshire
    Eugene Powell Letters, Antietam Collection
    J. M. Smither Letter
    B. H. Witcher Letter
    Charles E. Smith Letter
    Unidentified 102nd New York Letter
Dennis Buttacavoli, Hasbrouck Heights, New Jersey
    Private Collection of Letters
DeWitt Historical Society of Tompkins County Ithaca, New York
    Henry Rudy Diary
Duke University Durham, North Carolina
    Joseph Diltz Papers, 1861-65
    Joshua and Merrit Comfort Papers
Emory University, The Robert W. Woodruff Library Atlanta, Georgia
    Luther L. Gates Letters

Florence Kring Lexington, Nebraska
> William Harrison Bowlby Diary (transcribed by Mildred Nadeau)

Fredericksburg and Spotsylvania National Military Park
> Edward D. Camden Diary, 25th Virginia Infantry
> Samuel R. Lusk Letter, Vol. 117

Gettysburg College, Musselman Library Gettysburg, Pennsylvania
> Papers of Ambrose Henry Hayward

Gettysburg National Military Park Library Gettysburg, Pennsylvania
> Taylor Elmore Diary
> William Gray Letters (Copy)
> George S. Greene File
> 137th New York Infantry File
> David Zable Paper

Hagley Museum and Library Wilmington, Delaware
> Frostberg Coal Mine Map (notes)

Henry E. Huntington Library San Marino, California
> George Gordon Meade Letters (Ni 849)
> Alexander Dallas Bache Papers
> George Sears Greene (EG Box 22)
> John Page Nicholson Papers (Ni 127)

Jeff Ollis Harleysville, Pennsylvana
> Oliver Ormsby Letters and Diary

Judy Coy San Anselmo, California
> Charles Engle Letters

Kennebec Historical Society Augusta, Maine
> Kennebec & Portland R.R. Papers, Nash Collection

Library of Congress, Manuscript Division Washington D.C.
> Nathaniel P. Banks Papers
> John Bigelow Papers

Massachusetts Historical Society Boston, Massachusetts
> Richard Cary Letters
> Edwin P. Farling Letters
> Charles F. Morse Letters
> Henry B. Scott Letter

Montana State University Bozeman, Montana

Lester S. Willson Letter, Merrill G. Burlingame Special
Collections
The Morgan Library, The GilderLehrman Collection New York,
New York
George S. Greene Letter
National Archives and Record Administration
Records of the Adjutant-General's Office, 1780's-1917,
Record Group 94
William B. Goodrich Military and Pension Records
George Sears Greene Military and Pension Records
Charles P. Horton Pension Record
Caius C. Lord Pension Record
Washington M. Postley Military and Pension Records
Hector Tyndale Pension Record
Neville Public Museum of Brown County Green Bay, Wisconsin
Lysander Welman Diaries
New Jersey State Archives Trenton, New Jersey
Will of Hannibal Day, Morris County
Will of George Sears Greene, Morris County
New York Historical Society New York, New York
Henry W. Slocum Letter
New York Public Library New York, New York
Francis Vinton Greene Papers
New York State Archves Albany, New York
137th New York Regt 1896, Regimental History Survey Files
New York State Library Albany, New York
Hiram Bloomer Letter
Oberlin College Archives Oberlin, Ohio
Jacob Dolson Cox Diary and Papers
Ogdensburg Public Library Ogdensburg, New York
Preston King Letters
Ontario County Historical Society and Museum Canadaigua, New
York
Merwin Eugene Cornell Papers
Rhode Island Historical Society Providence, Rhode Island
George Sears Greene Papers

The William and Marion Sluys Collection of Greene Family Manuscripts

St. Lawrence County Historical Association Canton, New York
Donald Brown Reminiscences (Copy)
George Elderkin Letter, Allen Civil War Letters Collection

South Carolinana Library, University of South Carolina Columbia, South Carolina
Robert Wallace Shad Memoir

Stockholm Historical Society Winthrop, New York
E. L. Crane Letter

Three Village Historical Society Setauket, New York
Charles E. Jayne Papers

Tioga County Historical Society Owego, New York
Spencer Jasen Diary (Copy)

United States Army Military History Institute Carlisle, Pennsylvania
William J. Burns "Civil War Diary," Robert L. Brake Collection
Steuben H. Coon, Civil War Miscellaneous Collection
Charles T. Greene, Civil War Miscellaneous Collection
Abel Goddard, Civil War Miscellaneous Collection
James S. Hyde Diary, Norwich CivilWar Roundtable Collection
Joseph A. Moore, Moore Family: PA "Save the Flags" Collection
Norton Brothers, Ralph G. Poriss Collection
Northern Commanders and Staff, Robert L. Blake Collection
Robison Papers, Pardee-Robison Collection
William M. Sayre Collection 1862-64
William H. H. Tallman Memoir

United States Military Academy Library West Point, New York
George Sears Greene File
Official Registar of the Officers and Cadets of the U.S. Military Academy 1820-1823

University of Virginia Library Charlottesville, Virginia
Diary of Francis V. Greene

Virginia Historical Society Richmond, Virginia

Benjamin Anderson Jones Memoirs
Western Reserve Historical Society Cleveland, Ohio
George Sears Greene Letters
Wistar Institute Archives Philadelphia, Pennsylvania
Issac Wistar Papers
Government Publications
United States Congress, Joint Committee on the Conduct
of the War, Reports. Washington D.C. 1865. 3 Volumes.
United States Department of War. The War of the
Rebellion: A Compilation of the
Union and Confederate Armies Government Printing
Office; 1880-1901 128 Volumes.

Newspapers

Army and Navy Journal
Army and Navy Register
Binghamton Daily Republican
Binghamton Leader
Brookfield Journal
Chicago Tribune
Cleveland Herald
Cleveland Leader
Erie Weekly Gazette
Gettysburg Star and Sentinel
Jerseyman
Kennebec Journal
Mobile Evening News
New York Times
Ogdensburg Advance
Ogdensburg Daily Journal
Potsdam Courier and Freeman
Poughkeepsie Eagle
Providence Journal
Rhode Island Pendulam
San Francisco Chronicle

St. Lawrence Republican
Syracuse Journal
Union County Gazette
Warwick Beacon
Washington Post
Windsor Standard

Books

_____, The Biographical Cyclopedia of Representative Men of Rhode Island National Biographical Publishing Co. 1881.

_____, History of St. Lawrence Co. New York L. H. Everts & Co. 1878.

_____, Letters Home: A Collection of Original Civil War Soldiers Letters Garden Spot Gifts, Inc. 1996.

_____, The New York Genealogical and Biographical Record Volume 30, No. 2, 1899.

_____, Thirtieth Annual Reunion of the Association of the Graduates of the United States Military Academy Seeman & Peters, Printers and Binders, 1899.

Banes, Charles H. History of the Philadelphia Brigade J.B. Lippincott & Company, 1876.

Bartlett, John Russell Memoirs of Rhode Island Officers who were engaged in the service of their country during the Great Rebellion of the South Sidney S. Rider & Brother, 1867.

Barziza, Decimus et Ultimus The Adventures of a Prisoner of War The University of Texas Press, 1964.

Bean, W. G. The Liberty Hall Volunteers The University Press of Virginia, 1964.

Blair, William Alan (ed) A Politician Goes to War: The Civil War Letters of John White Geary The Pennsylvania State University Press, 1995.

Bond, Natalie Jenkins and Coward, Osmun Latrobe (ed) The South Carolinians: Colonel Asbury Coward's Memoirs Vantage Press, 1968.

Boyle, John Richards Soldiers and True: The Story of the 111th Pennsylvania Veteran Volunteer Infantry, 1861-1865 Eaton & Mains, 1903.

Brandy, James P. (ed) Hurrah for the Artillery! Knap's Independent Battery "E," Pennsylvania Light Artillery Thomas Publications, 1992.

Brodie, Fawn M. Thomas Jefferson: An Intimate History W.W. Norton & Company Inc., 1974.

Busey, John and Martin, David Regimental Strengths and Losses at Gettysburg Longstreet House, 1986.

Caldwell, Willie Walker Stonewall Jim: A Biography of General James A. Walker, C.S.A. Northcross House, Publishers 1990.

Cavanaugh, Cam In Lights and Shadows: Morristown in Three Centuries The Joint Free Public Library of Morristown and Morris Township 1986.

Clark, Walter (compiler) Histories of the Several Regiments and Battalions from North Carolina in the Great War 1861-1865 E. M. Uzzell, Printer and Binder, 5 Volumes 1901.

Clarke, Louise Brownell The Greenes of Rhode Island: With Historical Records of English Ancestery, 1534-1902 The Knickerbocker Press, 1903.

Cleaves, Freeman Meade of Gettysburg University of Oklahoma Press, 1960.

Coddington, Edwin B. The Gettysburg Campaign: A Study in Command Charles Scribner's Sons, 1968.

Collins, George K. Memoirs of the 149th New York Infantry, 3rd., 2nd Div., 12th and 20th A. C. Published by the author, 1891.

Cozzens, Peter The Battles for Chattanooga: The Shipwreck of their Hopes University of Illinois Press, 1994.

Crowell, Joseph The Young Volunteer Nova Publications, 1997.

Cullum, George W. Biographical Register of the Officers and Graduates of the U. S. Military Academy Houghton, Mifflin and Company 1891.

Cunningham, D. and W. W. Miller, (ed) Report of the Ohio Antietam Battlefield Commission Springfield Publishing, 1904.

Curtis, Newton Martin From Bull Run to Chancellorsville: The

Story of the Sixteenth New York Infantry together with Personal Reminiscences G. P. Putnam's Sons, 1906.

Dawes, Rufus R. Service with the Sixth Wisconsin Volunteers Press of Morningside Bookshop, 1991.

Eddy, Richard History of the Sixtieth Regiment New York State Volunteers, from July 1861 to January 7, 1864 Crissy & Markley, Printers, 1864.

Editors of Time-Life Books Voices of the Civil War: Antietam Time-Life Books, 1996.

Editors of Time-Life Books Voices of the Civil War: Chattanooga Time-Life Books, 1998.

Editors of Time-Life Books Voices of the Civil War: Second Manassas Time-Life Books, 1995.

Eggleston, George Cary A Rebel's Recollection University of Indiana Press 1959.

Foote, Shelby The Civil War: A Narrative-Fort Sumter to Perryville Vintage Books, 1986.

Foster, G. L. The Past of Ypsilanti: A Discourse delivered on Leaving the Old Presbyterian Church Edifice, Lord's Day, September 20th 1857 Fleming & Davis, Book Printers, 1857.

Fox, William F. (ed) In Memoriam Henry Warner Slocum 1826-1894 J. B. Lyon Company, Printers, 1904.

_____ New York Monuments Commission of the Battlefields of Gettysburg and Chattanooga. Final Report of the Battlefield of Gettysburg. J. B. Lyon Company, Printers, 3 Volumes 1900, 1902.

Freeman, Douglas Southall (edited by Richard Harwell) Lee: An Abridgment Charles Scribner's Sons 1961.

Furgurson, Ernest B. Chancellorsville 1863: The Soul of the Brave Alfred A. Knopf, 1992.

Galusha, Diana Liquid Assets: A History of New York City's Water System Purple Mountain Press, 1999.

Goldsborough, W. W. The Maryland Line in the Confederate Army 1861-1865 Guggenheim, Weil, and Co., 1900.

Grant, John and Lynch, James and Bailey, Ronald West Point The First 200 Years The Globe Pequot Press, 2002.

Greene, Albert R. "From Bridgeport to Ringgold by way of Lookout Mountain." MOLLUS Collection, 1890.

Hattaway, Herman General Stephen D. Lee University Press of Mississippi, 1976.

Howard, Oliver Otis Autobiography of Oliver Otis Howard, Major General United States Army Books for Libraries Press, 2 Volumes 1971.

Huyette, Miles C. The Maryland Campaign and the Battle of Antietam Hammond Press, 1915.

Jessup, Harlan R. (ed) The Painful News I have to Write. . . . Butternut and Blue, 1998.

Johnson, Allen and Malone, Dumas (ed) Dictionary of American Biography Charles Scribner's Sons, 16 Volumes 1931.

Johnson, Robert Underwood and Buel, Clarence Clough (ed) Battles and Leaders of the Civil War Thomas Yoseloff, 4 Volumes 1956.

Jones, Maudwyn The Limits of Liberty, American History 1607-1980 Oxford University Press, 1983.

Jordan, William B. (ed) The Civil War Journals of John Meade Gould 1861-1866 Butternut and Blue, 1997.

Kaminsky, Virginia Hudges (ed) A War to Petrify the Heart: The Civil War Letters of a Dutchess County, N.Y. Volunteer Richard T. Van Wyck Black Dome Press, 1997.

Klunder, William Carl Lewis Cass and the Politics of Moderation The Kent State University Press, 1996.

Krick, Robert K. Stonewall Jackson at Cedar Mountain University of North Carolina Press, 1990.

Leon, Louis Diary of a Tar Heel Confederate Soldier Stone Publishing Company 1913.

Livingstone, Charles Brandegee Charlie's Civil War: A Private's Trial by Fire in the 5th New York Volunteers Dury'ee Zouves and 146th New York Volunteer Infantry Thomas Publications, 1997.

McClendon, William A. Recollections of War Times by an Old Veteran Paragon Press, 1909.

McCullough, David John Adams Simon & Schuster 2001.

McIntosh, W. H. History of Ontario County, New York Everts, Ensign, and Everts, 1876.

McKim, Randolph H. A Soldier's Recollections: Leaves from the Diary of a Young Confederate Zenger Publishing Co., Inc., 1983.

Meade, George G., Jr. The Life and Letters of George Gordon Meade Charles Scribner's Sons, 2 Volumes 1913.

Mixson, Frank M. Reminiscences of a Private J. F. Fox, Inc. 1990.

Monroe, J. Albert "Battery D, First Rhode Island Light Artillery at the Battle of Antietam September 17 1862"

MOLLUS Collection 1886.

Nevins, Allan (ed) A Diary of Battle: The Personal Journals of Colonel Charles S. Wainwright, 1861-1865 Stan Clark Military Books, 1992.

_____ Grover Cleveland: A Study in Courage Dodd, Meade & Company, 1932.

North, James W. History of Augusta Clapp & North 1870.

Pfanz, Harry W. Culp's Hill & Cemetery Hill The University of North Carolina Press, 1994.

Priest, John Michael Antietam: The Soldiers Battle White Mane Publishing Company, 1989.

Published by the authority of the state of New York, under the supervision of the New York Monuments Commission In Memoriam: George Sears Greene, Brevet Major-General, United States Volunteers, 1801-1899 J. B. Lyon Company, State Printers 1909.

Quaife, Milo M. (ed) From the Cannon's Mouth: The Civil War Letters of General Alpheus S. Williams Wayne State University Press, 1959.

Quint, Alonzo H. The Record of the Second Massachusetts Regiment Infantry 1861-1865 James P. Walker, 1867.

Raab, Steven S. (ed) With the 3rd Wisconsin Badgers: The Living Experience of the Civil War Through the Journals of Van R. Willard Stackpole Books, 1999.

Rawley, James A. Edwin D. Morgan 1811-1883: Merchant in Politics Columbia University Press, 1955.

Sauers, Richard A. (ed) Fighting Them Over-How the Veterans Remembered Gettysburg in the Pages of the National Tribune Butternut and Blue, 1998.

Scharf, J. Thomas History of Western Maryland; Being a History of Frederick, Montgomery, Carroll, Washington, Allegany, and Garrett Counties from the Earliest Period to the Present Day; including Biographical Sketches of their Representative Men L.H. Everts, 1882.

Sears, Stephen W. Landscape Turned Red: The Battle of Antietam Ticknor & Fields, 1983.

Skinner, George W. Pennsylvania at Chickamauga and Chattanooga: Ceremonies at the Dedication of the Monuments Erected by the Commonwealth of Pennsylvania to mark the Positions of the Pennsylvania Commands Engaged in the Battles William Stanley Ray, State Printer, 1900.

Swanberg, W. A. Sickles the Incredible Charles Scribner's Sons, 1956.

Swift, Lindsay (ed) The Great Debate Houghton Mifflin Company, 1898.

Swisher, James K. Brigadier General Micah Jenkins C.S.A. Prince of Edisto Rockbridge Publishing Company, 1996.

Swords, Robert S. Historical Sketch of Company "D," Thirteenth Regiment New Jersey Volunteers, Part of the 3d Brigade, 1st Division, 12th Army Corps D. H. Gildersleeve & Company, Publishers, 1875.

Tevis, C. V. and Marquis, D. R. The History of the Fighting Fourteenth Brooklyn Eagle Press, 1911.

Thackery, David T. A Light & Uncertain Hold: A History of the Sixty-sixth Ohio Volunteer Infantry The Kent State University Press, 1999.

Toombs, Samuel Reminiscences of the War, Comprising a Detailed Account of the Experience of the 13th Regiment New Jersey Volunteers, In Camp, the March, and in Battle Journal Office, 1878.

Toomey, Daniel Carroll The Patapsco Guards, Independent Company of Maryland Volunteer Infantry Toomey Press, 1993.

Walsh, James J. (ed) The Catholic Encyclopedia Robert Appleton Company, 15 Volumes 1912.

Wiley, Bell Irwin The Life of Billy Yank, the Common Soldier of the Union Louisiana State University Press, 1952.

Wilson, Lawrence Itinerary of the Seventh Ohio Volunteer Infantry, 1861-1864 Neale Publishing, 1907.

Wisely, William H, The American Civil Engineer 1852-1974; The History, Traditions and Development of the American Society of Civil Engineers founded 1852 American Society of Civil Engineers 1974.

Wood, George L. The Seventh Regiment: A Record James Miller, 1865.

Wyckoff, Mac A History of the Second South Carolina Infantry: 1861-65 Sergeant Kirkland's Museum and Historical Society, Inc. 1994.

_____ A History of the Third South Carolina Infantry 1861-1865 Sergeant Kirkland's Museum and Historical Society, Inc. 1995.

Articles

_____, "Early Presidents of the Society." Civil Engineering Volume 6, No. 10 October 1936.

Balch, William M. "Did General S. Greene win Civil War at Battle of Gettysburg?" The National Tribune August 20, 1931.

Bertolf, G. D. "The Twelfth Corps. The Part they took in the Big Battle of Gettysburg." The National Tribune May 11, 1893.

Clemens, Thomas G. (ed) "The Diary of John M. Stone." Maryland Historical Magazine Vol. 85, No. 2 Summer 1990.

Coco, Gregory A. "Wasted Valor: The Confederate Dead at Gettysburg." The Gettysburg Magazine No. 3, July 1990.

Cornet, Joseph L. "The 28th Pennsylvania at Antietam." Grand Army Scout and Soldiers' Mail September 22, 1883.

Coski, John M. and Ruth Ann "Many are Delighted: Two Confederate Diaries from the Last Weeks of the War." North & South Vol.3, No. 4.

Elmore, Thomas L. "Courage against the Trenches: The Attack and Repulse of Steuart's Brigade on Culp's Hill." The Gettysburg Magazine No. 7, July 1992.

Ethier, Eric "King of the Hill." Civil War Times Illustrated Magazine Vol. 36, No. 6 December 1997.

Greene, George "Story of a Brigade." United States Services Magazine IV October 1865.

Jones, Jessie H. "A Pair of Breastplates." The National Tribune June 6, 1901.

_____ "Lookout Mountain: An Account of the Battle by a Fighting Parson." The National Tribune October 21, 1889.

_____ "Save the Day." The National Tribune March 7, 1895.

Jorgensen, Jay "Holding the Right: The 137th New York at Gettysburg." The Gettysburg Magazine No. 15, July 1996.

_____ "Joseph W. Latimer, The 'Boy Major' at Gettysburg." The Gettysburg Magazine No. 10, January 1994.

Lewis, William C. "Greene's Brigade." The National Tribune November 19, 1908.

Long, Roger "The Confederate Prisoners of Gettysburg." The Gettysburg Magazine No. 2, January 1990.

Martz, Jason A. "It was not a happy time: What the Civilians of Gettysburg saw and heard during the Battle." The Gettysburg Magazine No. 18, January 1998.

Motts, Wayne E. "To Gain a Second Star: The Forgotten George S. Greene." The Gettysburg Magazine No. 3, July 1990.

O'Brien, Kevin E. "A Perfect Roar of Musketry: Candy's Brigade in the fight for Culp's Hill." The Gettysburg Magazine No. 9, July 1993.

Pontius, Phillip (ed) "Uncle Jake in the Civil War" Bridgebuilder, The National Pontius Association Magazine February 1968.

Ryan, George F. "Greene's Brigade at Culp's Hill." The National Tribune November 29, 1923.

Schroyer, M. S. "Snyder County Historical Society Bullentins." Vol.2, No. 2 1939.

Shotwell, Mike and Sword, Wiley "Two New York Swords in the fight for Culp's Hill: Col. James C. Lane's and Capt. Nicholas

Grumbach's." The Gettysburg Magazine No. 10, January 1994.

Smith, James O. "My First Campaign and Battles, A Jersey Boy at Antietam-Seventeen Days from Home." Blue and Gray 1 1893.

Stakem, Patrick H. "The Mount Savage Iron Works: Western Maryland's Industrial (little) Giant." Western Maryland Chapter, NRHS, Inc.

Swineford, George W. "On Culp's Hill" The National Tribune August 3, 1916.

Sword, Wiley (ed) "Wiley Sword's War Letters Series-Army General George Greene Attempts to Solve Problem With Rebel Torpedoes" Blue & Gray Magazine Volume XIX, No. 4

Topps, David "The Dutchess County Regiment." The Gettysburg Magazine No. 12, January 1995.

Zollinger, William P. and Hollyday, Lamar, Howard, D.R. "General George H. Steuart's Brigade at the Battle of Gettysburg." Southern Historical Society Papers Vol. 2, July 19, 1876.

Thesis, Dissertations, and Miscellaneous Papers

_____, "In Memoriam. George Sears Greene." MOLLUS Papers January 31, 1900.

Armstrong, Marion V. "Sumner at Antietam." Antietam National Battlefield Park.

Bowen, Mary "Mt. Savage History." (Speech presented to the Homemakers Club) 1953.

Congressional Medal of Honor documents of John P. Murphy and Jacob George Orth.

Fennell Jr., Charles C. "The Attack and Defense of Culp's Hill: Greene's Brigade at the Battle of Gettysburg, July 1-3, 1863." Dissertation, West Virginia University 1992. WWW. Familysearch.org website: "George Sears Greene."

Gray, John (Reverend) Information compiled on Stephen Kenneth Gray, 66th Ohio Volunteer Infantry.

King, John R. "My Experience in the Confederate Army and in

Northern Prisons." Stonewall Jackson Chapter No. 1333, UDC 1917.

Mieyal, Timothy J. "A Story of Valor: The Seventh Ohio Volunteer Infantry." MA Thesis, Kent State University 1998.

Redington, J.C.O. "Greene's Brigade. The Thirtieth Anniversary: 1863-1893, Souvenir of the Reunion, July 1-3, 1893, of Greene's Brigade, 3rd Brigade, 2nd Division, 12th Corps, the 60th, 78th, 102nd 137th and 149th New York Volunteers, Who alone at Culp's Hill in the Days' Battle Saved the Right at Gettysburg." 1893.

Stinson Jr., Dwight E. "Analytical Study of Action of Greene's Division." February 2, 1961 Antietam National Battlefield Park.

Correspondence

Mr. William A. Blair to Author January 1, 2001.

Mr. Tom Brooks to Author June 22, 1999.

Mr. Mark H. Dunkelman to Author February 8, 2000.

Mr. Logan Hill to Author June 12, 1999.

Mr. Wilber D. Jones to Author November 26, 1999.

Mr. Don Nelson (interviewed by Stan Maine) to Author May 11, 2001.

Mr. Terry Reimer to Author August 9, 2001.

Mr. Stephen W. Sears to Author August 15, 2000.

Mrs. Shelley Wallace to Author November 14, 2000.

Index

Acquia Creek 112-113, 127, 135

Acquia Landing, VA., 112, 116, 135, 137

Adams, John 28

Adams, Julius W. 45

Alabama 140, 221

Albany, NY., 25, 53, 116, 239

Albany & Susquehanna Railroad 44

Alexandria, VA., 29, 137, 219, 235

American Society of Civil Engineers and Architects (ASCE) 45, 47, 238, 241

American Telegraph Company 65

Anderson, William 91

Andover, MA., 34

Anthony, H.B. 232

Antietam, Battle of 80, 96-101, 107, 117, 121, 129, 137, 195, 209, 236, 250, 255

Appomattox, VA., 235

Army & Navy Register 247

Army of the Cumberland 220

Army of Northern Virginia 72, 207

Army of the Potomac 17, 20, 77, 79, 88, 94, 106, 113, 115, 132, 139, 143-145, 207, 209, 216, 221

Army of Virginia (Union) 71

Ashby's Gap 213

Asheville, NC., 35

Astor Hotel 265

Atlanta, GA., 234

Atwater, Edward 90

Augur, C. C. 245

Augusta, ME., 41-43

Ayres, J. W. 45

Bach, William M. 17

Bachelder, John B. 250

Ball's Bluff, Battle of 139

Baltimore, MD., 22, 53, 59, 62, 70, 220

Baltimore & Ohio Railroad (B&O) 36, 38-40

Baltimore Pike 143, 145, 147-148, 163, 200, 203, 205

Banks, Nathaniel 66-67, 71-72, 74-75, 77

Barnum, Henry A. 155, 196, 229

Batcher, James 227

Bath, ME., 41-42

Bealton Station, VA., 217, 220

Bean, James B. 263

Bellair, OH., 220

Benning, Henry I. 223, 227

Berryville, VA., 104

Bingham, O. 201

Blue Ridge Mountains 213

Bolivar Heights, VA., 102-103, 105-
106
Borgardus, Jr., Stephen H. 81
Boston, MA., 21, 26, 29, 34, 41-42,
44, 245, 260
Boston & Providence Railroad 41-42
Bowdoinham, ME., 41
Bowlby, William H. 236
Boyd, Ebenezer 239
Boyd's Corners, NY., 238-239
Bragg, Braxton 220, 234
Brandegee, Charles 56
Brandy Station, VA., 220
Brandywine, PA., 55
Bridgeport, AL., 222
Bristol, RI., 247
British Navy 22, 30
Brown, Donald 52, 81, 96, 121, 200
Brown, John 49, 102
Brown's Ferry, TN., 224
Brown University 23
Brunswick, ME., 41, 43-44
Bryant, William C. 39
Buck, L. L. 260
Buckley, Oliver 125
Bull Run, Battle of 61
Bunker Hill, VA., 67, 105
Burnside, Ambrose E. 20, 106, 111,
113
Butterfield, Daniel 134, 261
Butts, Charles E. 199
Camden, Edward D. 200
Canada 30
Cantine, John J. 159, 162
Canton, MI., 46
Carmen, Ezra 92

Cary, Richard 67
Casad, J. 196
Cass, Lewis 30, 33
Catocin Mountains 141
Cattlets Station, VA., 214
Cedar Mountain, Battle of 73, 76, 96,
98, 100, 104
Cemetery Hill 158
Cemetery Ridge 147, 149, 203, 206
Century Club 244, 248, 255
Century Magazine 250
Chaffin, Jere G. 86
Chancellor House 119-120, 126, 129
Chancellorsville, Battle of 119, 128,
130-131, 134, 137, 144, 146,
220, 237, 245
Chantilly, Battle of 77
Charleston, SC., 35,50, 132, 218
Charlestown, MA., 34-35
Charlestown, VA., 102-104, 106
Chattanooga, TN., 220, 223, 226,
228, 231
Chesapake (ship) 22
Chesapake & Ohio Canal 37, 140
Chicago, IL., 260
Chickamauga, Battle of 221
Cincinnati, OH., 35
Clark, Samuel 91
Clarke, Louise B. 261
Cleveland, Grover 255, 257
Collins, George K. 104, 138, 148,
198, 205, 216
Comey, Henry 69
Comfort, Joshua 129, 218
Confederacy 104, 109, 217, 234
Confederate Army 195, 231

Connecticut 25, 31-32, 258

Cooke, John R. 91

Coon, Steuben H. 137, 150, 153

Cornell, Merwin E. 78, 83

Cornell, Stephen S. 78

Couch, Darius N. 131

Coventry 22

Coward, Asbury 225

Cox, Jacob D. 234

Cox, John 163

Cozzens, Peter 226-227

Crampton's Gap 209

Crane, E. L. 57

Craven, Alfred W. 45, 47, 238, 240

Cresson, William 157

Crittenden Mills, VA., 118

Croton Aqueduct 45, 47-48, 52, 75, 238, 240, 248

CSS Virginia 61, 111, 247-248

Cuba 259

Culpeper Court House, VA., 72

Culp's Hill, PA., 17, 20, 144-147, 149, 152, 155-156, 160, 162, 164, 196, 198-199, 202-203, 205, 232, 244, 250, 256, 261-262

Cumberland, MD., 37, 39-40, 221

Cumberland Coal & Iron Co., 36

Cumberland Mountains 35

Curtain, Andrew 98

Curtis, Newton 257

Dana, Samuel 34

Daniel, Julius 196

Darby, William 87

Davis, Jefferson C. 235

Dawes, Rufus R. 162

Day, Hannibal 27, 242, 245, 252

Day, Murray S. 242

Deckert Station, TN., 222

Democratic Party 50

DeWitt, W. R. 230

Diltz, Joseph 95

Dinsmore Wood & Co., 47

Dix, John A. 233

Drainsville, VA., 138

Duncan, Robert H. 153

Dumfries, VA., 107, 110-112, 136

Dunker Church 80, 87-89, 92, 121

East Cemetery Hill 152

East Greenwich, RI., 257, 260

Eastport, ME., 30

East Woods 83-85

Eddy, Richard 54-55, 101, 107-109

Edwards Ferry, VA., 139

8th South Carolina 95

18th Kentucky 235

82nd Illinois 155-156

Elderkin, George E. 59

Eleventh Corps 118-119, 121-122, 124, 127, 140, 155-156, 164, 215, 220, 222-223

Ellicotts Mills, MD., 54

Elliot, Thomas 129

Ellis Ford, VA., 216

Ellmore, Taylor 112, 140

Emmett, Thomas A. 45

England 21-22, 30

Engle, Charles 103-105, 113, 132, 136, 158, 213, 217, 219

Eutaw Springs, SC., 55

Ewell, Richard S. 149, 196

Fairchild, Walker, Coleman & Co., 76

Fairfax, VA., 136
Fairfax Court House 106, 136
Fairfax Station, VA., 106-107, 110
Fairmont, WV., 221
Fairplay, MD., 210
Falling Waters, MD., 67
Falmouth, VA., 132
Farling, Edwin P. (Failing) 211, 218-219, 230
Farmington, John 103, 147
Field's Point, RI., 242
15th New York 134
15th Louisiana 152
Fifth Corps 71, 141, 149, 155, 214
5th New York 56
5th North Carolina 83
5th Ohio 78, 84-86, 215
5th South Carolina 225
5th Texas 84
5th US Artillery 148
50th New York Engineers 140
50th Virginia 152-154
53rd North Carolina 196
First Corps 80-81, 140, 145, 148, 155-156, 160-161, 164, 205
1st District of Columbia 72-73, 75, 78
1st Louisiana 152, 154
1st Maryland Battalion 152, 156-157, 164
1st North Carolina 152,164
1st South Carolina 228
Fishbeck, Simon 54
Florida 52
Flower, Roswell P. 256
Follett, Edwin R. 165

Fort Donelson 58
Fort Evans 139
Fort Independence 30
Fort Monroe 28, 62
Fort Sullivan 30, 32-33
Fort Sumter 51, 218
Fort Wolcott 30
48th Virginia 152-153
45th New York 156
44th Virginia 152-153
42nd Virginia 152-153
14th Brooklyn (84th New York) 155, 158, 162-163
Fourteenth Corps 235
14th Louisiana 152, 154
14th Ohio 235
Fowler, Edward B. 163
Fox, William 68
Fraley, Peter 85
France 22
Franklin, William B. 94
Frederick, MD., 78, 142-143, 209, 212, 239
Fredericksburg, VA., 106-107, 113
Front Royal, VA., 66, 69
Frostberg, MD., 36, 38-39
Futch, Charles F. 163
Gardiner, Edward 45
Gardiner Hotel 41
Gardiner, ME., 41-42
Gates, Luther L. 59, 62
Geary, John W. 18, 73-74, 101-102, 105-106, 108-109, 114, 118, 120, 124, 126,129, 133, 137, 145-146, 148, 150-151, 164-165, 195, 198-199, 202, 205,

208,210, 213, 218-220, 224-225, 229

Georgia 129, 132, 234

Germania Ford, VA., 119

Gettysburg, Battle of 17, 19-20, 143-144, 147, 203, 206, 208, 229, 237, 245, 250-251, 255-256, 261-262

Gilmore, Quincy A. 248

Goddard, Abel 137, 153, 200, 203

Goldsborough, NC., 234-235

Goldsborough, William W. 157

Goodman, H. Earnest 243

Goodrich, William B. 53, 55, 63, 65

Goodwin, Daniel 260

Gordon, George H. 67-71, 91

Gorsuch, Robert B. 45

Goud, John 53

Grafton, WV., 221

Grand Army of the Republic 257

Grant, Ulysses S. 20, 233, 250

Gray, Stephen K. 200

Gregg, Joseph H. 160-161

Greene, Albert R. 225, 227

Greene, Anna M. 40, 59, 76, 132-133, 135, 242-243, 245, 261

Greene, Caleb 21-24, 45

Greene, Carleton 246

Greene, Charles T. 38, 40, 61, 70, 94-95, 128, 133, 135, 215, 217, 231, 238-239, 255-256, 260

Greene, Christopher 21

Greene, Francis Vinton (child of first marriage) 31-32

Greene, Francis Vinton (child of second marriage) 7, 43, 50, 57-58, 60-61, 76, 109-110, 132, 135-137, 142, 144, 212-213, 215-217, 226, 233, 239, 242, 246-247, 252, 255, 257, 259-261

Greene, George Sears 17-20, 22-24 ; a Cadet 25-27; Professor at West Point 28-29; Regular Army 30-33; Civil Engineer 34-40; Railroads and other projects 41-46; Croton Aqueduct, Family and Politics 47-51; Civil War Colonel 52, 54-64; Brigade command and Cedar Mountain 65-76; Antietam 77-81, 83-84, 86-94, 96-97; Winter in Virginia 98-112; Rest and Reorganization for Campaign in Spring 113-117; Chancellorsville 118-130;

Greene, George (child of second marriage) 31-32

Greene's Family and march into Pennsylvania 131-144; Gettysburg (Culp's Hill) July 2nd 145-165; July 3rd 195-207; Return to Virginia and transfer to Tennessee 208-223; Wauhatchie and end of Civil War 224-237; Civilian life 238-249; a Nation Remembers 250-263, 265

Greene, George Sears (child of first marriage) 31-32

Greene, George Sears (child of second marriage) 35-38, 71, 133, 230-231, 239, 242-243, 246, 249, 255, 260

Greene, James 43

Greene, John 21
Greene, Martha Barrett (Dana) 34-35, 37-38, 43, 59, 61-62, 76, 132,135, 231,239, 242, 245-247, 252
Greene, Mary V. 31-32
Greene, Nathaniel 21-22, 24, 28
Greene, Samuel Dana 37, 40, 49, 57, 60-61, 66, 110-111, 132, 134, 242, 247
Greenleaf, Halbert S. 252
Greenwich, VA., 215
Grove Church, VA., 118
Gum Springs, VA., 106
Hagerstown Turnpike 80, 83, 86, 88, 91
Halleck, Henry W. 19
Hallowell, ME., 41-42
Halltown, VA., 102, 104
Hammerstein, Herbert Von 151
Hampton Roads, VA., 61 247
Harlem River 48, 241, 248
Harper's Ferry, VA., 49, 62, 72, 98-99, 101-102, 111, 141, 147, 211-212, 221
Harris, Ira 232
Hartwood Church, VA., 118
Harvard College 48
Hastings, Hugh 262
Hawley, J. R. 252
Haymarket, VA., 215
Hayne, Peter 194
Hayne, Robert 35-37, 40
Haywood, Henry 88, 93
Hazel Grove 123
Herbert, James R. 157

Hill, D. H. 79, 85
Hill, John W. 154
Hillsboro, VA., 212
Hite, John 198
Hood, John B. 250
Hooker, Joseph H. 20, 80, 113-114, 116-120, 122, 127, 131, 134-135, 141, 220, 229
Hopkins, Charles 92
Horton, Charles P. 71, 95, 159, 207
Howard, Oliver O. 20, 101, 155-156, 158, 223-224, 229, 244-245, 249, 260, 262
Hudson River 24, 26, 53, 244
Hunt, Henry J. 145
Hunter, David 27
Hyde, James S. 141-143
Inches, Martin B. 44
Indiana 35, 221
Indianapolis, IN., 221
Ireland, David 123, 158-160, 162, 213, 225-226
Jackson, Stonewall 66-67, 72-75, 77, 122, 125
Jacobs, Henry 23
James River 62
Jasen, Spencer H. 135, 221
Jayne, Charles E. 74
Jefferson, MD., 141, 209
Jefferson, Thomas 22-23
Jeffersonville, IN., 221
Jenkins, Micah 224-225, 228-229
Jennings, Hudson 157
Jerseyman, The 246, 255
Jessup, Thomas J. 32

Johnson, Edward 149, 164, 196-197, 202, 206
Johnston, Albert S. 27
Johnston, Joseph E. 250
Jones, Jessie H. 146, 152
Jones, John M. 152, 154, 200
Kane, Thomas 20, 133, 145, 151, 155, 164, 256
Kansas 49
Keedysville, MD., 79
Kelly's Ford, VA., 119, 216, 219
Kelton, J. C. 253
Kennebec Journal 41
Kennebec, ME., 42
Kennebec & Portland Railroad 41-44
Kentucky 35, 217, 221
Kershaw, Joseph 86-87, 95, 98
King, Preston 50, 56, 64-65, 108-109, 116, 265-266
Kingston, NC., 234-235
Knap's Pennsylvania Independent Battery 90, 148, 224-229, 251
Knight, William 54
Knoxville, MD., 141
Lafayette (Marquis) 28-29
Lamont, Daniel S. 257
Lane, James C. 85, 121, 123, 128, 134, 154-155
Latimer, Joseph 148
Laurie, James 46
Lee, Robert E. 29, 77-79, 84, 88, 94, 96, 117-121, 127, 135, 139-140, 143-144, 195, 202-204, 206, 208, 210-211, 233-235
Lee, S. D. 89

Leesburg, VA., 106, 138-140
Leesburg & Alexandria Railroad 138
Leigh, Benjamin W. 202
Lexington, KY., 35
Lewis, John 91
Lewis, William C. 147
Libby Prison 131
Lilly, William C. 197, 229-230
Lincoln, Abraham 50, 115-117, 131, 139, 220, 234
Lincoln, Robert T. 243-244
Little Round Top 143, 206
Littlestown, PA., 142-143, 208
London 241
London Star 217
Lord, Caius C. 123
Longstreet, James 92, 149, 224, 251
Lorick, Soloman 87
Loudon Heights 99-100, 103, 139
Louisiana 199, 204
Louisville, Cincinnati & Charleston Railroad Company 35
Louisville, KY., 221
Lowe, Thaddeus 102
Lower Trent Road 234
Lusk, Samuel R. 124-125
Lynde, R. D. 229
Mahan, Dennis H. 27
Maine 30, 34, 41, 43, 73, 75, 77, 258
Mansfield, Joseph K. 27, 77-78, 80, 82
Marietta, GA., 129
Marsh, Luther R. 76
Marshall, James 91

Martinsburg, VA., 221
Martinsburg Pike 105
Maryland 36, 39-40, 53, 66, 77-78, 132,139-142, 144, 157, 163, 209, 239
Maryland Mining Co., 36
Maryland & New York Iron & Coal Company 39
Massachusetts 30, 34, 55, 67
McArthur, Sullivan F. 131
McClellan, George B. 20, 66, 77-79, 88, 91, 94, 96-97, 100, 102
McGilvery, Freeman 73
McGregor, Wesley 99
McKim, Randolph 164
McQuire, James 163
Meade, George G. 17-20, 141, 144-149, 164, 195, 198, 203-204, 206, 208, 210, 215, 232, 251
Mealy, William 49
Messereau, Dudley 123
Miantonomah 21
Michigan 46, 240
Miles, Dixon S. 26, 61, 63-64, 99
Mill Creek, VA., 105
Miller's Cornfield 83
Mississippi 210
Mitchell's Station Road 73
Mollus (Loyal Legion) 227, 244, 253, 260
Monitor (ship) 57, 60-61, 110-111, 132, 168, 247
Monmouth, NJ., 55
Moore, Henry 154
Moore, Joseph A. 89

Mordecai, Alfred 245, 249
More, J. Addison 93
Morell, W. H. 46
Morgan, Edwin 52, 54-55, 64, 101, 108
Morgan, John F. 200
Morrisania Station, NY., 239
Morris Aqueduct 254
Morris, Robert E. 248
Morristown, NJ., 245-246, 252, 254-255, 259-260
Morse, Charles F. 68
Mumma Farm 85, 88
Murfreesboro, TN., 222
Murphy, John P. 85
National Museum of Civil War Medicine 263
Narragansett Bay 251
Nashville, TN., 221-222, 230, 234
Naval Academy (Annapolis) 46, 58
Nelson, Robert 204
Newbern, NC., 234
New Hampshire 247
New Jersey 46, 245, 251, 260
Newport News, VA., 62
Newton, VA., 69
New York 25, 45, 50, 52, 56, 63-64, 70, 101, 108, 201, 233, 238-239, 245, 260-262, 265
New York Battlefield Commission 261
New York City 23-24, 26, 46-49, 64, 85, 133, 217, 230-232, 238-240, 242-243, 245, 251, 254, 259, 265
New York Genealogical & Biographical Society 244, 255
New York Historical Society 244

New York Times 49, 75, 257

Nichol, David 90

Nicholson, John P. 243

19th Virginia 160

North Carolina 35, 110-111, 163, 217, 234-235

Norton, Perry 151

Ocoquan River 107, 110-111

Ogdensburg Daily Journal 265

Oglesby, R. J. 232

Ohio 35, 221

Ohio River 221

Old Point, VA., 61

O'Neal, Edward 196, 199, 206

111th Pennsylvania 78, 85, 87, 98, 111, 115, 164

157th New York 156

150th New York 199

149th New York 101, 103-104, 111, 114, 122-123, 126, 128, 133, 138-139, 145, 148, 152, 154-156, 163, 196-198, 204, 211, 213, 216, 218-219, 224, 228, 230

147th New York 155, 158, 161

147th Pennsylvania 133, 143

109th Pennsylvania 78, 80, 101

106th Pennsylvania 158

137th New York 101-103, 105, 110, 112, 122-125, 127, 133, 135, 140-145, 147, 151, 155-163, 197, 202-203, 205, 209, 213, 216-217, 221, 224-225, 227-229

102nd New York 74, 78, 83, 85, 93, 101, 121, 123-126, 128-129, 134, 145-146, 149, 154, 222

124th Pennsylvania 81

122nd New York 197

Orange & Alexandria Railroad 214, 220

Orange Culpeper Road 73

Orange Plank Road 119, 125

Ormsby, Oliver 103, 105, 120, 123

Orth, Jacob G. 88

Oswego, NY., 46

Otto, August 156

Palmer, J. G. 201

Parsley, William M. 164

Patapsco Guards 54

Pennsylvania 98, 100-101, 140, 142, 144, 209, 212

Petersburg, VA., 234

Peterville, MD., 141

Philadelphia, PA., 26

Philippines 259

Piedmont, VA., 213

Pile, George 160

Piltortan, Charles 143

Pitney, H. C. 254

Pittsdon, ME., 41

Poffenberger, J. 80, 83

Points of Rocks, MD., 141

Pomfret, CT., 31-32, 258

Pontius, Jacob 235

Poolesville, MD., 78, 141

Port Hudson, LA., 210

Portland, ME., 41

Portland, Saco, & Portsmouth Railroad 42

Portsmouth Naval Yard 247

Post, S. S. 46

Postley, Washington W. 211

Potomac River 62, 78, 112, 141, 208, 210-211

Powell, Eugene 84, 87, 196, 200-201

Providence, RI., 23, 43-44, 240-242

Purnell Legion of Maryland 72, 78, 81, 83, 91-92, 98

P. W. & Balt. Railroad 58

Quincy, MA., 29

Quint, Alonzo 67

Raccoon Ford, VA., 219

Raines, Charles A. 157

Raleigh, NC., 235

Randall, William H. 128, 155, 228

Rapidan River 119, 219

Rappahanock River 62, 112, 118-119, 126-127, 216, 219

Redington, John C. O. 57, 60, 81, 115, 124-125, 128-129, 148, 150

Reimar, Terry 263

Rhinebeck, NY., 26

Rhode Island 21, 25, 30-32, 43-44, 232, 240-241, 247, 251, 257, 260-262

Rhode Island Historical Society 261

Richmond, VA., 62, 144, 234-235

Ringgold, GA., 230

Rock Creek 145, 147-148, 150, 156, 203

Roebling, W. A. 127

Rogers, Hiram C. 149-150

Rose, Elderkin 63

Rowan, Samuel 87

Rudy, Henry 143, 151-152, 197, 203, 213, 227-228

Ruggles, George D. 257

Russia 242

San Francisco, CA., 260

Sayre, William 95

Schurz, Carl 156

Scotland 52

Sears, George 22

Second Corps 71, 149, 159, 212, 214

2nd Maryland 156

2nd Massachusetts 67-70

2nd South Carolina 87

Seekonk River 242

7th Indiania 148

7th Ohio 78-79, 84-86, 90, 94, 137, 204

7th South Carolina 87-88

78th New York 72-73, 75, 78, 99, 101, 114, 128, 131-132, 145, 148, 151, 154, 205, 212, 218, 220, 222, 224, 229

71st Pennsylvania 158-160, 162

74th Indiania 235-236

Shand, Robert 87

Sharpsburg, MD., 91, 209, 211

Shedd, J. Herbert 241

Shelbyville, TN., 222

Sherman, William T. 245, 250

Sickles, Daniel 256, 261

Sidell, W. H. 46

Sigel, Franz 20

Sixth Corps 141

6th Georgia 84

6th Maine Battery 72-74, 96

6th Wisconsin 155, 158, 162

60th New York 52-54, 56-57, 61-63, 72, 78-79, 81, 96, 101, 104, 108, 111-112, 115-116, 118, 121, 123-126, 128-129, 134, 137-139, 145-147, 150, 152-154, 165, 195, 198, 200, 203-204, 223, 260

61st Ohio 156

66th Ohio 78, 84, 87, 89, 95, 107, 196, 200-201, 205

Slocum, Henry W. 18-20, 62, 106, 110, 127, 133-134, 139, 141, 146, 149-150, 196, 206, 210, 213, 220, 234, 245, 253, 256-257

Smith, Hugh 129

Smith, James 92

Smith, Richard P. 158-159

Smith, Wallace 63

Smith, William F. 253

Smoketown Road 80

South Carolina 35-36, 50, 140, 218, 225

South Mountain 79

Spain 259

Stafford Court House, VA., 116, 118

Stanton, Edwin 108, 232, 237

Stegman, Lewis R. 146, 155

Stevenson, Adali 255

Stevenson, TN., 18

Steuart, George H. 152, 156-157, 160, 164, 196

St. Lawrence Republican 55, 224

St. Lawrence River 239

Stone's River 222

St. Petersburg 242

St. Peter's Episcopal Church 260

Sugar Loaf Mountain 139

Swayne, Wagner 253

Sweet, Owen J. 160-161

Swineford, G. W. 164

Talcott, W. H. 46

Taneytown, MD., 142

Taneytown Road 143

Taylor, Willam P. 260

Telegraph Road 118

Tennessee 18, 221-222, 234, 243

Tennessee River 35

10th Louisiana 152

10th Virginia 152, 161-163

Thayer, Sylvanus 23-26, 28-29

3rd Arkansas 91

Third Corps 121-122, 140-141, 145, 149, 214

3rd Delaware 72, 78

3rd Maryland 78

3rd North Carolina 152, 156-157, 163-164

3rd North Carolina Artillery 234

3rd South Carolina 87-88

3rd Wisconsin 67, 203

13th Alabama 85

13th New Jersey 91-92, 96

38th Ohio 235

37th Virginia 152, 160

33rd Virginia 199

Thomas, Lorenzo 27

Tompkins, John A. 86-87

Troy, MI., 240

Tullahoma, TN., 18, 222

Tweed, 'Boss' 240

12th Alabama 206

Twelfth Corps 17-19, 68, 77-80, 98-99, 106-108, 111-112, 114, 118-119, 121-122, 133, 136-137, 139, 141-143, 146-148, 150, 152, 154, 162, 164, 195-198, 202, 204, 208, 211, 215, 220-221, 231, 252, 255

12th Georgia 125

28th Pennsylvania 78, 84-86, 88-90,

93, 95, 243, 251

25th Virginia 152, 200-201

29th Ohio 78, 80, 123

29th Pennsylvania 67, 69

21st Virginia 152

27th Indiana 67, 79, 91, 95

27th North Carolina 91

23rd Virginia 152, 157, 160

Two Taverns, PA., 143

Tyndale, Hector 89-91, 93

Union Army 66, 72, 109, 111, 114, 122, 149, 262

United States Ford 126-127

Upperville, VA., 214

U.S. Congress 20, 30-31, 34, 63-64, 227, 252-257, 260

U.S. First Artillery 27 U.S.

Navy 134, 242

USS New Hampshire 247

USS Vandalia 242

U.S. Third Artillery 27, 30

Van Buren, William H. 233

Van Cleve, Horatio P. 253

Vicksburg, MS., 132, 207

Vinton, David H. 27, 31

Vinton, Elizabeth 31-34, 37, 258

Virginia 23, 28-29, 61-62, 66, 71, 94, 103, 115, 139-141, 157-158, 204, 208, 213, 217, 234, 236

Wadsworth, Craig 158

Wadsworth, James S. 145, 148, 152, 155, 160-162

Wainwright, Charles S. 152, 205

Walker, James A. 149, 196

Walker, John G. 92

Walkersville, MD., 142

Walton, Simeon 157

Warren, ME., 44

Warrenton Junction, VA., 215, 217

Warrenton Post Road 118

Wartrace, TN., 222

Warwick (Apponaug) RI., 21-22, 24, 32, 247, 260-261

Washington DC 19-20, 50, 55, 58, 60-65, 67, 69-72, 77, 100, 109-110, 114, 116, 137, 139-140, 217, 231-232, 236-239, 243, 250, 260

Wauhatchie, Battle of 223, 243, 251

Webb, Alexander S. 262

Weed, Thurlow 265

Welman, Lysander 106, 111

West Point (US Military Academy) 19, 23-31, 34, 47, 52, 54, 61, 66, 99, 101, 147, 242, 244, 249, 252, 257-259

West Woods 83, 86, 88-90, 98

Whalen, H. A. 65

Whitecomb, F. B. 260

White Plains, VA., 214

Whiteside, TN., 223

Whitman, Walt 109

Whittingham, William R. 37

Wicks, Sarah R. 22

Wiggins, Jr., Edward 74, 96

Willard, Van R. 203

Williams, Alpheus S. 18-20, 78-80, 82, 88, 90-91, 94, 96, 108, 118, 126, 135, 138, 149, 195-196, 211

Williams, Jesse M. 152, 154-156, 199

Williams, Oscar C. 196

Williams, Roger 21

Williamsport, MD., 66-67, 210-211

Willson, Lester 59

Winchester, VA., 66-68, 75, 105, 137, 214

Witcher, B. H. 84

Woodburn (Woodsboro), MD., 142, 209

Wrentham Academy 23

York River 62

Yorktown, VA., 28

Ziegler, C. W. 261

CPSIA information can be obtained
at www.ICGtesting.com
Printed in the USA
BVHW032333100620
581243BV00003B/46/J